Policing, Politics, and Faith

"This diary is a remarkable record of an extraordinary time. The entries from 2020 alone—charting the first lockdown, the pressure on policing, the ethical dilemmas of emergency powers, and the human stories woven through each week—show Alan Billings at his most thoughtful and grounded. His reflections provide a valuable record of leadership under pressure, written with compassion and a profound sense of public duty."

—Abtisam Mohamed, Member of Parliament for Sheffield Central

"Alan Billings is probably a unique figure in British politics. He is certainly the only person who could have put together such a fascinating piece of social history . . . [This diary] was contemporaneous—put together in this book, it remains fresh and has not been 'curated' years later."

—Andrew Lockley, Solicitor, Chair of the Independent Monitoring Board, HMP Moorland, Doncaster

"[This diary] is essential reading alongside Baroness Hallett's excoriating report in November 2025 on Boris Johnson's government's decision-making and governance. . . . As the country was led into the unknown, Dr. Billings understood with great clarity his duty to ensure the police in his area retained the trust and confidence of a public being asked to accept the extreme curtailment of daily life in unprecedented circumstances. He charts the challenge in granular detail."

—Michael Lewis, Former Chair, South Yorkshire Police Independent Ethics Panel

"What makes this book extraordinary is not simply its record of political and policing turbulence, but the humanity threaded through every page. Dr. Billings listens—to victims, officers, faith communities, young people, professionals and the unheard—and he invites us to listen with him. . . . A vital read for anyone who cares about justice, leadership or the fragile bond between police, faith, and community."

—Derek Pamment, Lead Police Force Chaplain

Policing, Politics, and Faith

A Police and Crime Commissioner's Diary from Lockdown to 2024

Alan Billings

FOREWORD BY
Lord David Blunkett

RESOURCE *Publications* · Eugene, Oregon

POLICING, POLITICS, AND FAITH
A Police and Crime Commissioner's Diary from Lockdown to 2024

Copyright © 2026 Alan Billings. All rights reserved. Except for brief quotations in critical publications or reviews, no part of this book may be reproduced in any manner without prior written permission from the publisher. Write: Permissions, Wipf and Stock Publishers, 199 W. 8th Ave., Suite 3, Eugene, OR 97401.

Resource Publications
An Imprint of Wipf and Stock Publishers
199 W. 8th Ave., Suite 3
Eugene, OR 97401

www.wipfandstock.com

PAPERBACK ISBN: 979-8-3852-6920-4
HARDCOVER ISBN: 979-8-3852-6921-1
EBOOK ISBN: 979-8-3852-6922-8

VERSION NUMBER 01/16/26

For my grandchildren: Rudy, Norah, Moses, and Celeste

Contents

About the Author

Dr. Alan Billings was the elected police and crime commissioner for South Yorkshire between 2014 and 2024, when he retired. He is also an Anglican priest. Prior to that, he had been, at various times, a parish priest in Sheffield and Kendal, vice principal of an Oxford theological college, director of the Centre for Ethics and Religion at Lancaster University, deputy leader of Sheffield City Council, and a board member of the Youth Justice Board for England and Wales. Before becoming the police and crime commissioner, he was a regular contributor to "Thought for the Day" on BBC Radio 4's *Today* program. He is an honorary canon of Carlisle Cathedral and a fellow of the Royal Society of Arts.

Foreword

My long-standing and close friend, Alan Billings, has done all of us a service in pulling together his diaries during the period from the first COVID-19 lockdown to his retirement in 2024. As he spells out in the preface, he was the police and crime commissioner for the Metropolitan area of South Yorkshire for ten years through some of the more difficult times for the force, not least because of historic events with which so many readers will now be familiar. His reflections touch on some of the most important issues of how the police relate to both the ever-changing demands of the community they serve, and the requirements cascading from central government. No more so than during the period when COVID hit the daily lives of us all.

Alan captures the way in which the police are often required to enforce contradictory and often confused demands made on them, and to disentangle the law from broad regulatory frameworks, codes, or even edicts backed up merely by the threat to introduce legislative requirements. He captures the essence of difficulties when two-way communication is stretched to the point where those at the top of the managerial and leadership tree have a very different view of what is actually happening on the ground to those at the sharp end. Communication from the top can be so confused and reinterpreted that genuine difficulty arises for those in neighborhood teams, and to those responding to incidents, as to what the law actually is and what is expected of them. In other words, the period covered in this book examines and reflects, in primary colors, on what faces the police service on a daily basis.

I have myself, more recently, led a review into police leadership, with recommendations for the home secretary, who supported the

College of Policing in establishing a commission to examine the way forward. Training, culture, and command and control communication can all be seen as crucial in navigating the ever-changing tide of opinion, the currents that make consistency and clarity extremely difficult, and the critical importance of listening and responding to both the community and those in the service, who wish their voices to be heard. That voice speaks through the pages of this book and can teach all of us a great deal as we seek to navigate the future.

Lord David Blunkett
Former Home Secretary

Preface

I was first elected as the Labour police and crime commissioner (PCC) for South Yorkshire in October 2014. It was a difficult by-election for the Labour Party and a difficult time for the police. A few months before, Professor Alexis Jay had published her report into child sexual exploitation in Rotherham, finding that the local authority and the police had turned a blind eye to the grooming and abuse of more than 1,400 girls by mainly Pakistani Asian males between 1997 and 2013.[1] The report shocked people in South Yorkshire and nationally. Locally, confidence in the police plummeted. My Labour predecessor as commissioner had been a member of Rotherham council during the time of the child grooming and abuse. In the face of growing public anger, he was compelled to resign. The party chose me, an Anglican priest, to be its candidate in the subsequent by-election, which Labour was not expected to win. But I did win and eventually completed two more terms before retiring in 2024.

The idea of a directly elected PCC overseeing the work of the police in each force area was first proposed in the Conservative manifesto for 2010. Theresa May, as home secretary, guided the legislation through Parliament and the first PCCs were elected in 2012. Their role was to ensure that the local force was run effectively and efficiently, and to hold them to account. They appointed, and if necessary, suspended or dismissed the chief constable, though the chief constable retained operational independence.

The scandals in South Yorkshire did not end with the Jay Report. In 2014–2016, fresh inquests were held into the deaths of Liverpool football supporters at the Hillsborough football ground in Sheffield in

1. Jay et al., "Report of the Independent Inquiry."

1989. The first inquest in 1991 had declared the deaths "accidental," but following a long campaign by the bereaved families, new inquests were ordered and South Yorkshire police were found responsible.[2] The officer in charge had ordered a gate to be opened at the Leppings Lane end of the ground to relieve pressure from supporters trying to get in, and when they then poured into the overcrowded pens immediately ahead, many were crushed. Ninety-six people died.[3] (A ninety-seventh victim died of his injuries some years later.) It was also clear that in the aftermath of the disaster, the police had fed the media false stories about the behavior of fans in order to deflect attention from their own. The new verdicts led to calls in the House of Commons for South Yorkshire police to be disbanded. Andy Burnham MP, the shadow home secretary, said that in terms of its leadership and culture, the force was "rotten to the core." In addition, later in the year, Her Majesty's inspectorate of constabulary, having previously rated the force as "good," now found it "required improvement" and sent it into "special measures."[4] Unsurprisingly, public trust and confidence in South Yorkshire police sank further, as did police morale.

South Yorkshire was also where the Miners' Strike of 1984–1985 began and where, at the Orgreave Coking Plant, one of the most significant events of the strike took place. This was a violent confrontation between police and striking miners in which both officers and miners were injured. Miners were arrested and charged with serious offenses. At the time, the police defended their actions but subsequently had to pay £425,000 in compensation to thirty-nine miners for wrongful arrest and malicious prosecution.[5] An investigation by the Independent Police Complaints Commission published in 2015 reached damning conclusions: there had been excessive police violence, officers had committed perjury, and senior officers had attempted to cover this up.[6] The

2. A comprehensive summary of all matter relating to the Hillsborough disaster can be found in Hillsborough Independent Panel, "Report."

3. Hillsborough Independent Panel, "Report."

4. Investigations by His Majesty's Inspectorate of Constabulary and Fire and Rescue Services by year and force can be found on the website: hmicfrs.justiceinspectorates. gov.uk.

5. Hillsborough Independent Panel, "Report"; an account of the actions at Orgreave and subsequently, from the miners' perspective, can be found on the Orgreave Truth and Justice Campaign website: otjc.org.uk.

6. Reports from the Independent Office for Police Conduct can be found on their website: www.policeconduct.gov.uk/ourwork/investigations.

Orgreave Truth and Justice Campaign lobbied politicians assiduously and the Labour Party committed to hold a public enquiry. Memories of these events run deep in South Yorkshire's former mining communities, and whenever confidence in the police becomes an issue, they quickly come to the surface again.

So, for much of my first few years as commissioner, I had to pay considerable attention to two elements of my role: holding the force to account and engaging with local communities.

Holding the force to account meant ensuring, as far as I could, that the police understood and accepted the mistakes of the past while, at the same time, supporting their determination to improve going forward. I appointed a new chief constable, Stephen Watson, whom I believed understood what had to be done and also appreciated the fragility of public trust that had resulted from past mistakes. (He was subsequently appointed by Andy Burnham, now mayor of Greater Manchester, to perform a similar task for police there, and his contribution was recognized in 2025 when he was knighted.) I then committed to speak and listen to as many organizations in South Yorkshire as I could, explaining what had gone wrong in the past and why, and seeking their help in getting things right in the future. The chief constable undertook a similar exercise. Sometimes, I went with police officers so they could hear directly what was said, but sometimes, the groups and organizations asked me to go unaccompanied by police. (This was often the case at first with victims of child sexual abuse.)

I got into a pattern of speaking with several organizations and groups each week. I met with civic bodies: parish councils, town councils, district councils. I spoke to community groups: Tenants' and Residents' Associations (TARAs), Police and Communities Together (PACT) meetings, youth clubs, football and boxing clubs, martial arts groups. I spoke in schools. I visited religious groups in gurdwaras, temples, mosques, and churches where I was welcomed as a priest, a person of faith, as well as the commissioner. I had long conversations with professionals in the public and voluntary sectors: independent sexual violence and domestic violence advisers (ISVAs and IDVAs), therapists and social workers, magistrates and court officials, crown prosecutors and defense barristers, probation and prison officers. And so on. This was a two-way process: listening to what people were telling me about policing and explaining to them what I was learning from the police.

One of the key groups I met with was a victims, survivors, and their families panel, which we had formed. I had been approached soon after becoming commissioner by a young women, who had been groomed as a child in Rotherham, and her father. They offered to help me form a panel of some of the victims of abuse so that we could learn directly from them how the grooming had happened and how the response of the police and local authority had been so woefully inadequate. At first, they had refused to meet with the police directly, but over time, we introduced them to officers who we believed understood how they had to be prepared to hear hard truths and to listen to what the women and family members—parents but also younger sisters—had to say. It is important to say that at this time, there was widespread ignorance among the general public about sexual grooming. The girls involved, regardless of age, were seen as willful young people who "knew no better" and were little more than "child prostitutes." It was these attitudes that professionals, such as the police, had to rid themselves of.

And every week, I met with the chief constable and other officers seeking to relay to them what people were telling me about their various encounters with the police. Given the nature of the mistakes the police had made over the years, these conversations had to be frank and robust, while remaining respectful and supportive.

During this time, I came to realize two things about communication within police forces. First, in hierarchical, command and control organizations like the police, bad news does not travel upwards easily. There are nine ranks between a police constable and a chief constable, and at every level, information that is not good tends to get filtered out when presented to those in more senior ranks. Officers tend to speak about everything in the best possible light or highlight only the good outcomes. The senior command team can be left ignorant of the true state of affairs on the ground, unless they take active steps to overcome this. And there are issues for downward communication as well. Information tends to be decontextualized in busy organizations that want to get on with the job. So, actions are tasked out, but the reasons why they are being tasked can be thinly explained or hardly explained at all. And the complexities of modern policing need officers to understand why they are being asked to perform certain tasks and to modify or adapt in the light of changing circumstances on the ground. This is less about process and procedure—important though that is—and more about the quality of the officers.

Then at the end of 2019, COVID happened, culminating in lockdown. I could no longer keep in touch with people and organizations in person. Gradually, we learned how to conduct business remotely. At the same time, I decided to keep a weekly diary and record some of the interactions I had with individuals and groups, the issues they were raising, and my thoughts on them. A member of my staff suggested I share the diary each week with as many people as possible across the county. Quite soon, we had a substantial readership. When *The Yorkshire Post* began to take some of the items from the diary and publish them as a column on Saturdays, we found we had expatriate Yorkshire readers in every part of the country and other parts of the world! By the time my term came to an end in May 2024, the diary/blog was being read by several thousand people in South Yorkshire and beyond.

So, these selected and abridged diary entries are offered as a small piece of social history: what one PCC and those in the criminal justice system were doing and thinking over this period of time, from March 2020 to May 2024, and as a way of stimulating continuing reflection on matters of policing, politics, and faith. Something to dip in and out of.

Alan Billings

Acknowledgments

While the opinions expressed in these diary entries are mine alone, the observations were made possible as a result of the many conversations I had over four years with people in all parts of South Yorkshire: in the police, in national and local government, in the voluntary sector, in the various parts of the criminal justice system, with chaplains and with members of the public.

I am grateful to Andrew Lockley and Michael Lewis, chairs of the Independent Ethics Panel of South Yorkshire Police; Chris Hartley (Crown Prosecution Service); Luke Shepherd (probation); Mick Mills (prison governor); Richard Caborn (former MP, minister, and supporter of many local young people's clubs); and the Rev. Derek Pamment, Ameena Blake, and Imam Sheikh Mohammad Ismail (police chaplains), for the many and varied dialogues we had.

I owe a particular debt of gratitude, however, to those who worked with me in the Office of the Police and Crime Commissioner (OPCC) and the Violence Reduction Unit (VRU). These include Michelle Buttery, chief executive of the OPCC, and Rachel Staniforth and Graham Jones, successive heads of the VRU. But also, Sophie Abbott, Erika Redfearn, Linda Mayhew, Marie Carroll, Cheryl Wynn, Sally Parkin, Julie Morley, Kathryn Whittington, Efe Eruero, Robert Jemilianowicz, Karl Robins, Stephanie Humphrey, Sarah Wood, Lydia Kaighin, Kelly Lycett, Andrea Chipchase, Charlotte Smith, Chantelle Allison, Hayley Marshall, Naomi Muchiti, Paige Shaw, Angela Greenwood, Jessica Adams, Mike Parker, Rachel Fletcher, Nancy Byrne, Albina Burdukovskaya, Ian Bailey, and Dave Cowley, all of whom had extensive contacts in policing and the justice system.

I am especially grateful to those who traveled with me to public meetings, not least the livelier ones, and those who ensured the weekly entries were completed on time: Fiona Topliss, Gemma Hyland, Katie Dearnley, Tracy Webster, Mel Staples, Fay Mills, June Renwick, and Sue Gladwin. I thank those like Kevin Wright, Sharon Baldwin, Alex Heeley, and Josh Keeling, who discussed ideas with me at water cooler moments, though they may not always have realized it. And I owe special debts to Neepa Bandyopadhyay at the VRU, Deborah Hall, and my two PAs, Linsey Jordan and Vanessa Rodgers, who always maintained calm amid the storms.

Diary for 2020 (March to December)

Life During the Pandemic

The First Lockdown

"From this evening, I must give the British people a very simple instruction—you must stay at home." —Boris Johnson, Prime Minister, March 23, 2020

April 20, 2020

Working from Home

As a result of the COVID-19 crisis, I am having to work from home, and so I am unable to visit all those different groups across South Yorkshire that I would normally meet. They include parish and town councils, tenants and residents groups, youth organizations, community associations, and so on. This is a great loss because this is how I learn about how the police are doing on the ground in communities. I have been able to continue almost all my regular committees and boards by conference call. These have included the Public Accountability Board, where I ask questions of the chief constable and senior officers about how the force is dealing with COVID; and where I receive reports from the South Yorkshire Violence Reduction Unit. There have been some gains in this: we have saved a lot of travel time and reduced our carbon footprint!

Responding to the Emergency

The police have responded now to two emergencies in short order: the floods before Christmas 2019 and now the coronavirus. In both, they have received praise from the public. My job is not, of course, to take operational decisions—that is for the chief constable. But it is to ensure that they retain public trust and confidence in what they do and the way they do it. In the present situation, they are asked to make sure that people follow the rules around staying at home and keeping social distance (six feet). They have done this by seeking first to persuade people and only taking enforcement action (such as fines) as a last resort. Where an individual officer has been a little overzealous, the force has apologized and learnt from it. My view is that with this emergency legislation, we are all feeling our way and there may be the odd misstep. We are all learning and that requires a degree of understanding on all our parts.

The force has a Gold group meeting regularly, chaired by an assistant chief constable, to manage the crisis. It gathers all the information needed and makes strategic decisions. It has to be very fleet of foot because the situation moves on so rapidly. It must also think ahead: what will happen as we move out of the lockdown? And it must be aware of the impact the disease is having on the health and well-being of the force as well. There are many officers and staff in very exposed or vulnerable situations. I have told the chief constable that the force must have whatever resources it needs to protect and keep safe police officers and staff.

The Emergency Legislation

The police have been given extraordinary and wide-ranging powers for a period of time to help the country combat the spread of the virus. I am satisfied that so far, they have used these in an appropriate and proportionate way, and as a result, the public support them. The force knows that these powers will lapse and "normal" policing will resume. When that happens, they need the confidence of the public to be there still.

April 2020

Letter to Chairmen of Mosques throughout South Yorkshire

Observing Ramadan in the Present Emergency

Dear Friends,

The holy month of Ramadan will soon begin. I know how important this is for you and your families. It is a time when you can deepen your faith and draw closer to God through prayer, fasting, and acts of charity. In normal times, you would also spend time in the mosque with fellow believers, hear verses from the Holy Qur'an, and do good in the community.

But these are not normal times. This year, we have been afflicted with a terrible disease, COVID-19. This is a worldwide pandemic, but the nations of the world are not at the same stage in the progress of the disease. Some are beginning to emerge from lockdown. But we have yet to face the peak of its impact in this country, which is expected to happen in the coming weeks.

If we are to overcome the disease with fewer people becoming ill and fewer dying, we need to observe the emergency measures the government has announced, especially in this next period of time. Those measures, as you know, are to stay at home except for getting food, medicines, and a little exercise, and for traveling to jobs that cannot be done from home. If we are out in public, we should keep two meters (six feet) from other people and never gather in non-family groups.

The job of the police is to ensure that we all do this and they may stop us and remind us of these measures if we are out in a public place. They will always seek to get us to cooperate freely; but if not, they will enforce the law. They can fine and arrest.

So, I write to you before Ramadan begins to ask you, this year, to observe Ramadan at home rather than by visiting the mosque—something that the Jewish and Christian communities have already had to do with Passover and Easter. This would be an act of charity for the sake of the health and well-being of the whole community.

When the crisis has passed, we can return again to our places of worship and give thanks to God for all his blessings to us.

Thank you for receiving this letter. I wish you a happy and blessed Ramadan.

Dr. Alan Billings
Police and Crime Commissioner for South Yorkshire

April 27, 2020

Share the Thinking

The science of pandemics is (like economics) all about modeling, and that depends on the data you have and the assumptions you make. We have little data around coronavirus because we have not been testing; so, we don't know how many in the population have had it or have got it, and we have to make assumptions about the rate of spread, which may or may not be true. Deciding when and how to come out of lockdown, therefore, can't be based on the science in the sense that there can only be one answer. Scientists will have different views and the final decision will have to be political. All the more reason, therefore, that the government share their thinking with us, like grown-ups. As I was told when I did my O Level GCE mathematics: always show your workings.

Corona

Incidentally, and coincidentally, St. Corona is the patron saint guarding against epidemics. She is commemorated on May 4, which may be around the peak of the pandemic in this country.

The Criminal Justice System

Last week, I took part in a conference call with other PCCs and the policing minister, during which a senior Home Office analyst gave us a summary of what had happened to police-recorded crime nationally during the first four weeks of the lockdown. Unsurprisingly, crime has fallen dramatically, especially acquisitive crimes such as house burglaries. This has been reflected in South Yorkshire, too. More surprisingly, the Home Office has no evidence of domestic abuse rising by much either, though some PCCs tend to think that this may not be revealed until the lockdown is over. All the more reason to welcome South Yorkshire police developing a new way for victims of abuse being able to contact them surreptitiously online through mobile phone, tablet, or laptop.

Attacks on Mobile Phone Masts

While everyone else in the crime and policing world is trying to base what they do on science and evidence, there are one or two people on social media who ignore the science altogether. They include those who think COVID-19 is spread via signals from mobile phone masts. There have been fifty-three attacks on masts, mainly in the North West and North East. One person has now been arrested in the West Midlands. Fear of the virus seems to affect some people as much as the disease itself.

May 4, 2020

Mental Health and COVID-19

There is nothing good about coronavirus. It has made some people very ill. It has caused many premature deaths. It has led to some people having to work incredibly long hours caring for the sick while causing others to lose their businesses and their jobs. It has brought worry to us all. As I write this, I am listening to someone on the radio talking about the impact this is having on people's mental health and well-being, especially where people are cooped up in a small flat or apartment. I don't doubt for one minute that this is so and can be very serious for some people. But there can be another side to this—for some.

My younger son is a case in point. He lives in a village near Winchester with his partner and three little children. His normal day would be this: he gets up at 5:00 am (while the family are asleep), cycles to a train station a few miles away, catches a commuter train into London (standing room only), then a couple of stops on the underground, and a short walk to his office. He does this in reverse in the evening, arriving home around 8 o'clock and just in time to say good night to the children. But for the last five weeks, he has had to work from home. As a result, he has been able to have all meals with the family, he has played with the children for part of the day and read them a story at bedtime. So, for him and his family, COVID-19 has perversely led to a big improvement in mental well-being. But it has also raised serious questions about the kind of life he will be going back to.

May 11, 2020

The Four Cs of Policing

I have evolved a theory of policing and reduced it to four Cs, each of which is challenged in present circumstances.

1. Policing is consensual.

Everyone agrees that British policing is grounded in Sir Robert Peel's principle of policing by consent. This works as long as what the police do is broadly what people expect and want and is what the law says. So far, people have been supportive of the lockdown and what the police have been asked to uphold. In fact, public opinion wanted these steps taken earlier and, if our emails are anything to go by, they wanted them more heavily enforced. People were emailing to tell us about their lax or willful neighbors who needed police attention! Far fewer have complained about police heavy-handedness. At the moment.

But the police have been in a potentially difficult place in that the government's guidance (heavily publicized) was stricter than the legislation itself. The public probably did not distinguish between guidance and law; but the police have to. If forces enforced the guidance of ministers rather than the legislation passed by parliament, they could find themselves challenging lawful behavior and that would undermine their legitimacy. One of the Peelian principles touches on this:

> To seek and preserve public favour, not by pandering to public opinion, but by constantly demonstrating absolutely impartial service to law, in complete independence of policy.[1]

There is a danger if forces appear to be too willing to do the bidding of ministers (or public opinion), however grave the emergency. Also, there may come a point where lockdown fatigue combines with mixed or confusing messages from the government around relaxation of the guidelines, to make consensual policing far more difficult. After all, the emergency legislation has turned normal social behavior into (potentially criminal) anti-social behavior. And no government in a democratic state can sustain that indefinitely. This is another way of saying that policing by consent also assumes that we have government by consent. In the present

---

1. Law Enforcement Action Partnership, "Sir Robert Peel's Policing Principles," no. 5.

climate, that requires the government to take us with them in their thinking by sharing it with us.

2. Policing is contextual.

What the police can do and how they do it will vary to some extent from place to place. This is one reason for having neighborhood teams, so that they can get to know their patch and its different communities. Whether we like it or not, policing in Hexthorpe is one thing, and policing in Wickersley is another. (This is why engagement and education in Page Hall, Sheffield, has involved asking for help from a Roma-speaking university student. He can explain to people, whose traditional recreation in the evening is to gather in the street, why this was not allowed during the epidemic. Without this, the police might have been tempted to embark straightway on enforcement.)

Or again, among one social group or demographic, the police may be seen as on your side, whereas with another, trust has to be won over time and with a settled presence of approachable officers. Nothing disrupts a neighborhood team more than constant change of personnel. Yet, there are many good reasons for moving officers around. Getting this balance right is challenging.

I believe this approach is right, yet it is not without its dangers and needs constant explanation and assessment. There will be some areas and people who will question the approach as building in unequal (and so, unfair) treatment and use of resources. And context is wider than the local. One aspect of the lockdown may be that more crime is going online, including traditional street-based crimes, such as drug dealing.

3. Policing is contingent.

This is not always understood, but what police can do and what they have to do, and how they do it, is affected all the time by things that lie outside their control. So, to take big and obvious examples, from 2010, we had almost ten years of austerity. Each year, the resources shrank. This required adjustments and changes. Most of this was done incrementally, because it had to be. It was salami slicing rather than working to a plan with an end point, because no one was able to predict how long the year-on-year cuts in funding would go on for. If you had been able to do this, you could have planned for a different (smaller and more focused force) accordingly. Then, almost out of the blue, austerity was reversed and there was a promise of increased resources. And absolutely out of the blue, we had the floods and then COVID-19. As far as COVID-19 goes, we cannot predict the end result: what will happen, for example, to both the economy and, as a result, the criminal economy as a consequence.

This also suggests that if a force is not to be caught out by those events and changes that can sometimes be foreseen, at least in part, they need the courage to try and anticipate them. Sometimes, that means making difficult choices, where to put resources, for example; and sometimes, it may mean taking what turn out to be missteps and learning from them. So, you need a police force that is dynamic, always looking around and thinking ahead.

   4. Policing is communicating.

My final C, which brings everything together, is communication. This has already run like a silver thread through all of the above. But if the force is to retain confidence in itself and the confidence of the public, it must be clear about what it's seeking to do and be able to communicate that both internally and externally to partner agencies and the public. If the police do not communicate, they leave a vacuum that will be filled by the speculation of others.

   That's my theory. Policing is consensual, contextual, contingent, and communicating. You have to be good at them all because they are all interlinked.

May 18, 2020

VE Day and COVID-19

A couple of weeks ago, we were commemorating the seventy-fifth anniversary of VE Day in that strange muted way that COVID-19 has driven us to. We probably didn't appreciate the irony of it at the time. We overcame Nazism so that we could keep all our democratic freedoms: to hold elections, to gather and assemble, to worship in our own way, to be able to criticise the government in the press without being censored. Yet, most of these freedoms, and more, we surrendered at the behest of government with hardly a squeak: the local and PCC elections were just suspended; we were forbidden to gather; churches, synagogues, temples, and mosques were closed; we were required to work from home; travel was restricted; and so on. Only the free press remained, though its survival is now threatened: they have less to report because little is happening, and there are no advertisements for non-events. In fact, they seem to survive only because the government chooses to place so many notices with them on a daily basis. Strange times indeed.

Joining the Dance

A visitor from Mars observing the social customs of people today would draw some pretty strange conclusions. If, for instance, the Martian were to stand on the balcony of my flat, she would overlook a playing field and some pathways. During the day and evening, she would see dozens of people walking on the paths and enacting a strange ritual. They walk towards one another but then step to one side, at quite a distance. Everyone smiles, some bow politely, but few talk. It's like watching a dance. I call it the choreography of COVID and we have all learned it. The question is, will we unlearn it? Or will the dance go on?

May 25, 2020

There's Science and Science

The government has been at pains all along to insist that decisions to overcome COVID-19, such as social distancing, lockdown, and so on, are based on the *science*. This is why, at the daily briefings, a minister is always flanked by medical and scientific advisers: it gives the appearance that the political decisions were not really political at all; they were what the science dictated. But the longer the crisis has gone on, the more we have come to realize two things about this decision-making based on the science.

The first is that the science in question is a mix of medical knowledge and modeling. There is the science of the virus itself, what the people in laboratories with petri dishes and microscopes are discovering—an exact science, we might say. But what the government is also calling science is something very different. This science is less like medicine and more like economics. Economists seek to model how economies will behave if particular policy decisions are taken; but this is not an exact science. We all know that different economists can use the same data and come up with different recommendations for policy. Only time will tell whether or not their calculations were right.

Policy decisions may rely on modeling but they are not dictated by it. The decisions of the policymaker take into account what the different views of the experts are, but in the final analysis, the policy decisions are theirs. Advisers advise, ministers decide. Every decision taken around what we should do because of this virus has been political in this way. This is no criticism of decision-makers. It's what we elect them to do. They have to make decisions because science cannot do it for you.

This brings me to the second point. If what I have said above is true, and if this virus is new and unique, then no one could have been absolutely certain about everything that needed to be done to keep us safe. When we start to come out of lockdown, the same will be just as true. And since we are not let into the conversations the different kinds of scientists are having with the ministers, we have to rely on what the ministers tell us. The entire strategy of the government needs us to trust them. If we trust them, we will obey the rules they ask us to follow. (Though we do need to see them obeying the same rules.) We have to trust their judgment, their competency.

Trust and Confidence

But something has now happened to damage trust and confidence. When the government decided to allow patients in hospitals to be transferred to care homes, they said testing was not necessary. We now know that was wrong. Some brought the virus with them from the hospital. As a result, no sector of the population has suffered more than elderly residents in care homes and those who look after them. If this decision were based on the science, then the science was an unreliable guide. Common sense alone would have got you to a better conclusion. So this has caused doubts in the public mind around competency, and that has damaged trust and confidence in both experts and ministers. Trust and confidence is something the police understand very well. A police force knows better than many organizations that once public trust and confidence starts to slip, it takes a supreme effort to get it back.

June 1, 2020

The Time of Trust

The issue of trust applies to government as much as police. We all want the government to succeed. We all need the government to succeed, especially in the next phase of the gradual relaxation of the restrictions. They have to keep our trust and confidence, but that has had a battering this past week or so. This is the real tragedy of the Dominic Cummings affair. (Dominic Cummings was the prime minister's senior adviser. He drove from London to Durham and then to Barnard Castle on May 26 during the lockdown, and subsequently tried to justify it. I was telephoned by a *Daily Mirror* journalist who wanted to know whether our police knew he was passing through South Yorkshire.) How differently that could have been handled. It could have been a moment for saying: "We got this wrong. Whatever the law said, these were journeys that should not have been made." That would have strengthened trust.

And trust is now at a premium because many are anxious about what happens next. Parents with children who will be going back to school are anxious. Those who will be returning to work are anxious. Those with underlying health conditions are anxious. And we in the north are anxious because we do not seem to be at the same stage as London and the south: we fear a second wave if we move too quickly.

So we look for clarity around what is and is not permitted. We, the public, need that, and so do the police if they are to continue to act in a measured way and, in turn, retain trust.

June 8, 2020

David Blunkett Is Right. And Yet.

I think the argument of the former home secretary, David Blunkett, was broadly correct when he wrote in the *Daily Mail* that police officers should not make their personal views known when policing demonstrations.[2] The job of the police is to enable peaceful protests to take place and to maintain law and order, whoever is demonstrating and whatever they are demonstrating about. As they do so, they must lay aside any personal views they may have, political, religious, whatever. It is not for them when on duty to take sides or express preferences. This is the role

2. Blunkett, "Why I Am So Uneasy."

of a police force in a democracy and one of the things that marks us off from totalitarian states.

So, I see the logic of saying that police officers should not have bent the knee and shown solidarity with the protestors last week. But on this occasion, I think we should be more relaxed. This was a simple and spontaneous expression of humanity in the face of a terrible wrong, a moving signal to the surrounding crowd that these police officers were also shaken by what had happened in Minneapolis and did not want to see that behavior here.

If only German police officers had done something similar in 1930s Germany before Nazism took root.

June 16, 2020

What They Did in the Seventeenth Century and What We Don't Do Now

As a former vicar, I have been dismayed that the bishops gave in to the politicians and ordered churches to be closed during this time when, arguably, places of worship could have been made places of sanctuary and consolation for some distressed people. I was even more dismayed that clergy were prevented from visiting their flock. The *Book of Common Prayer (1662)* has this rubric for the priest taking the sacrament to the sick:

> In the time of the Plague, Sweat, or such other like contagious times of sickness or diseases, when none of the Parish or neighbours can be gotten to communicate with the sick in their houses, for fear of infection, upon special request of the diseased, the Minister may only communicate with him.[3]

Times have changed, along, it seems, with job descriptions.

June 23, 2020

Statue Toppling: A Footnote

I used to live in Bristol, not far from the statue of Edward Colston (1636–1721), the slave trader, which was unceremoniously dumped into the river by Black Lives Matter protestors a week or two ago. Everyone in Bristol knew about Colston, how he made his fortune, and what he did

3. *Book of Common Prayer (1662)*, "Communion of the Sick," 5th rubric.

with some of the money. His name is everywhere: Colston Street, Colston Avenue, Colston Hall, Colston School, Colston's Almshouses. Bristolians passing his statue would all know where the money came from as well as his charitable bequests. And, knowing this, they would read what it says on his plinth about his generosity with a wry smile.

But there is another statue in Bristol that also commemorates a figure from the days of empire: Ram Mohan Roy (1772 1835). This is in a very prominent place on College Green. Roy was an Indian, ultimately, a subject of the crown in British India. He is remembered because he was a vocal and early advocate of empirical science and various liberal reforms. He argued for freedom of speech and religion, he condemned the caste system and the practice of suttee (burning widows when their husbands died). He is known as the "Father of India" and is commemorated in Bristol because he was welcomed there when he came to Britain. He is, in fact, buried there and has an impressive mausoleum.

Now that Colston has been toppled, we are left with this extraordinary paradox. The statue that reminded people in Bristol of the shame of empire has gone, leaving the statue that reminds us of the emergence of liberal values in India. If we are not careful, our urban iconoclasm will leave us with false memories as we keep the bits of the past of which we approve and airbrush out the criminal record.

Ah, the law of unintended consequences.

June 30, 2020

Disruptions and Working Practices

Coronavirus has disrupted everything. Public bodies of all kinds have had to adapt rapidly to the new circumstances caused by the spread of COVID-19. Some changes will be reversed as soon as it is safe to do so, but others may remain in some form. The crisis has made everyone look again at working practices.

The courts are a case in point. There were no jury trials in South Yorkshire between the end of March and the end of June. This is because social distancing made it almost impossible to hold a trial in the existing Crown Court. The building has had to be adapted by using more court rooms, two or three, for each trial. It's not just the court room itself. An assembly room is needed that can accommodate enough potential jurors, two meters apart, from which twelve can be drawn for a trial. When the trial gets under way, the twelve jury members will need to be seated two meters apart while they hear the case and two meters apart in the jury room as they deliberate. There have to be ways of ensuring social distancing when people move around the court building, hygiene and distancing when they go to the toilets, and so on. The more defendants there are, the more barristers, the trickier it all becomes.

But some changes have proved interesting. Solicitors now speak to their clients in the custody suites by phone. Some remand hearings have been held remotely, using video links to custody suites. The judges and court administrators, like all of us, as they think about the changes that have been forced upon them, will also be thinking about which of them could become permanent features.

Last week, the recorder of Sheffield, HHJ Jeremy Richardson QC, spoke (remotely, of course) to the Local Criminal Justice Board, which I chair. (This brings together representatives of the Crown Prosecution Service, the courts, the police, probation, prisons, youth offending teams, and so on.) He talked about some of these changes. But he ended by saying how more remote working is making us all very tired. And it is true.

The normal working day is broken up in all sorts of ways, small and large. We go to the kitchen to make tea or coffee and have a brief chat with someone as we pass their desk. We leave a building and travel to a meeting elsewhere. But remote working means we fit in more meetings in a day, often back to back or move swiftly from one to another, never leaving the table we use as the office at home. And because we are not seeing each other for those informal and impromptu chats, we send emails, more emails.

The modern technology, emails, that was to save us from so much drudgery, which it does, has nevertheless, with the virus, taken us back to the nineteenth century: we are once again slaves to machines.

Social Care

The police noticed what was happening in care homes very early in the crisis because they were being called out when there were deaths in them. Yet, it seems to have taken a long time before the government acknowledged what was happening: older people were being discharged from hospitals into care homes to make beds available for coronavirus sufferers, but all too often, they were themselves already infected and then infected others.

But we also realized something else. Because the homes were often part of a chain of private care homes, when many deaths occurred at the same time in a home, and as it became impossible to bring new residents in, the businesses became unviable.

This is surely an area where, like the probation service, it really does not make sense to have it operated through the private sector. The business model is not resilient enough when a major crisis of this kind happens. This is not to make an ideological point but simply to say that there are some services that really do need to be provided by the local state in the spirit of public service. In other words, like the NHS.

From July 4, local lockdowns were in force.

July 7, 2020

From Tribal to Consensual Politics

That is the journey the Labour MP Harriet Harman has had to make in order to help victims of domestic abuse. As an opposition MP, she wanted to see new legislation, but that meant working with those whose politics she did not share. Last week, the Domestic Abuse Bill successfully passed through the House of Commons and made its way to the Lords. Once it is law, it will transform the way victims of these horrible crimes are helped. It needed MPs from across the House to work together.

Those of us who are old enough to remember the time when police officers turned away from "domestics" know what an extraordinary journey we have all been on in understanding what this form of abuse is and how it has caused so much suffering, not just for adults trapped in abusive relationships but for so many children as well.

There are times when politics is rightly consensual and not tribal.

Sitting in a Garden

Do people become more creative out of the office than in? Sir Isaac Newton (1642–1727) was forced to leave his office in Cambridge because of bubonic plague and spent more time in his garden in Woolsthorpe, Lincolnshire, watching apples fall. As a result, he worked out his theory of universal gravitation. All our office are currently working from home, so I am expecting great things. But creative thinking is one thing; knowing how it might have application can be quite another. The Incas invented the wheel. But they only used wheels on children's toys. They never grasped their wider potential.

July 20, 2020

Assaults on Officers

Each Monday, I meet with the Senior Command Team and we go through the incidents that have occurred over the previous weekend. It's mainly a list of depressingly familiar crimes, from theft to murder, with some good results being noted as well. But recently, I have found it quite shocking to hear about a growing number of assaults on officers.

At first, this seemed to be COVID-related, with detainees spitting and coughing into officers' faces. But lately, the assaults have become much more physical and aggressive. It is hard to know what this is all about. It may be partly related to the lifting of restrictions and some frustrated people venting their anger against the police. It may be a carryover from the highlighting of incidents in the US where there has been some shocking police conduct. Whatever it is, we need it to stop and that requires the collective effort of all of us. We need to make it clear that this is not how we want our police to be treated. If they fail to live up to the standards of their own calling, that can be dealt with. But attacking police officers (and other emergency service workers) who are simply doing what we ask them to do on our behalf should not be tolerated. This gratuitous violence towards the police has no place in our county.

July 27, 2020

Who Enforces the Law?

I was made to think about this last week when broadcasters and journalists asked me to comment on the new requirements for wearing face masks in shops. Who should ensure that we did it? The story they were pursuing, for which there was very little evidence, was that many people would flout the law and shopkeepers would be forever sending for the police.

The reality is that the law is enforced every day, first of all, by each one of us. We enforce the law by complying with it. If we all took the law into our own hands, any kind of normal life would be impossible. And by complying, we put social pressure on our neighbors to do the same.

But we do have to be convinced that the law makes sense, and sometimes, it takes time for us to accept that. Wearing seat belts in cars is an example. When the law first came in, I recall how scornful some people were: an infringement of my liberty. What is the evidence? Over time, we were convinced, probably because the evidence began to accumulate of how horrific injuries in vehicle collisions could be lessened by wearing a seat belt.

The trouble with face coverings is that there is no time to conduct random control testing, and so, the evidence is not there. What the government is doing, and probably should have been doing before, since they applied the same principle some time ago to traveling on public transport, is taking a precautionary view.

What about day-to-day enforcement in shops? I heard some shopkeepers saying they couldn't be expected to enforce the law; that was for the police. In fact, shopkeepers have been enforcing the law ever since social distancing came in. My local shops have evolved ways of keeping people six feet apart with signs in the widow, restriction on the number of people who come in, and a one-way system. And as far as I can see, this has worked. I can't see why face coverings will be any different. The police only need to be involved if a situation arises where someone creates a major row that the shop can't handle alone. But there is nothing new about that.

So, who enforces the law? We do, in the first instance, by willingly complying, which puts pressure on those around us to do the same. Then, the shopkeepers with clear notices and signage. The police are the last resort. But that is no different from how it always is. What helps is clear and consistent messaging from the government and a greater transparency around what is science and what is precaution.

August 3, 2020

The Real World

As we have come out of lockdown, the police prepare for a second wave or possible spikes in the coronavirus as it becomes clear that we are far from on top of COVID-19. We have seen, since Leicester was suddenly locked down and then Greater Manchester and parts of West Yorkshire, how decisions can be taken at the center with little or no warning. There seems to be some mismatch between national statistics and local ones, such that local public health officials can be taken by surprise as much as the general population. But each new set of restrictions puts the police increasingly at the center if the guidance is confusing or people (or a community) feel they are not fair and begin to resist the measures. And we need to bear in mind that over the coming months and years, there will be increasing numbers of relatively inexperienced officers on the streets trying to enforce the law in this ever-changing landscape. With large-scale unemployment among the young now in prospect, I fear that we may be facing a very bumpy period indeed.

Brexit: Getting Oven-Ready

We have, between now and December, to put in place alternatives to all the protocols and agreements around data sharing and the handling of criminals, suspects, and missing persons that came with membership of the European Union and fell out when we left in January. These made it possible for us to send back people wanted in some other parts of Europe and vice versa, and to exchange information on those suspected of criminal or terrorist activities, missing people, and so on. Whatever replaces all of these might be good, but they will undoubtedly involve more bureaucracy and form-filling. And we all know what can so easily happen when that is the case.

August 10, 2020

Retention as Much as Recruitment

Retention may turn out to be harder than recruitment. This is my guess about the future of the police force. I say this first as a general comment, as the police become an all-graduate profession. Today's police officer will either join the force as a graduate apprentice, working for a degree from a provider university (Sheffield Hallam in South Yorkshire's case) or join with a degree already. This means that the men and women who make up the modern police force will have very marketable and transferable skills, as some already have.

They will be computer literate and very adept with modern technology. They will be skilled in analysis of data and problem solving. They will be confident and competent leaders. Pay and conditions will have to recognize that or people will vote with their feet and leave the organization.

But retention may also be harder than recruitment when it comes to getting a better representation of officers from minority groups, including ethnic minorities. Until new recruits actually become part of an organization, they cannot know for certain that what the organization says about itself is true. So, forces will say they welcome LGBTQ+ people or those from ethnic minorities, but whether people from those groups feel included is a judgment they can only make from the inside.

I know this is something the force wants to get right. As far as ethnic minority officers are concerned, the current position of just under 5 per cent is about half of where the force needs to be. That percentage looks as though it will be exceeded among the recruits coming through. But once they are doing the job, they will need to feel valued and included if working for the police is to feel more like a vocation than a job.

Policing Education Qualifications Framework (PEQF)

Last week, I met (by Skype) with those who are overseeing the move to the all-graduate profession and their proposals to ensure greater diversity and inclusion. Their enthusiasm and commitment to make this work well in South Yorkshire was very encouraging. But I note one thing here, which is important. It has been agreed with Sheffield Hallam University to remove the criterion that candidates will have to have an A level or equivalent qualification to join the course. Relevant experience can also count. If we want to attract those from disadvantaged backgrounds, that may be very important.

Comprehensive Spending Review (CSR)

Last week was very busy! We also had to turn our minds to the CSR. This is an exercise the government does in which it looks ahead over the next three years and sets out the spending parameters for every department of state. This is then the financial envelope that each must stick to.

The CSR task is massive. It is led by the Treasury and each department has to have its detailed spending plans approved. It's very important, therefore, that everything is captured and nothing missed.

Last week, police and crime commissioners had a Skype meeting with Patricia Hayes (director general for Crime Policing and Fire in the Home Office), the senior civil servant who will be making the case for policing to Treasury officials.

Among many other things, we made these points:

- If the government is to remain committed to raising the number of police officers by 20,000, it must also include in the plans provision for 6,500 support staff (people in finance, HR, analysts, call handlers, and so on), otherwise those officers will not be able to do their jobs.

- Provision must be made for pay and pensions and their likely increase over the CSR period (inflation).

- Provision must also be made for income that will be lost from local council tax because the council tax base is being eroded due to the collapse of so many businesses as a result of coronavirus.

- The newly established Violence Reduction Units must be funded over the whole period, since it is a long-term preventative program.

- I made a specifically South Yorkshire observation that we must have help towards the massive legacy costs of civil claims arising from the Hillsborough football disaster and Rotherham CSE cases, and the cost of the National Crime Agency investigations of non-recent CSE in Rotherham.

If these and other matters are not supported in the CSR, then the funding for police budgets will not be enough to cover costs; savings and/or cuts will once again have to be made. The government will, no doubt, make great play of the fact that there are more police officers, but this will have something of a hollow ring to it if the implication is that other parts of the service—police staff—will have to be cut to pay for them.

Ethical Dilemmas of Coronavirus

I have two adult sons. Both said they could never leave the north with the moors, the hills, the dales, the coastal walks. Both work in finance in the City of London and are, or were, daily commuters. They have been working from home since March and realized that now we have the technology for remote videoconferencing as well as the internet, they can work anywhere, and the company does not need big expensive offices in London or any other city. Their companies are thinking about what all this might mean. The idea of working permanently from home with occasional trips to a venue for face to face meetings has its attractions.

One returned to work last week to find virtually no one on his normally packed commuter train and tube. The streets were deserted, the cafes, restaurants, and theaters closed. Yet, if his company is to thrive, they need these enterprises great and small, whose money they handle, to thrive as well. But if his firm and all the others give up their London offices, there will be no more commuting, shopping, eating, and going to the theater. It's a dilemma. The ecology of an economy is subtle and complex. Yet, thousands of individual decisions, taken in isolation, will be made over the coming months that will either strengthen or potentially destroy that balance.

August 17, 2020

Helping Victims of Sexual Assault

Rape is an appalling crime. We want those who are victims to know that if they find the courage to speak to the police, they will be sympathetically treated and find justice. Yet in 2018–2019, while 58,657 allegations of rape were made in this country, only 1,952 successful prosecutions followed. This is a bleak picture. As the chief inspector of the Crown Prosecution Service (CPS) said in a report, "something must be wrong." Indeed. But for victims of rape, this is not just a bleak picture but one that is likely to cause them to think twice before reporting to the police. What victims of this crime need as much as anything is confidence in the system to deliver justice, and these figures do little to instill that confidence. So, what is going wrong?

There is a review underway that, hopefully, will have an answer. Or more likely, a series of answers, since if there was only a single cause, it would surely have been fixed by now. There is no doubt that the years of austerity have had an impact with fewer resources for both police and the CPS. But many women's and victims' groups have also alleged that in 2016, the CPS made a conscious decision not to pursue what they regarded as weak cases in order to boost the number of convictions. A weak case might be one where there was little forensic evidence, and the verdict was going to turn on whether a jury believed the victim or the accused when they give their accounts in court, a subjective judgment rather than one based more on physical or digital evidence. The chief inspector did not think the CPS had told prosecutors to increase the conviction rate by rejecting less certain cases, but it would not be surprising if, at a time when resources were tight, the CPS felt the need to maximize the number of more assured prosecutions and, in the process, became more risk averse. This would not need to be a conscious decision. But changing that mindset, if it exists, would be.

Whatever the reasons for the relatively small number of prosecutions and convictions compared with the number of allegations, as we wait for the review to conclude, I must do what I can to make it as easy as possible for rape victims to get help, and then to support them if they decide at any point to report the assault to the police.

This is why we set up in 2016 the Sexual Assault Referral Centre (SARC) for South Yorkshire at Hackenthorpe Lodge, a former police station in Sheffield that we refurbished. The SARC is as welcoming as any building could be for people who have suffered such a terrible experience as rape. There are two forensic examination rooms, a family room, and areas where people can just sit and talk. And there are sympathetic support workers who will advise victims, explain the criminal justice system, and give them support, should they decide to involve the police and pursue a criminal charge against their abuser. There is also a video link to the courts, which they can use if being in a court building just feet from the person who abused them is likely to cause yet more fear and distress.

There could scarcely be a more traumatic crime than rape. We all have to do everything we can to close that wide gap between allegations and convictions.

The Police During the Lockdown

An important part of my role is to hold the force to account. This doesn't mean constantly finding fault with what they do but ensuring, by asking questions and observing, that what they do is effective and ethical and in line with the priorities in the Police and Crime Plan. This work goes on all the time. But occasionally, something out of the ordinary happens and I need to get reassurance around that: how did the police respond and are there any lessons to be learned? The advent of coronavirus and the enactment by the government of emergency powers to deal with it presented just such a challenge to the force.

So, I asked my Independent Ethics Panel to look back over the period of the lockdown to see how the police had responded. Did they understand the powers they had been given and exercise them correctly and proportionately, including Fixed Penalty Notices (fines)? Did they distinguish between requirements that could be legally enforced and government guidance that was only that: guidance? Above all, did they retain the trust and confidence of the public throughout?

The broad conclusion gave me reassurance: "Our assessment . . . is that the public generally has a high level of trust and confidence in SYP in the COVID-19 context and that there is widespread consent for the manner in which the county is being policed." It could have been very different.

August 24, 2020

Whose Voices Are We Missing?

We had a second meeting with supporters of Black Lives Matter (BLM) last week. (The local Black Lives Matter group had contacted us after the death in the USA of George Floyd. He had died after a police officer in Minneapolis had arrested him and then knelt on his neck when he was on the ground. The officer was subsequently found guilty of murder. BLM wanted to talk about attitudes to race in the South Yorkshire criminal justice system.) Someone from the youth offending service and the deputy chief crown prosecutor attended, all remotely, of course. We spent time discussing criminal justice matters, not least why the disproportionality of black young people worsens the further they go in the criminal justice system, and therefore, the need to prevent them getting into it at a young age in the first place. The prosecutor also had to make it clear that sentencing was not something any of us could directly influence; this was a matter for the judges, who were independent.

But as we talked, I recalled a meeting I had last year with a group of mainly Asian young Muslims who wanted to chat about policing. They were all teenagers; but what was so unusual was that they were all girls. Most of the meetings I am asked to go to are dominated by older (and sometimes younger) males.

As I started to talk about what I thought might be the issues they were concerned with, they stopped me. No, they insisted. This wasn't their agenda. I had been listening to the boys and the men. Their priorities were different. As far as stop and search was concerned, that was a boys issue. They didn't like it if it was done insensitively, but as girls, they were glad if weapons and drugs could be taken off boys and off the streets. Knowing that boys might have blades made them feel unsafe. And also, as one said, "As a Muslim, I don't want boys doing drugs and trying to involve me in it. I'm glad the police are trying to stop it."

They then went on to talk about what did concern them. The issues here ranged from not always feeling safe when traveling on public transport to having racial comments made about them in the street if they wore the hijab. But they all said they would find it hard to talk to the police about it, whether the police were black or white, male or female. And no, they didn't think of the police as a possible career.

We are all trying hard at the moment to hear other voices—voices that may not have been heard as they should have been in the past. Those of ethnic minority teenage girls has to be one of them.

August 31, 2020

She Wanted a Varied Career

From time to time, I hear about things that police officers do that are not quite in the normal line of duty. Recently, I was told about an officer in the Barnsley district who rescued a woman who had wandered by night into a large pond and was soon out of her depth and in trouble. The officer and a colleague answered the call for help. While his colleague guided him with a beam of light from a torch, the officer waded into the water and then swam to the struggling woman. He brought her safely back to the bank, probably saving her life.

I also heard about an officer who had only been in the force for a few months but found herself with a colleague in a house where a woman went into labor. The officer delivered the baby. When I congratulated and thanked her, she told me that she had joined the force because she wanted "a job with a bit of variety"!

We take it for granted that police officers will deliver babies and save people from drowning. This is part of our culture. Not all the world's police forces would look at it that way. Policing is a varied career and no day is ever the same as the next. But to all those new officers now joining, I would say, "Just be careful what you wish for."

Oh, Dear . . .

One of our senior officers told me about a certain police force that issued a document called "Getting it right first time. 6th edition."

September 7, 2020

Anger Management

We seem to be getting more angry as a society. On the odd occasions when I look at comments posted on social media, people often seethe with rage, and even the letter columns in our local newspapers seem to tolerate levels of abuse that I don't remember in the past. From police video footage that I see from time to time, road rage is all too common, as are attacks on emergency service workers (ambulance, fire service, and police); and when police are called to domestic incidents, the anger and levels of violence that is often revealed, both verbal and physical, is shocking. Meanwhile, on the streets, while fighting often featured in the past when the pubs turned out, we are now seeing levels of anger that seem to result in serious violence far more often.

One of the more worrying parts of all this is that many children and young people are being routinely exposed to it and, as a result, are seeing angry behavior as "normal," within the home and in the community. As I write this, we are just beginning to discover how much anger some children witnessed between the adults in their lives during the long period of lockdown. And we know from research how adverse childhood experiences, such as seeing violence in the family or being subjected to angry behavior, have lasting effects. The conclusion is simple: we need to protect children from anger and to steer others away from it. The solutions are going to be far more difficult.

There are some good practices developing. Before the schools closed, South Yorkshire police were ensuring that if they attended incidents of domestic abuse where children were present, the school would be informed at the start of the next school day, so that the children could be supported as necessary. I have also funded charities that help perpetrators change their behavior. Some of this work can be embedded in normal police practice, but some will be dependent on the relevant parts of the voluntary sector being able to continue their work on a long-term basis. But who knows what the future holds for them when so many charities have seen their income collapse these past months.

And perhaps, there is a job for us, too. Don't we all need to ensure that our public conversations remain courteous and civil, recognizing that living together means we can't always get everything we want, and sometimes, compromise is a virtue.

Who Are You Kidding?

One of our local newspapers reported a criminal trial at the Crown Court. The defendant was about to be sentenced for being the go-between who enabled a firearm to be passed from one person to another. His barrister, making a plea in mitigation, said of his client, "He is a father of five children. He is a very caring man outside of his criminality."

"Outside of his criminality," I expect a lot of offenders are, though why being a criminal was thought to be setting a life-enhancing example to the five children was not made clear. So, this is a portmanteau mitigation that can be hawked from trial to trial and applied to offender after offender—and perhaps is, for all I know. Why anyone would think it would ever carry any weight whatsoever with a judge is beyond fathoming.

The offender got a long prison sentence. The barrister was spared.

September 12, 2020

COVID and Cables

My small flat is beginning to resemble a branch of PC World. This is the effect of working from home. As well as the two computers and two printers my wife and I already have for personal use, I now have from the office a laptop, a tablet, another printer, and several miles of cable, all on or around a dining table.

I am not alone in this. When I have video conference calls, I see people at kitchen tables, jammed between the toaster and the coffee machine, or squeezed into lofts with old university trunks and eyeless teddy bears, or in conservatories surrounded by geraniums. Although the technology allows some to display a fake background, such as a Caribbean beach or a clinical looking office, we all know they are actually perched on a stool in the children's bedroom. (With the children making faces behind the camera.)

If working partly from home is to become the new norm for many people, that will affect the sort of houses we build in the future. We shall want an office, like vicarages. That will become as normal as a kitchen. And that will have implications for crime and policing. Such houses will make rich pickings for the determined burglar who just wants some high value, easily carried item like a laptop or tablet. We have been warned.

Permanent Secretary's Visit

Matthew Rycroft, CBE, the permanent secretary at the Home Office (i.e., the top man), visited the Violence Reduction Unit at Shepcote Lane, Sheffield, last Friday. This was quite something, as he has only been in post a matter of months. But the department does seem to think we have a VRU that is beginning to make a mark. He talked to Rachel Staniforth and Superintendent Lee Berry, who lead, and the team. He heard about the work of the Navigator projects.

Navigators work in the A&E Department of the Northern General Hospital and the police custody suite. They meet people who have been involved in a violent incident—such as stabbings—and who, as they lie in a hospital bed or sit and contemplate in a cell, may be helped to realize that they need to turn their lives around, or next time, it might be the mortuary they visit. And some respond.

If they are in custody, this is not an alternative to the justice system, but it can be a reachable or teachable moment. The Navigators act as mentors and stay with the men for as long as it takes, to get them off alcohol or drugs, to get them into training or a job. Just one of the many schemes that form part of the VRU's preventative approach to violence.

From September 14, the "Rule of Six" was in force: people could gather, but no more than six at a time.

September 19, 2020

Heads, Hands, and Hearts

Do you work with your head, hand, or heart? David Goodhart has written a book called just that: *Head, Hand, Heart.* Its subtitle is *The Struggle for Dignity and Status in the 21st Century.*[4] The thesis is that at one time, we thought the future of work lay in preparing as many young people as possible for jobs in the knowledge-based economy (the "Head" in

---

4. Goodhart, *Head, Hand, Heart.*

the title). This was why there was a big push to get more and more into universities at the end of school. These were people who, during the lockdown, found themselves working from home. However, what the lockdown revealed was just how dependent we were on people doing manual jobs ("Hand" in the title) and care jobs ("Heart" in the title). But during the years of university expansion, we stopped valuing these hand and heart occupations, to our cost and, perhaps, shame.

Although Goodhart's analysis is a simplification, I'm sure there is something in it, and we need to reevaluate some of those who worked using their hands and their hearts: the hospital porters and the care workers. They have been undervalued but are actually crucial in any civilized society. They need greater recognition, not least in pay.

When I think about the police force, what I think is happening is that modern policing is having to bring all three together, head, hand, and heart. There was a time when police officers were literally on the streets, pounding the pavements by day and night. It was a very physical occupation. Now, as well as that, we need officers who can problem solve, using their heads, and understand data to make a difference to crime in their patch. But as they come across more vulnerable and frail people, we also need officers who have all the softer skills as well. The modern force is about head, hand and heart.

September 26, 2020

Well, I Never . . .

The judge who rejected the appeal of the drunken Liverpudlian woman, who claimed she had been assaulted because officers had cleaned her up in the custody suite, began the summary of his judgment with words that were as unusual as they were arresting:

> Cheryl Pile brings this appeal to establish the liberty of inebriated English subjects to be allowed to lie undisturbed overnight in their vomit soaked clothing. Of course, such a right, although perhaps of dubious utility, will generally extend to all adults of sound mind who are intoxicated at home. Ms Pile, however, was not at home. She was at a police station in Liverpool having been arrested for the offence of being drunk and disorderly.[5]

There are times, though, when you think the police simply cannot win.

5. Turner, "Ms Cheryl Pile v Chief."

October 5, 2020

Keeping the Rules

"If the Prime Minister can't get it right, what hope have the rest of us got?!" That was how someone put it to me after the last set of local coronavirus restrictions were announced for the North East, and many others have said the same. Mind you, it has not always been easy to keep up with the national rules, as we made the journey from complete lockdown to the "Rule of Six" with various iterations in between. My office had been preparing to return after working from home since the end of March, but all is changed again. Now we are faced with the prospect of a patchwork of local restrictions across the country. No wonder people become confused and fatigued.

One group of people who cannot afford to get this wrong is the police. They have to enforce the law. But they need to do it in a way that does not alienate them from the public they are seeking to serve. This is why the force has followed the four Es approach. They first seek to Engage with people who may not be observing the restrictions, then to Educate and Encourage them to behave correctly, only Enforcing the law if they believe people are being willful and reckless.

So far, this has worked as well as one could hope. The police have, by and large, kept the trust and confidence of the public. But, as I have repeatedly argued, policing by consent in the circumstances of coronavirus crucially depends on governing by consent. People have to be able to trust the government.

There are two situations in which this might change very quickly. First, if local restrictions are imposed in some parts of South Yorkshire and not others, that has the potential to create confusion for the public, not least if people live in one place, work in another, and have family or friends in a third. That will need very careful messaging, and to do that well, all the authorities (councils and police) as well as businesses and schools will need as much warning as possible. Too many of these rule changes have been imposed with little or no advance notice to police or local authorities, and, on at least one occasion, by social media late at night. You need time to get the messaging in place and understood.

Second, the trust and confidence of the public in the police will remain as long as what we are asked to do by government, and what the force is asked to enforce, makes sense to us. If we understand what the overall government strategy is, and how any new rules fit in with that, the public will support the police as they seek to gain compliance.

Yet, this is the area where, at the moment, the government seems to struggle. They tend to make the case only in terms of following the science. But we know that these decisions are not just about the science. They cannot be; science alone cannot tell you what to do. Decisions are made after taking into account a mix of factors: the science around the behavior of the virus; the very different science around how people behave when certain restrictions are imposed; and a judgment about how far you can let the economy suffer for the sake of health needs and vice versa.

What we don't always know is quite how the government is calibrating that difficult balance. What is the science and other calculations that produce the "Rule of Six" and the 10:00 p.m. curfew, for example? We need the government to level with us more as we face fresh outbreaks. Otherwise, asking the police to break into private homes to enforce the rules, if that is where we are heading, may be a step too far.

Prioritizing Domestic Abuse

During the period of lockdown, we were concerned about what was happening to those who had become victims of domestic abuse (DA). How were they faring as a result of being confined to the house with an abusive partner? What about the children? We gave financial help to organizations that support victims and the police took steps to enable victims to make contact surreptitiously through the internet and with silent calls to the emergency number.

Now the Violence Reduction Unit is making the prevention of DA one of its priorities for the present financial year. We are funding groups across South Yorkshire who are working to prevent or reduce abuse in domestic settings. Initially, we made £190,000 available but were overwhelmed with forty applications for grants that came to £760,000. So we have increased the original pot of money to £200,000, and a small panel (that included local authority DA leads) has now awarded grants to thirty projects.

The projects are very diverse, though many have a focus on younger people. In2Change, for example, will seek to change the attitudes of young people who are already showing signs of aggressive behavior that may lead to future negative relationships, including domestic violence. There is funding for a women's refuge to help their work with the children and for a project working with the Roma community in Doncaster to develop children's understanding of what healthy relationships look like.

Domestic abuse lay hidden for decades. We now recognize it as a major issue for our society. The Violence Reduction Unit brings together a wide range of partners to reduce it, not least by seeking to prevent it in the first place.

Surely Not . . .

I am writing this against the backdrop of breaking news about the American president, Donald Trump, having coronavirus. A spokesperson for the president says that he has been taken to the Walter Reed Military Hospital as a precautionary measure.

I may be mistaken, but I thought wearing masks, social distancing, and not holding large public gatherings were the precautionary measures. One hears the sound of stable doors being bolted.

October 12, 2020

The Scourge of Drug Addiction

"Why do you bother?" A man asked me this at the end of a meeting. I had said that I commission services to help people who are addicted to drugs or alcohol break the habit. "Why do you bother?" was more of an exasperated comment than a question. He could see no good reason for doing anything for people who, in his view, simply lacked the will to change their way of life and, in one way or another, sponged off the rest of us. So, why do we bother?

The first response has to be a human or humane one. This is a fellow human being who, for whatever reason, is now in the grip of a powerful addiction and, as a result, is throwing their life away. We want to help them make something of themselves and their lives.

But when that falls on deaf ears and an unmoved heart, I talk about the cost of not helping. In every town and city across South Yorkshire, there will be a few people like this who are well known to the police and other agencies. They call them prolific offenders because, in order to fund their addiction, they will be involved in some form of criminality repeatedly.

Let me briefly set out the costs to all of us of the prolific offender. (We have been looking at a few cases.)

Person A is a drug user. She shoplifts to fund her habit. She has been doing this since childhood. Fining her is a waste of time because she immediately shoplifts again in order to pay the fine. In 2019, she committed forty-four recorded offenses and spent time in prison. In that year, she cost the South Yorkshire taxpayers about £132,000 in quantifiable costs. These included benefits, the cost of courts, custody (about 20 percent of the total), probation, and police, as well as costs to businesses trying to keep themselves secure. She is not without qualifications, but her drug problem means she doesn't hold jobs down. The costs are even higher if you factor in her children who, when young, had to be cared for. Over a lifetime of offending, this totals to something like £2.3 million.

So, in answer to the question, "Why bother?" one answer is, "Because over the next five years, if we can get this person off drugs and into steady work, we will save £662,000 for the public purse." This is why I fund programs to help people break these habits of substance abuse. And we have a happier human being.

Modern Slavery and the Clewer Initiative

We all know that slavery was not abolished in the nineteenth century. It simply took new forms and became less visible. We meet the modern slave unknowingly all the time. Many, though by no means all, are from overseas, trafficked here by organized gangs.

I came across one when I went with police as they broke into a house in Rotherham where cannabis was being cultivated. The gardener (the one tending the plants) had been brought from North Africa by organized criminals. He had no English and traveled on a fake passport and other forged documents. He spent all day and everyday watering the plants and living in squalid conditions in the kitchen. Every other room was full of plants. As far as the gang was concerned, he was expendable.

I don't know what hold the gang had over him. Perhaps he was in debt to them. Perhaps they threatened harm to his African family. He was undoubtedly breaking the law. But he was also a victim, living the most wretched of lives. Others are brought to this country to be domestic servants or for sexual purposes or to eke out their days in warehouses, nail bars, factories, farms, and car washes. We pass them in the street; they are hidden in plain sight.

Some years ago, I was the vice principal of an Oxford theological college where Anglican clergy were trained. Recently, a group of nuns relocated to the college, selling their house in Clewer, near Windsor Castle. Their order had been founded in the nineteenth century to help women leave lives as prostitutes, where they had lost all autonomy and dignity. The sisters wanted the proceeds from the sale of their property of over £1 million to be used for some similar purpose today. The modern forms of slavery seemed an obvious situation to address.

So, the Clewer Initiative was launched and Sheffield Diocese is one of the areas taking it forward. I was pleased to be at the local launch in the cathedral a year or two ago. The Clewer Initiative seeks to raise awareness of modern slavery and support projects that will help people escape safely from miserable lives. But we all recognize that the shackles that bind the modern slave are not visible and not so easy to break apart.

Antislavery Day is kept on October 18.

October 19, 2020

Police Overtime

I worry when I see police overtime increasing, as it is with the coronavirus. Overtime has in part gone up because the police have been asked to do not only their "normal" job but extra duties that come with enforcing the restrictions or covering for colleagues who are unwell or having to self-isolate. This causes me concern for two reasons.

First, there is the impact on the budget. When the COVID crisis first began, Home Office ministers told police and crime commissioners (in our weekly video conferences) to spend all we needed to, and we would be fully reimbursed. As the months have gone by, the ministerial mood has changed and become far more cautious. "We are having robust conversations with colleagues in the Treasury about COVID spending" is the latest. If we are not reimbursed, we shall be overspent by the year end (March 31, 2021), and that is not a good starting point for the next financial year.

But more worrying is what overtime is doing to officers and staff. A little extra in the monthly pay packet is welcome, but the more overtime people work, the more tired and eventually sick a workforce becomes. Tiredness can lead to errors. Absence through sickness puts even greater pressure on those still working. The longer it takes for us to suppress the infection, the more this situation will continue, and that makes me anxious.

Thanks to the Specials

So, a big thank you to the special constables. Specials are people with a day job who have trained and qualified as police officers and who give their time voluntarily each month to work alongside other police colleagues. If they had stepped back from volunteering as a result of the coronavirus, we could quite understand it. But when I look at the monthly activity of the specials, they have done the opposite. In September alone, 126 specials contributed 4,136 hours. They attended 650 incidents, including 30 that were COVID-related. This was an average of 33.3 hours per officer.

That all helps to relieve some of the pressure the force is feeling as a result of COVID, that results in overtime. So, as I say, a big thank you to the specials.

October 26, 2020

Feeding the Children

Marcus Rashford, the footballer, is not someone any politician would want to contradict or disappoint at just this moment. So, by the time you read this, I expect the government will have found a way of feeding hungry children during the school half-term holiday.

But there is also an important point here for those of us concerned with crime and policing. It is a reminder that one effect of the pandemic is to increase disadvantage in our communities as people are laid off, businesses fold, and unemployment rises.

We know that gangs are actively targeting children and young people, seeking to draw them into their criminal activities, particularly moving drugs around county lines. Young people in struggling families, where there is little money, are very vulnerable to the promise of friendship and cash in hand that the gangs offer, which is a type of grooming. Whatever helps to make families more resilient, and their children and young people less vulnerable to the gangs, has to be supported, and that includes ensuring that they have a decent meal each day.

This is why driving down crime cannot be a policing matter alone.

Surely Not

My worried granddaughter asked me what the restrictions were for Santa Claus as he entered South Yorkshire and Tier 3 territory. "If he doesn't wear a mask, will your police officers arrest him?"

Perhaps, I should find out in good time what they have been briefed.

November 2, 2020

Supporting Witnesses During COVID-19

Coronavirus is impacting every aspect of life, including the working of the criminal justice system. I chair the Local Criminal Justice Board and among our many current concerns is that of the witness support scheme.

If a witness fails to show at court, a trial can easily collapse. Even in normal times, witnesses can find the experience daunting, and for many reasons:

- The court buildings are likely to be unfamiliar.
- Some witnesses have to attend very difficult trials—such as child sexual abuse (CSE), murder, or drugs cases.
- In some instances, they may be open to intimidation.
- They may find giving evidence distressing—as when a CSE victim appears as a witness in another CSE trial, where terrible incidents in the past have to be revisited.
- We can now add to that anxieties around coronavirus.

The Witness Service is designed to help witnesses overcome their lack of knowledge of the court system and their anxieties. It's an opt-in service, provided in South Yorkshire by Citizens Advice, giving free, practical help, emotional support, and information so that witnesses are in the best place to give their evidence.

Many of those involved in witness support are volunteers, some 2,700 across the country. They contact the witness before the trial and, if they want it, show them the court. They will keep the witness up to date on timings and progress and meet them on the day of and after the trial.

But COVID-19 has meant the service has had to do many things differently. Much of the support is now online or on the phone. In addition, many of the volunteers are older people, and they have had to think carefully about whether they can do face-to-face work.

Witnesses can fall away and the coronavirus is not helping. It has taken a while for the courts to become COVID secure and some trial dates have been put back. (There was a backlog even before the pandemic.) But we know that the longer witnesses are kept waiting for a trial to start, the greater the chance that they will give up. Even if they do turn up, the longer they have waited, the more they may struggle to remember what happened; and then their evidence looks less reliable. And some witnesses now worry that they will be infected by coming to court.

So, we owe the Witness Service a debt of gratitude for the support they give and the way they have responded in this very trying time of the pandemic.

Whatever Next

I was sent a letter last week by a university business school. It was a wonderful example of how to fail in your marketing. The letter began, "Dear Ms Billings." It then went on to say, "Have you ever considered taking your career as Police and Crime Commissioner to the next level?"

I can't say I have.

The second national lockdown came into force on November 5.

November 27, 2020

Restorative Justice

Last week, I met (by video call) several victims of crime, some direct victims and others indirect. The direct victims included someone who had been burgled and someone who had been abused within the family since the age of twelve. The indirect victim was someone whose brother had been murdered. But whether direct or indirect, all had suffered and all had been helped by restorative justice (RJ). As one put it, "I have got my life back again."

All these stories were told to me in short fifteen-minute interviews as part of a week of activity raising awareness about restorative justice. In South Yorkshire, I commission the organization Remedi to run the RJ service for us.

The woman whose brother had been murdered had come forward to ask for RJ twenty-four years after the murder. She wanted to confront her brother's killer directly. She was a deeply thoughtful person. I asked her why it had taken so long for her to want this. She said it would have been impossible to do this before because she had been close to her brother and remained so very angry for so long. She would have got nothing from any earlier encounter because her rage would have got in the way.

But now, she was ready. She met the offender in the prison where he is serving his long sentence. For two hours, she was able to ask all the questions that had been troubling her for so long—Why my brother? Why so brutal? And in turn, he was left in no doubt about the impact this had had on her life down the years.

"Did it help you?" I asked. Again, she was so thoughtful. Yes, she had her questions answered up to a point, though she knew full well that he might be lying; he would likely have an eye to parole hearings. But the main thing was that the shadow that had sat on her shoulder all those years and had always been present when she thought about her brother had lifted, and meeting the murderer, as he now is "older and balder," made her realize he had no control over any part of her life any more.

A second set of interviews was with a prolific burglar and then one of his victims in Rotherham District.

The burglar had been involved in criminality since he was a boy. He had been in and out of prison countless times. But one day, he realized that unless he did something radical, the rest of his life would be a repetition of what had gone before. He described his life as a dark world in which he was lost in drugs. His probation officer put him in touch with Remedi, and through them, he met one of his victims who, he said, "saved my life."

She also told me her story. She was a deeply thoughtful and compassionate person who was willing to listen to what the man who burgled her house had to say about his crime against her. In turn, she told him what the burglary had done to her and the effect on her of losing items of small monetary value but considerable sentimental value, such as the loss of photographs of her late mother. He had been deeply moved by this. "I broke up," he said.

I was very impressed and moved by the victim. Remarkably, she took the view that if she could help turn this person's life around, even though he had caused her grief, she should do it. Thinking about his life and hers, she said, "I've been lucky in life." She ended by quoting Vivian

Greene: "Life isn't about waiting for the storm to pass. It is about learning to dance in the rain."[6]

People sometimes say to me that PCCs should spend every penny on policing. Most pennies are, of course. But the PCC role is about crime as well as police and that includes the victims of crime. Restorative justice is not an alternative to the criminal justice system. Criminals have to serve their sentences. But RJ offers a way of bringing some satisfaction or healing to the lives of those who have been distressed by criminal acts perpetrated against them. It can also lead to some criminals turning their lives around, and that, ultimately, will save public money.

All in all, I met some extraordinary ordinary people last week.

December 7, 2020

Police Well-Being

A couple of years ago, I visited the Police Treatment Centre at Harrogate. It offers support and treatment for officers suffering from physical or psychological problems arising from their work. They can be residential. It is very well-equipped and I had a tour of the hydrotherapy pools, the gyms, treatment rooms, and so on. It is, however, a charity, and I had given them some funding.

What I found most interesting was an observation by the chief executive. He said that there was a definite shift in recent years towards treating those with emotional and psychological issues. Even when officers had come in for help with physical strains and stresses, emotional matters often presented as physical, and the charity was investing increasingly in building up its counseling capacity.

These are some of the realities of modern policing and the dominant theme of 2020, the coronavirus, will not have helped.

December 14, 2020

The Virus, Crime, and Borders

Organized criminality and the coronavirus have this in common: they bring misery to individuals and communities and they pay no regard to boundaries or borders. This is why, as far as the virus is concerned,

---

6. Aminlogic, "My Quote Review."

our whoops of joy at being the first country to secure the vaccine will be short lived if the immunity it gives is very time limited and if other parts of the world are not able to secure their citizens against the disease as well. International travel and trade requires global and not just local solutions. We are in this together.

Similarly with crime. Whatever measures we take here, unless we can work successfully across borders, we can still be impacted by criminals operating elsewhere. This is why I have to keep asking the chief constable what the police have in place, nationally and locally, for when we exit the European union on December 31st.

Fortunately, the police and security services have been planning for this, as far as they can, because the situation was going to be like this, deal or no deal. The National Police Chiefs' Council established the International Crime Coordination Centre (ICCC) to find alternative solutions, which they have largely done. But the alternatives are more cumbersome, more manual, more time-consuming, less automated, and therefore less real-time. As a result, forces will have to be far more proactive; and therein lies the risk. This is why I need reassurance that the force's Gold Group understands what will have to happen from the New Year.

The virus and the criminal will both exploit any complacency or lack of preparedness, and, crucially, neither recognizes borders.

December 21, 2020

Christmas Message 2020:
Between Hope and Fear

Just over a year ago, I was talking to a police officer who was on duty in the Doncaster District during the floods. He had been standing at the end of a flooded road for some time, directing traffic away. It was getting dark and cold, and he had forgotten his gloves. I had just come from homes that had been made uninhabitable by foul-smelling water. There was little reason to be cheerful. So, I said that we must look forward to something better next year.

Who could have imagined the arrival of COVID-19 and the harm and damage it has done? People have been made very sick. Hospitals have been overwhelmed. Some have died. The emergency services have been stretched. And we are all left a little anxious. The one ray of light in this darkness is the possibility of a vaccine for all during the course of next year. As Christmas approaches, then, we are left suspended between hope and fear.

Although we might not be able to sing Christmas carols in churches or pubs this year, no "Chiming Christmas Bells" (a local Sheffield carol), we should not lose sight of the Christmas message, which is shared by people of every faith and none: the importance for our lives of love within families and between neighbors. If anything, we have seen this strengthened during the weeks of the pandemic. We have learned to value again the things that really matter to us, which the Christmas story epitomizes.

And as we celebrate Christmas in a more subdued way, perhaps we can also remember for a moment those who will be working over this period to keep us safe, not only the men and women in the NHS but also those working in the emergency services: Yorkshire Ambulance, South Yorkshire Fire and Rescue Service, and South Yorkshire Police. It would be a wonderful Christmas if none of those in these services had to be called out over the festive season. If, for instance, none of them had to attend a road traffic collision because someone decided to have a drink, get into a car, and drive home while none of us stopped them.

So, while this won't be a normal Christmas, let's make it a happy one nevertheless, for ourselves, our families and friends, and also for those who will be working as well. This year, more than ever, we need a bit of cheer.

So, That's Alright Then

One of my granddaughters, just aged nine, cheered me up. She said she thought her presents would get through alright at Christmas because her parents had assured her that "Santa is in our bubble."

Happy Christmas.

Diary for 2021

A Year of Virus and Violence

The third national lockdown came into force on January 3.

January 4, 2021

In the Eye of the Storm

We begin the new year in the eye of the perfect storm. A new, more infectious variant of the coronavirus is spreading rapidly across the country, the NHS is in danger of being overwhelmed, the new vaccines are a long way yet from getting us to the point of herd immunity, where 90 percent or more of the population is immune, and we are in lockdown again. Ministers have drawn up a priority order for the vaccine and it is right that those most at risk are vaccinated first. But where should the police figure in this order?

My own view is that we need those on the front line to be protected as soon as possible. I have said this publicly and police and crime commissioners have said it collectively to ministers.

Frontline officers come into contact with the public on a daily basis. Where there is a domestic incident, for example, they may have to enter a house where there may be children as well as adults. When someone is arrested and taken to a custody suite, they and the custody officers will be in close contact while processes are gone through. Officers are sometimes sent out of area to help other forces (mutual aid), places where the virus may be more virulent. In these and many other instances, officers run the risk of contracting the virus and passing it to their colleagues, families, and members of the public. It is not in the public interest to have a police force that is seriously debilitated by illness. We rely on the police not only to maintain law and order but also to be there when emergencies of all kinds arise, and we cannot predict what or when that may be. We need a force that is immune from coronavirus.

January 11, 2021

Recalibrating for 2021

The coronavirus has affected everything, including how criminals have been operating and what the force has to do to meet the different challenges. This, in turn, has meant that I will be recalibrating where my own holding-to-account arrangements will focus between now and the PCC election in May. I will give one example: cyber crime.

We know that lockdowns are likely to accelerate the growth of crime online, not only fraud but also the exploitation of children. The reasons for this are not hard to see. The closures and the restrictions on movement have led to more viewing of the internet by adults and children alike, and this has given the digitally aware criminals their opportunities. But these are issues that cross boundaries and borders, so it is essential that whatever we do locally, we need to know that robust measures are in place both regionally and nationally. We are, in fact, part of a North East seven force cyber collaboration: South, West, and North Yorkshire, Humberside, Durham, Cleveland, and Northumbria.

We also need to know that the force is doing everything it can to support individuals and businesses in protecting themselves from the internet criminals. As far as fraud goes, I have been to too many breakfast meetings where business leaders have admitted to being ignorant about their own company's cyber security arrangements or have confessed that they have not reviewed them for years. I have been to too many presentations at the Lifewise Centre where victims of fraud have told their stories, and we have all winced as we realized that there, but for the grace of God, any one of us might have gone. So increasing our cyber awareness has to be part of the recalibration for 2021.

January 18, 2021

Being Safe and Feeling Safe

When I ask people whether policing should be evidence based, everyone says yes. We all seem to agree that what we ask the police (and partners) to do should have the outcomes we want to see, whether that is deterring crime and antisocial behaviors or bringing criminals to book. We want to know what works. We want to put our money into measures that make a difference and that means we need ways of evaluating the impact that something is having. Likewise, when the government gives us additional funding for, say, tackling serious crime, they want to know what outcomes we will be looking for and how we intend to evaluate them. There is no point in throwing money at activity that has little or no effect. I agree with this, though I am not sure it is always as simple as it sounds.

Take road safety. I had a very interesting conversation last week with a local authority officer who has responsibility for road safety, including advising on traffic calming measures, speed limits, road signs, and the like. His budget is very limited and every change brings a cost: the cost, for instance, of putting up a new speed limit sign and the annual cost of keeping it in good order. So, he has to prioritize; he builds an evidence base. He often starts with the number of accidents there have been along a stretch of road. This makes residents very cross. They say, not unreasonably, "So, we have to have someone killed before we can get the speed limit reduced?" He also knows, again, part of his evidence base, that what slows drivers is not so much a reduced speed limit, for the evidence suggests that makes 1 mph difference, but what drivers see ahead of them. If the road is straight and devoid of hazards, they tend to put their foot down, whatever the signs say. But if they see parked cars ahead, or the start of a more built-up area, or an island in the center of the road, they automatically slow down.

When a request comes from a village or part of a town for a reduced speed limit, he thinks about this evidence for what causes drivers to slow down. He knows that a sign will have minimal effect, even though residents are overwhelmingly in favor of it. In other words, they might feel safer, though there is little or no empirical evidence that says they will be safer. The decision to change a speed limit is often, therefore, a political one, not one that is evidence based.

Or is it? My Police and Crime Plan is quite explicit. It says I want people in South Yorkshire not only to be safe but also to feel safe. There is no reason why measures that help people to feel safe cannot be part of an evidence base. After all, we can measure empirically whether people feel more safe after a speed limit has been reduced from 40 to 30 mph, say, just as much as we can measure how many accidents there have been.

January 25, 2021

Domestic Abuse and Children

There was a time, some years ago now, when domestic abuse (DA) was hardly taken seriously. The authorities, including the police, were reluctant to get involved. "It's only a domestic." Not anymore. So much so that some forces found over Christmas that DA accounted for more than half of all crime.

All abuse starts with the attempt by someone, usually a male, to control others in the household. We tend to think that must involve some form of physical force or violence, but psychological and emotional manipulation can be just as powerful as a means of control. The police in each of our district commands have teams of officers who are specially trained in understanding and dealing with DA and all frontline officers are being given training as well. (This in itself can be quite harrowing.)

Our attention is, rightly, focused on the victims. But who are the victims? We need to think more widely. Officers who answer calls for help realize very well that in many households, there are children. They may not always be the direct recipients of abusive behavior, but they witness what is happening. They hear the shouting and see their mother crying.

In South Yorkshire, we have an important partnership between police and education called Encompass. This allows the police, when they have attended an incident of DA where children have been present, to inform the school before the start of the next school day. Teachers can then look out for the children and give them any support they may need, both that day and subsequently.

I think this is a brilliantly simple way of making an early intervention to safeguard, as far as possible, vulnerable children. What distresses me is the scale of the issue. In 2020, the number of children who were referred through Encompass were 398 in Sheffield, 388 in Doncaster, and 186 in Rotherham. My Police and Crime Plan has protecting vulnerable people as one of the three priorities for South Yorkshire police. I think Encompass is one way in which the police meet that priority.

February 1, 2021

Leadership

Two conversations I have had recently have caused me to think a little about what makes for good leadership. The first was with one of the assistant chief constables, who, for most of the week, had been interviewing candidates for the rank of inspector, one of the key leadership roles in the police service. The second was with Kate Josephs, who has just become the chief executive of Sheffield City Council. I was struck by what she said about leadership as something that radiated out from the person in the leadership position. It impacted those around as well as those above or below in an organization. What also occurred to me as I thought about what she and the assistant chief constable said were two other things.

First, leadership is found at every level of an organization. If we stay with policing, leadership is something that involves a police constable as much as a chief constable. Whatever your rank or position, at some point, your words and actions are going to have impact and influence on others, for better or worse. From the PC who has to deal with a disturbance in the town center on a Friday night, to the senior officer who takes charge of a serious collision on the motorway, all are offering leadership, which made me wonder what the common factor might be in all these leadership roles and leadership moments. What makes for good leadership?

I think a good leader is someone who can see the wood for the trees. When others are distracted or obsessed by some detail, the person who can stand back and take in the situation as a whole, who can appreciate the wider context in which things are taking place, will bring the perspective needed to make the best decisions. This is why the modern police service needs people at every rank who are curious and thoughtful about the world around them, who see the bigger picture, the developing patterns, the wood and not just the trees.

Oh, Dear

In recent weeks, I have attended (remotely) a number of parish council meetings, from Ecclesfield to Braithewell and Micklebring. All the meetings were well chaired: everyone had their chance to speak and all were respectful and good humored, unlike Handforth Parish Council, a recording of whose shouty and disrespectful December meeting went viral on the internet last week. In contrast, in South Yorkshire, the only time I heard a mildly raised voice was when the chair said, "You're on mute.... You're on mute! ... YOU'RE ON MUTE!!"

February, 8 2021

Why Democracy Is Precious and Fragile

Democracy is a fragile thing. So said Joe Biden at his inauguration as president of the United States on January 20. He had particular reason to speak about democracy's fragility because only a few days before, protestors loyal to the former president had stormed the Capitol building and came within a whisker of a successful, if accidental, insurrection.

Security was lax. But at least the few law enforcement officers present seemed clear that their primary duty was not to the man who was trying to hang on as president but to the institutions of the democratic state, which some of his followers were trying to subvert. There are lessons to be learned here.

The new President speaks of bringing people together and healing. This seems a mammoth task. Eighty one million people voted for Joe Biden, the biggest vote in American history, but seventy-four million voted for Donald Trump (51 and 46 percent). Rather like our Brexit vote, which was about much more than Brexit (52 percent for leave and 48 percent for remain). Each nation is left divided.

If you think about that, it means that whatever enables a democracy to hang together, it cannot be shared values. In the west, we live now in countries that are plural and we have to learn to live with difference. In the US, this is what many find difficult: unity for them means a common culture, a common religion, a common set of values, and for some, even a common ethnicity. In the UK, it is why the search for Britishness or British values of a few years ago was doomed to fail: we are plural. When we look back at that period, it seems like another world.

Norman Tebbit thought that to be British was really to be English. It was about the cricket team you supported—England, not Pakistan or India. John Major's suggestion seems even more strange. Britishness was about long shadows on country cricket grounds (what is it about cricket?), warm beer, invincible green suburbs, dog lovers, and pools fillers. Gordon Brown insisted on the need for Britishness but couldn't define it.

These are all potentially dangerous projects. Enforcing shared values is what dictators do. It seems to me that in a plural democracy such as ours and the USA, if we are to hang together, it cannot be through shared or common values. We don't have them, at least not wholly so. We will only hold together if we acquiesce in, what I would call, the ground rules of democracy. This then enables us to live together with our many differences: different values, ethnicities, religions, cultures, political beliefs. But without acquiescing in these ground rules, a plural state descends into chaos. The ground rules of democracy are respect for the rule of law, equality of all before the law, democratically elected government, freedom of speech, assembly and worship, the freedom to live as you would wish, subject only to not interfering with the rights of others, and tolerance and respect for those who differ from us. And the job of law enforcement is to uphold and defend those ground rules.

We see now why democracy is fragile. But also, as the new president said, why it is precious.

Dear Secretary of State . . .

Last week, I wrote a letter, not to the home secretary, but to the secretary of state for transport. I had just read the findings of the inquests into the very sad deaths of two men who had been killed on a stretch of the M1 in South Yorkshire, which is called a smart motorway. This is near Meadowhall, where the number of lanes has been increased by bringing the hard shoulder into use as a permanent live lane. The men had been involved in a minor collision, pulled into the nearside lane, and stopped in order to exchange insurance details. They were struck by a lorry traveling in that lane and died. The coroner said that the lack of a hard shoulder had contributed to the deaths. This was an important moment because the coroner has looked at all the evidence and reached an unequivocal conclusion.

What has seemed odd to me throughout has been the stance of Highways England, who are responsible for the motorway. They reject the suggestion that smart motorways were built as a cheap way of increasing capacity where traffic was heavy. And they say that the safety record of smart motorways is no worse, and may even be better than that of conventional motorways. I don't doubt this because conventional motorways don't have gantries regulating speed according to traffic conditions as the smart motorways do. So, the true comparison would not be between a smart and a conventional motorway but between a smart motorway with gantries but no hard shoulder and one with gantries and a hard shoulder. So, Dear Secretary of State . . .

February 15, 2021

Police as Carers

From time to time, I get emails and letters from people saying they support the police in cracking down on crime, but not when they become social workers or therapists. This is not what they pay for.

I agree that social work should be done by social workers and therapy by therapists; the police are not trained to be either. But increasingly in their work, the police are called upon to show skills that are often not dissimilar to those of the caring professions. I had an email last week, for example, from someone whose elderly father had been the victim of a telephone scam. He lost around £3,000. She wanted to thank the officer who had called and helped her father and the family. The advice he provided her father, and them as a family, was invaluable.

The officer had helped the father regain his self confidence; he had been burdened by the thought that he had been uniquely foolish in falling for the fraudster. And the officer helped the family to see what they could do to ensure nothing like this happened again. The officer, she said, was so caring, compassionate, and understanding, and treated her father with kindness, more like a friend than a victim of crime.

No, not social workers or therapists, but not automata either.

March 8, 2021

Ex-Offenders and Their Families

Last week, I was part of a discussion between the four PCCs in Yorkshire and the Humber together with some of those responsible for our prisons and the prison service. What struck me about the conversation was that, while we spent a lot of time talking about the needs of offenders on release, we had little or nothing to say about one crucial group who must have a key role in their rehabilitation: the partners and families to whom many will return.

One of the lessons I learned from the child sexual abuse crisis in Rotherham was that those impacted by these crimes were not just the immediate victims but their families and the families of the abusers, including their children. Families where men come back from prison may likewise struggle. If the men have continuing problems with drugs or alcohol, the families need to be able to recognize the signs and know who to contact for help. But I am not sure how much support and advice is available specifically for them.

Helping ex-offenders is never a popular cause. People sometimes write to me to say they begrudge every penny spent on them. Yet, if we are to reduce re-offending, we need to think seriously about how practically we can make a difference, and helping the families may be one way.

Leadership Again

One or two people were in touch with me following my recent comments on leadership. These words in particular summed up the matter really well. They were from someone who has held senior leadership positions in the NHS: "I always said to staff that leadership was about doing the right things, and management was about making sure the right things were done. I also used to say leadership was a leasehold and not a freehold, i.e., it was for a finite period of time."

March 15, 2021

Sarah Everard, aged thirty-three, was kidnapped, raped, and murdered by Wayne Couzens, a serving police officer, in London in early March. The women's group Reclaim These Streets was denied permission to hold a vigil for Sarah on Clapham Common on Saturday, March 13 because of COVID restrictions. Women gathered nonetheless and there were struggles with the (many male) police and arrests.

Sarah Everard

Last week, International Women's Day, and all its associated events, was overshadowed by the shocking news of the kidnap, rape and, murder of Sarah Everard by a serving police officer. Its somber shadow fell across Mothering Sunday (Mothers' Day) as well. We inevitably wondered what turmoil of emotions Sarah's mother might be experiencing.

Every aspect of what we have come to know about the crime has been horrible. And there is no way of protecting her family as each new detail emerges. At times such as this, we appreciate all the more the largely hidden but vital role of the police family liaison officers.

But just as last year, the death of George Floyd in the USA awakened in many African Americans memories of their own daily experiences of abuse, something similar seems to have happened for many of this country's women with the death of Sarah. In one event I attended (remotely) to mark International Women's Day, speaker after speaker told of sexual abuse they had been subjected to from predatory men at one time or another in their lives. Some older women said they had never felt able to speak about this before. This is clearly a moment of catharsis and significance, with big implications for policing and criminal justice. Issues are emerging that we are only partly addressing: abuse online, abuse in the workplace or in public places, low levels of convictions for rape, reluctance to report, and so on. There is also a growing consensus that there must be a focus on men's behavior, otherwise, in those instances where women are subject to violent assault, we will go on making women feel either ashamed or responsible for what happens to them at the hands of men. This is wrong and is one of the major problems we have to address.

I commission support and counseling services for victims of sexual violence. We have a Sexual Assault Referral Centre (SARC) where it is made absolutely clear to victims that it is not them but the offender who is responsible for what has happened to them. Training is given to front-line police officers so that they recognize and understand what domestic abuse is and what they must do about it. I also fund a program that seeks to work with perpetrators of abuse to prevent further offending. But much of this support and intervention is after the event. We need to prevent sexual abuse happening in the first place. This is why I give grants to groups that work with young people, teaching them to be respectful towards one another. It is also a prime focus of the Violence Reduction Unit. They have been working on a program that trains young people to be mentors to their fellow students in violence prevention. I saw this in operation in Glasgow. Young people were taking classes and engaging with their peers in how they could cease to be bystanders when unacceptable behavior happened around them.

And as with most big societal issues, this will need more than a single initiative. If there is a continuum between lower level abuse and serious violence, we need to find ways of making early interventions if we are to stop rapes and homicides, because the serious and violent assaults take place in a more general climate in which certain behaviors by men towards women are thought acceptable. And here, we all have a part to play in making our communities safer, not least by teaching our children what safe, respectful relationships are.

Between a Rock and a Hard Place

On the one hand, the police do not want to alienate the public they are here to serve. On the other, they must enforce the law. Most of the time, this does not result in conflict. When it does, or has the potential to do so, the police have to think very carefully about their options. It's not just a matter of what they do, it is how they do it and how they talk about what they do: the narratives that explain actions are just as important as the actions themselves. What is said has to be convincing. Words have to be chosen with care. Tone matters.

The police have been under a lot of pressure recently from the home secretary and ministers to step up their enforcement of the law around people gathering together because of the risk of increasing infections and prolonging the lockdown. We all understand that.

We also understand why many women felt a compulsion to hold a vigil for Sarah Everard on Clapham Common. That was obviously going to present a problem given the rules about leaving home and gathering. It was essential that a compromise was found because if it wasn't, it was clear that some people, perhaps many, would seek to gather anyway. And public support for police action might not be so understanding.

Of all forces in the country, the Met could least afford to lose support. Its use of stop and search has already brought criticism from the black community. It could hardly afford to alienate women as well. That is most of the population of London.

But the police don't make the rules around coronavirus, politicians do. So, politicians who make the rules also need to do some explaining about what they think the police should have done last Saturday. It is hard to believe that ministers could not have intervened and found a way to make the holding of a socially distanced and managed vigil, policed by female officers, on this occasion and in this place an exception under the rules.

Even so, we ask our police to act in ways that are measured and proportionate. Yes, the Met were between a rock and a hard place, but what finally transpired was the worst of all worlds.

March 22, 2021

Police Speak

As PCC, I have learned a lot of police speak. Among the latest is problem-solving policing (PSP). Or, a better term in my view, problem-orientated policing (POP). You don't always solve a problem, but you may mitigate it or improve on it.

Problem-solving policing is something that all South Yorkshire officers are now trained in, and it's very important. It's a recognition that if we are to reduce or do away with crime and antisocial behavior, we are never going to do it by police action alone. PSP teaches police officers to see crime and antisocial behavior in its wider context and ask questions about causes and, so, cures. When you do that, you realize that solving or mitigating the problem might involve others and not just the police.

There is nothing new about this approach, of course. Some years ago, I brought together a group of local residents to do just this as we thought about our community and how it could be improved. We began by thinking about what was good and what was bad about the place. To help our thinking, we did a little exercise, writing down on a flip chart ten good and ten bad things about our neighborhood. We called this "ten for sorrow, ten for joy." The speed with which we came up with the relevant ten spoke volumes about whether we felt this was a relatively good or bad place to live. Then, we thought about what we needed to do to strengthen the good, remove the bad, and how we could bring this about.

Problem-solving policing follows a similar process. It requires officers to take these steps:

1. Identify a specific problem, such as ASB by young people at a local shopping center, or house burglaries in a particular group of streets.

2. Analyze the problem, using local intelligence and police data to ask questions such as, "What are we seeing happen and why here?"

3. Formulate a specific, bespoke response, which may need others to be involved, such as the local authority. How can we prevent or mitigate this?

4. Evaluate the effectiveness of the response and learn from it. What worked and what didn't?

This is the way South Yorkshire police approach crime and ASB. Yes, they have to respond to incidents as and when they happen. But they are also being more than just reactive. If we are to drive down crime and ASB, we also need to think our way to solutions that are more preventive, get to the roots of why things happen in the first place, and how we can make changes for the better; and that involves working with other partners and residents. We need problem-solving policing.

Smart Motorways

Last week, the issue of smart motorways loomed large in our correspondence and media interest. (Smart motorways are where the hard shoulder is replaced by a live lane with occasional refuges. I have always regarded them as inherently dangerous.) I was contacted by journalists from the *Sunday Telegraph*, the *Daily Mail*, and the *Sun*, and I spoke on the *Today* program on BBC Radio 4 and Radio Berkshire, where part of the M4 is being made into an all-lane running motorway (ALR).

Two things have struck me about all of this. Usually, if you express a point of view, you quickly discover, if you didn't know already, that not everyone thinks as you do! But as one of the journalists and one of the broadcasters said to me, no one seems to think ALRs are a good idea, let alone a smart one.

The other thing I noticed was the way both ministers and Highways England seem to think that the repetition of a familiar mantra about how safe they are is a sufficient justification for continuing with the rollout of smart motorways, even when so much disquiet has been expressed. So, for instance, in a letter to me last week, the minister wrote, "Overall, evidence shows that in most ways ALR motorways are as safe as, or safer than, conventional motorways, but not in every way." (I did worry and wonder about that "but not in every way," but the minister did not elaborate.) I know the statistics, but it seems more likely to me that better safety figures are because ALRs have gantries and speed regulation, not because they have no hard shoulder.

My question to those who are pushing on with the program is this: If you were to break down in your car with your family in a live lane on the ALR stretch of the M1, would you be thinking, "At least we are as safe as, if not safer than, on a conventional motorway"? I think I know the answer.

We should be designing dangers out, not building them in.

Well, I Never: Blue Light Elephants

One of my nine year old granddaughters drew me a picture of an elephant with a blue light on its head. She told me that, as well as police horses, we should also have police elephants. They would be better for crowd control because they could swish people out of the way with their trunks. I have yet to put the idea to the chief constable.

April 19, 2021

Quads

If I were to look through the emails I receive from the public to see the word that came up most often, it might well be quads. For as long as I have been PCC, there have been complaints about nuisance quad bikes, but in the last year or two, they have risen exponentially. It is an issue across the country as well as in South Yorkshire, and in both rural and urban areas. In the countryside, I hear from farmers who tell me about the destruction of crops, the breaking of fences, and the pursuit of animals. In urban areas, I have reports of people driving furiously and recklessly along pavements, creating anxiety and noise as they go. But catching people who suddenly appear and take off across fields is not easy. So, how has the force responded?

Imaginatively, I think we could say. In April 2020, they established a central, off-road bike team of six full-time riders. They are supported by a further fifteen officers in the districts who can assist as and when needed. Their weekly operations are based on intelligence and demand and the plans are circulated to the districts.

This is a summary of some of their activities between April 2020 and February this year.

Number of deployments	313
Offenders reported on summons	60
Warning notices issued	256
Bikes seized for antisocial use	27

Seized for no driving license/insurance	114
Value of bikes seized	£177,000
Stolen bikes recovered	88
Value of stolen bikes recovered	£181,000
Arrests made	19

Of course, the police bikers cannot be everywhere and calls on them exceed their capacity to respond to every request. But as the table shows, they are making a difference, and this year, they hope to increase the number of trained district-based riders from fifteen to twenty-one.

April 26, 2021

Vulnerable Youth

Some young people, we know, are as troubled as they are troublesome, as sinned against as sinning. The police know very well that officers need to understand that the young people they come across can be at one and the same time both a victim and an offender. Otherwise, opportunities may be missed to make interventions that will make a difference to the way a young life works out in the future. We don't want to criminalize the young if we can possibly avoid it.

Seeing the vulnerability and not just the offending was one of the points made last week by David Urpeth, one of the South Yorkshire coroners, at the conclusion of the inquest into the death by stabbing of Sam Baker. Sam died during a street fight at the age of fifteen, a brief life in which he had come to the notice of numerous agencies innumerable times. He had gone missing from home, missing from school, and had become involved in violence and drugs. But despite this, the coroner believed, his serious safeguarding needs had not been fully recognized. That was in 2018, and it made me look at what had changed. Were we in a better place now for picking up the signs when young people start to get into difficulties?

I think we are. To take one example, since Sam died, we have seen established in each district Multi Agency Child Exploitation (MACE) meetings. The MACE is not led by the police but by a senior manager from the local authority children's services. All relevant agencies are represented, including the police. The MACE seeks to stop child exploitation and the serious risk of vulnerable young people being groomed and recruited by organized gangs. It meets weekly.

Each agency represented (youth offending team, probation, police, health, education, drug and alcohol services, local authority, and so on) can flag up concerns they have for particular children who have come to their notice. Some children are known by several agencies and it is important to establish which will take the lead, otherwise each may think the other is doing what is needed. In addition, it prevents the young people being overwhelmed by encounters with multiple agencies. The MACE decides what intervention is needed and who is best positioned to take matters forward. The interventions may include the need to disrupt the involvement in the young person's life of, say, a criminal gang.

As I talked about the work of the MACE meetings last week, I was concerned about one area where we may need to do more, an unintended consequences of schools becoming academies. Academies are independent of the local authority, and this makes it harder to know what is happening to those young people who are not expelled but leave an academy and go off roll, as when a parent decides to home educate. Who are the off-rollers? Where are they? What education are they now receiving? Who is keeping tabs on them?

The Importance of Friends

I have been reading a book by a psychologist about friendships. If he is right, the social support network that friendships bring is vital for our health. We recover better, for instance, from heart attacks and strokes if we have friends. This is also true of our mental health.

But we can only sustain so many close friendships. Many of us will have up to one hundred-fifty people we know and might class as friends in general; but within that, there will be smaller groups, including some family members, and most critically of all, about fifteen people who are our inner sympathy group. About 60 percent of our social effort will be needed to keep the bonds within this group in good order.

We have now had a year in which many of the usual occasions that enable us to maintain those social bonds have been closed down. Zooming is a poor substitute. We can, therefore, expect an impact on people's mental health.

We knew before the pandemic that police officers were having to deal more and more with people in mental health crises. We must assume that will not get any better if social support systems have been so disrupted. We must also assume that the threat to mental health applies to all—including police officers and their families, including ourselves. Well-being has to feature largely on all our risk registers going forward.

Elections for police and crime commissioners, deferred from 2020, were held on May 6, 2021, and the diary entries were suspended during the pre-election period.

May 10, 2021

The Big Decisions

Last week, I was elected for the third time as police and crime commissioner. Although I stood as the Labour and Co-operative Party candidate, the following day, I took an oath in the magnificent, wooden-paneled reception rooms of Barnsley town hall to work for the good of everyone in South Yorkshire, whoever they are, wherever they live, without fear or favor. And that is what I will try to do.

It was a very good election result for me. I was elected on first preference votes (which is not true of every PCC) and by bigger margins than previous elections. This gives me some confidence in thinking that I must have been given credit for getting some decisions right, perhaps the big decisions. And there are few bigger decisions than appointing a chief constable. Five years ago, I asked Stephen Watson to lead South Yorkshire police. At that time, the force was in poor shape: morale was low, there had been poor inspection reports, and public confidence in the police had taken a knock following the Jay Report into child sexual exploitation in Rotherham.

I remember meeting the chief informally shortly after the interview in an Italian restaurant in Sheffield. I said I thought there was a mountain to climb. He was very clear: there were many good men and women in the organization who could be motivated if given a sense of purpose and direction. He promised that SYP would become a good force by the time his contract came to an end, which was this year. And so it has turned out. He took the force to where it is today: one of the top-performing forces in the country.

Last week, we said an emotional farewell and thank you to him at police headquarters as he left to undertake a similar task for Greater

Manchester Police, where the elected mayor, Andy Burnham, has police responsibilities. We wished him well on the other side of the Pennines. But it does mean that I shall have to make another big decision and appoint a new chief constable to take us forward. I didn't want a big gap with no substantive chief, so the process is already well under way.

The task now will be no less challenging. But it will be less about rescue and more about maintaining and improving a force now rated as good by Her Majesty's Inspectors, and outstanding in terms of its ethical leadership.

What Next?

One of the first things the new Chief Constable will have to do is make some assessment about what will happen to crime and anti-social behavior as we come out of the lockdowns.

Last week, the Office for National Statistics published data about crime in 2020. Overall, crime fell in South Yorkshire by 8 percent. Some crimes fell dramatically: thefts by 25 percent, burglaries by 24 percent, and robberies by 16 percent. Even knife crime fell by 12 percent, despite the media-fueled perceptions that it was rising.[1] I have no doubt that the lockdowns were a big factor in these statistics. Burglars, for instance, were a little too obvious out on deserted streets at night and houses were rarely without occupants. So, crime fell. But what happens next? Will crime return to normal levels and patterns? Or have things changed in the last twelve or so months?

There is almost certainly more online crime now. But how much more and what sort of crime? We can also expect a rise in public order offenses as nighttime economies function again. We often talk about lessons learned. We certainly want a police force that learns lessons. But we need more than that because a totally lessons learned approach would tend to keep us rooted in past behaviors, as if what had happened in the past was going to happen again. But the past does not repeat itself exactly and sometimes not at all. So, we need a police force that not only learns from the past but also one that thinks ahead and figures out how things are changing. We want dynamic policing because life is dynamic. Society is not a kind of Madame Tussauds with moving parts.

1. Office of South Yorkshire Police and Crime Commissioner (OPCC), "Big Falls in Crime."

June 7, 2021

A New Chief Constable

We have a preferred candidate for chief constable, Lauren Poultney. I cannot call Lauren the chief constable yet because my proposal has to be confirmed by the Police and Crime Panel at a meeting in June. The Police and Crime Panel is a statutory body and consists of councilors from each of the four districts plus independent, non-councilor members. The panel has to scrutinize the selection process, to ensure that it was fair, and consider the candidate I propose, to ensure I have made a sound choice.

Choosing a chief constable is arguably one of the most important decisions a PCC has to make. Of course, a police force is more than a chief constable, more than a senior command team; but if you have a good team at the top, that can make all the difference, one way or another. And there have been far too many anecdotes about dysfunctionality in some forces over the years. So, I am pleased that we not only have the right chief constable but we can also see a strong and cohesive leadership team building around her. There is continuity with this appointment as well as change.

What the leadership team does is to provide two things: first, a clear and consistent sense of direction and purpose; and second, motivation. If the people at the top model in their own professional lives the values and commitment they want (and we need) throughout the organization, people will respond to that.

Chief Constable and Commissioner

The selection process for the new chief constable extended over two days and was quite rigorous, and quite exhausting. Candidates were grilled by two panels of people: one drawn from various communities from across the county (including young people, those from minority groups, and those working in the voluntary sector) and the other consisting of representatives of the workforce (trade unions, staff associations, a women's group, LGBTQ+ group, and so on).

The candidates were also tested on their ability to handle media interviews. They were asked to envisage an incident where the police had dispersed people gathering in defiance of coronavirus rules. They were then interviewed about the police response by a professional journalist, being filmed as if on TV. This latter exercise was important because anyone who aspires to be a chief constable has to be able to think on their feet and deal effectively with questions from broadcasters and journalists. All these results came together at the final interview, where I was assisted by a recently retired, and very successful, chief constable and the chair of our Independent Ethics Panel.

As we chatted after the interviews, the retired chief constable told me that, in his view, the most successful police forces were those where a good, professional relationship had been established between the chief constable and the PCC. So, the appointment has implications for me as well, and I will work hard to establish that relationship. As I see it, my role is to give support and encouragement to the police, while also being a critical friend, the holding-to-account role. If we can get that right, the next three years (my term of office) should be as fruitful as the term that just ended.

June 14, 2021

The Perils of Social Media

Last week, more public figures found themselves in trouble for things they had posted on social media in the days of their youth. How they regretted the foolish things they had said and done then. But the damage was done. So, how do we stop young people doing things that could come back to haunt them in later life?

While parents and teachers will do what they can, young people are less likely to listen to adults than they are their peers. Perhaps this is one of the lessons to learn from what has happened with climate change. Children and young people have listened to Greta Thunberg in a way they would never have listened to any adult, even the adult scientists on whom Greta relies. (Of course, part of Greta's appeal was that she reversed the normal order of things: this was a child telling adults how to behave responsibly.) Now we need a teenage Anders Andersson who will warn his peers about the dangers of doing foolish things on social media. They might listen to him.

Children are the messages we send into a future we shall never see. But our children are posting their own messages for that future, which they and many others will see, and sooner than they think.

Just When We Thought Hot Desks
Were a Thing of the Past

Coronavirus has had some interesting as well as utterly devastating consequences, not least in the area of employment. I think we all know that older patterns of people being either at work or at home have been seriously eroded. We have discovered what some always knew: it is possible for many of us to work at home, for some of the time, at least. This is why the police are looking hard at what it will mean for the workforce in a post-coronavirus world.

This mainly concerns police staff. Clearly, there will always be some jobs in the force that cannot be done from home. A custody suite cannot be run remotely. But what about call handling? For this reason, the force is currently taking a long hard look at which jobs are possible to be done at least some of the time from home. My own office is doing the same.

Of course, some people want to come back to the office, at least for some of the time. It's important for their own mental health and well-being. If we work from home, we have to be very disciplined about when we are working and when not. I have seen too many emails arriving with a send time in the small hours. We can't all be insomniacs, and even if we are, I don't think opening up the laptop is the way to overcome it. Stick to camomile tea. On the other hand, working from home seems to have been good for many people's physical health: the sickness rate fell during the lockdowns, an efficiency saving if not a cashable one.

We have also realized how much business is actually transacted informally in casual encounters and conversations. It would be tedious if everything had to be done via a video call or an email all the time. But we may not need everyone in the office all the time, and that has implications for desks and computers and buildings. So, as far as workforce planning goes, the virus has got us to a place which we might have reached eventually, though not this quickly. However, reconfiguring the office is one thing, refashioning the mindset and the culture will be more demanding and take longer.

June 28, 2021

An Acted Apology

Sorry is the hardest word to say, or so it is said. And sometimes, a government will only say sorry by what it does, not by what it says. I don't think we shall ever hear a minister say that cutting police numbers by twenty thousand between 2010 and 2019 was wrong and they apologize. But restoring the twenty thousand, which is being done, is the apology—the recognition that a mistake has been made and is being rectified. I call this an acted apology.

As with the police, so with the probation service. This was split in two by the government in 2014, against the advice of almost everyone. High-risk offenders remained with the publicly run National Probation Service while low to medium-risk offenders became the responsibility of a series of privately run companies called Community Rehabilitation Companies (CRCs). Many who worked for the old probation service had to compete for their jobs and some left the service altogether. The CRCs had to recruit and train new staff very quickly, and then retain them, as well as meet targets on which their funding depended. It was soon discovered that some offenders who were deemed low-risk became high-risk and should have had the closer supervision of the probation service. Two hundred went on to commit serious offenses, including murder, and 24 percent re-offended.[2] As HM inspectors and parliamentary committees pointed out, it was a recipe for disaster.

The government abandoned the reform and from this week, the two services have been made one again. We now have a new, publicly managed and accountable National Probation Service. An acted apology if there ever was one. But at such cost, human and financial.

Community Payback

Something the new probation service will have to get on with very quickly is to restart the community payback scheme. This is where an offender is sentenced to undertake hours of supervised, unpaid work in the community as an alternative to prison. You may have seen offenders in high-visibility jackets at work in this way. But the scheme came to a halt as a result of the lockdowns and the associated restrictions. So, there are many offenders whose unpaid work in the community needs to be done as soon as possible.

2. My analyst provided me statistics like this from Office of National Statistics (ONS) reports: www.ons.gov.uk.

Hoarse Whispering

Last Friday, I went to the launch of a book by Helen Jackson, a former MP for Sheffield Hillsborough, about the municipal politics of Sheffield between 1970 and 1992. David Blunkett was the main speaker. The launch was held in Millennium Square, by the Peace Gardens. As I came away, I bumped into two police officers and their horses from the mounted section. I took pity on one of the horses, Treeton (they are all named after places in South Yorkshire), who looked rather down in the mouth. We had a chat, a bit one-sided, and as I had just been talking rather a lot, I was a bit croaky, a little hoarse. So, I tried to cheer him up with an extra strong mint, always a favorite with the horses. If he was won over, he didn't let on.

But what was so noticeable was the number of people of all ages who were drawn to the horses and, as a result, chatted to the officers. I doubt whether there would have been the same interaction if two non-mounted officers had walked along the same stretch of road. The horses, of course, don't speak, at least not in a language anyone over the age of nine understands. You need approachable and personable officers as well.

But wherever they go, the horses facilitate engagement. This might not be their primary job, and the following day, they were on crowd control duty in Batley and Spen. But this engagement is so valuable. People who would never normally seek out a police officer cross the road to speak to the mounted officers, and all this helps to build positive relationships between public and police. There are very few police forces now with a mounted section, I think about eleven out of forty-three. Many were lost during the era of austerity. Our mounted section is now back at a refurbished Ring Farm, Cudworth, and I hope everyone in South Yorkshire recognizes their value.

July 5, 2021

Crime and a Deer Farm

It's not everyday that I talk crime in a walled garden on a deer farm. And most residents of South Yorkshire living in a city, a town, or other urban area probably never associate crime with the countryside anyway. Woods and fields, rivers and meadows are where we go for pleasant walks at the weekend and to get away from the darker aspects of urban life. So what was I doing?

I joined local farmers, South Yorkshire police officers, and the rural adviser for the Country Land and Business Association (CLA) North to talk about wildlife and rural crime. Being a sunny day, we sat outdoors, with a herd of ivory-limbed and brown-eyed deer (Oscar Wilde) just over the wall, looking on quizzically. Although most of our crime happens in urban areas, we also have crimes in rural areas and the farms within them; and since farmers also pay council tax, they must have their fair share of police time and resources.

Libby Bateman from the CLA led a conversation about wildlife crime, from hare coursing to deer poaching. And rural crime, from theft of agricultural machinery to fly tipping and livestock worrying. Our focus was on what can be done to bring perpetrators to justice and to safeguard farming families. We also noted that during the last year, after an initial fall, there were probably more people in the countryside than ever before.

But until the last year or so, police resources have not really been adequate to deal with much wildlife and rural crime. Some farms are quite remote and the police in rural areas were often pulled away to tackle incidents elsewhere. There is now, however, a serious attempt to do more, and we discussed this. At our meeting was a sergeant (Mark Gregory) and two officers (Amanda Brundell and Rachel Attwell) who have expertise in rural crime and are based at Ring Farm, Cudworth, with the Mounted Section. More will join them later this year and next to create a dedicated rural crime team. In addition, officers more generally and call handlers have been trained to understand better the issues raised by crime and antisocial behavior in the countryside, and some forty officers are now accredited wildlife crime officers, carrying out this role alongside their other duties.

What will make the real difference will be the ability of the rural crime officers to work closely with the local authorities and other specialist officers in the force. This will enable them to deal effectively with those organized gangs who carry out some of the most serious crime. These other units include roads police officers, the off-road bike team, and the armed response teams, as well as the local neighborhood teams. I detect a new and real determination to make a substantial difference in the years ahead.

We have agreed to meet again with the CLA in six months time to check progress. In the meantime, I am left with an abiding memory of the deer with their half-curious, half-anxious look, a projection of animal vulnerability that makes them so appealing.

Money, Money, Money

Meanwhile, the word from Whitehall is that work is beginning in the Treasury on the Comprehensive Spending Review (CSR). The CSR is the government's spending plan for each of its departments for the coming three years. This is vital information for every organization in the public sector because we shall then be able to see how much we are likely to receive each year in grant, one of the core elements of our funding. For policing, that mainly means understanding what funding the Home Office will get and give.

The Association of Police and Crime Commissioners (APCC) is represented in talks with the Home Office and ministers by a Conservative lead PCC (Roger Hirst, Essex) and a Labour deputy. I have just been asked to be the Labour deputy. This arrangement allows PCCs to have some say in the submissions the Home Office will make to the Treasury in the CSR process.

It will be a great relief to get away from single-year financial settlements, where you never knew from one year to the next what the grant would be: reduction, flat cash, flat cash plus inflation. It will also be good to get away from what the government has been doing for the past year under the pressures of coronavirus, giving a whole series of extra pots of funding for which bids had to be made. Government ministers have been like someone who, after years of living frugally, wins the lottery and starts to give cash away to equally impoverished friends and family.

July 12, 2021

Driving Under the Influence

Last week, a roads police officer showed me a very scary video. He and his colleagues had been out along South Yorkshire's motorways in a tall vehicle, like the front of an articulated lorry. It had been borrowed for a few days from Highways England. The vehicle had cameras on each side and an officer in the cab holding another. They had been recording instances of dangerous driving: the videos would be very compelling evidence for any action they subsequently might take. The advantage of this vehicle from an enforcement point of view was that it lifted up the officers so that they could see clearly into cabs of a similar height and they could look down into cars and small vans.

In the video I saw, the police were traveling behind a car on the inside lane of the motorway. The car swayed somewhat and, as the police started to overtake, it came very close. I assumed we were watching someone under the influence of drink or drugs. When the police drew alongside the car, they could film what was happening. A young woman was driving at speed while texting on her mobile phone. She was barely in control and was quite oblivious to everything going on around her, including the police officer with the camera.

When the woman was stopped, she at first denied texting, until she was confronted with the filmed evidence. Then, she wanted the police to deal leniently with her because she already had points and could lose her license; and her job was dependent on being able to drive.

I was left wondering. If the prospect of losing your license, your livelihood, and your life was not enough to persuade someone to drive responsibly, what was?

July 19, 2021

The Baader Meinhof Effect

We are all likely to suffer from it. I first recognized it in myself when I became police and crime commissioner. After years of living without noticing police officers or police vehicles, I began to see them everywhere and started to think that they must be out and about more. But it was all to do with my job. It raised my awareness of the police and created the illusion that there were more of them than before. But it wasn't that there were more in actuality, just that I noticed them more. It was a case of the Baader Meinhof Effect, also known as frequency illusion, when increased awareness of something creates the illusion that it is appearing or occurring more often.

It happens all the time with crime. If a crime is committed, especially some act of serious violence, this generates a lot of media attention on TV, radio, social media, and in newspapers. It can create the illusion that murders or stabbings are on the increase, and that is very hard to counter. The fact may be that such incidents are decreasing, but if an incident is intensively reported, it perpetuates the illusion that something is getting worse.

I am beginning to think that dog theft is a case of frequency illusion. In the first few months of this year, stories began to appear in the national media about dog thefts during the period of the lockdowns. It was said that with more people wanting dogs to take for walks, the price of canines had gone up, and kidnapped pets became a lucrative source of income for criminals, which may be true. A few people began to speak about their stolen pet and the distress it caused. Rather more spoke about near misses as people tried to snatch them, or so they thought. Others said someone they met had told them about people who had lost a dog. One excitable PCC started a national campaign and one of our local MPs said the police should have a dog theft lead (no pun intended, I think) in South Yorkshire.

There are always going to be some thefts of dogs, but looking back over last year, there is no evidence in our county that numbers had gone up dramatically, if at all. And as time has gone by and more things are beginning to happen for the media to report on, stories about dog thieving have started to die away. It was a case of frequency illusion. So, it's just as well we didn't set on a dog theft lead. They would have little to do for most of the week.

July 26, 2021

When Is a Child Not a Child?

Nothing seems to divide opinion quite as much as the age at which we think children should be held responsible for any crimes they commit. I get emails from people who are outraged when a young person is not prosecuted for a crime and emails from people who are outraged when they are.

Of course, the problem starts with our understanding of childhood itself. The point at which a child is thought to be an adult is different from society to society and from age to age. It is not so long ago that children were regarded as little adults and sent up chimneys and down mines. My mother left school at fourteen and worked (literally) for the rest of her life in a factory; she died in her early fifties. Even today, we have different ages for treating people as mature enough to take on certain responsibilities: getting married, driving a car, taking out a mortgage, fighting for the country, and so on. And judging by the way many children are now dressed (think of the growing trend for school proms), we seem to want to abolish the distinction between childhood and adulthood altogether.

I have young people telling me they don't want to be treated like children and adults telling me we must not criminalize the young. I think you could say we are confused.

But the age of criminal responsibility is ten, and children do commit crimes, including quite serious ones, and the police have to deal with them. If we were clearer about childhood, we might make better decisions about how we deal with those who are involved in criminality.

In South Yorkshire, when children are sentenced to serve time in either a young offender institution (our local young offender institution is at Wetherby) or a secure children's home, such as Aldine House, Sheffield, our Youth Offending Services start to work at once to prepare them for their return to the community. They treat them as children and know that they are often more sinned against than sinning, themselves the victims of abuse or neglect. The danger is that these children write themselves off, even as they have so often been written off, and see only a life of criminality ahead of them. Time in secure accommodation can be used well to encourage them to think differently about themselves and their future, and to plan and prepare carefully for it. A difference can be made, and I have met those who have been helped to have a different view of themselves and have turned their young lives around.

The key is to get them to believe in themselves. And that often starts by having people around them who believe in them first. Of course, this is all easier said than done. But done it can be, and I support those who work with these young people in every way I can.

Making Ends Meet

If you are a government, you can decide that balancing the books is a problem for another day. That has been the government's stance for the past year and a half as they have borrowed eye-watering sums of money to combat the coronavirus. They have had little choice, but, currently, it would need tax rises of about £8,000.00 per household to pay down the debts we have run up during the pandemic.

We can't take that approach with the police budget. As the chief constable and I start to put together next year's budget, I know that what we want to spend must be matched by income, and if we don't have the income, we must cut our coat according to the cloth.

The principal sources of funding are, of course, government grant and council tax. But the ratio between them differs widely from force to force, and in some cases, very widely. In some wealthier and usually more rural parts of the country, they are less dependent on government grant. In Surrey, for instance, 56 percent of funding is from council tax and 44 percent from grant. In North Yorkshire, it is 48 percent council tax and 52 percent grant. Whereas, in South Yorkshire, it is 26 percent from council tax and 74 percent from grant. The contrast is even starker in Northumbria, where 18 percent of funding comes from council tax and 82 percent from grant.[3]

What this means is that if government grant is cut by x percent, that has a much bigger impact on the resources available for policing in South Yorkshire than in Surrey. It also means that any losses can be made up from a smaller rise in council tax in Surrey, where property values are higher, than in South Yorkshire.

But the public, who will not know about these different ratios, will assume that a rise or fall in government grant will affect everyone equally and will not understand why a PCC in a rural area may only need to impose a small rise in the precept (council tax), whereas a PCC in a more urban area may have to raise the precept more.

I have yet to find a simple way of explaining any of this.

Good Work of Note

Each morning at about 6 o'clock, I read an email from the police headed "Chief's Log." This captures some of the more serious incidents that officers have had to deal with in the previous twenty-four hours. After listing the daily accounts of robberies, break-ins, drug offenses, assaults, and so on, there is also a space for senior officers to record instances of good work of note. This always catches my eye, and I am sorry the public are not able to glimpse this as well. It can be a real eye-opener into some of the things that officers do during the course of their everyday duties that are a bit special.

Last week, I noticed that doctors from one of our hospitals had written to the force. They had been dealing with a man who had an arterial bleed. Two officers had gone to the incident and their tactical medical training (TACMED) enabled them to apply a tourniquet to his arm. Their quick action had stabilized the victim and saved his life, the doctors wrote.

---

3. My chief finance officer provided me notes on these statistics.

One can only imagine the scene with so much blood and the need to act with speed and without panic. But for our officers, it's all in a day's work.

August 9, 2021

The PM and I

Recently, I was able to speak directly to the prime minister, Boris Johnson, in Downing Street. Directly, but remotely! The PM had invited PCCs from across the country for a discussion around the government's Beating Crime Plan. I stayed in South Yorkshire but was able to join by video link. Now that we know we can hear and see really well by these remote links, I find it harder and harder to justify at taxpayers' expense long (and expensive) journeys for meetings that may last, as this one did, less than an hour. (Though it would have been interesting to see inside No. 10!)

Amongst the various topics discussed, the PM made a point that I have previously made in the diary, that leveling up cannot just be about economic leveling. Or, putting it another way, economic leveling up will also depend on other kinds of activity, including getting crime and anti-social behavior down. It's a simple but obvious point. If you can locate your business anywhere in the country, why would you choose to go where serious crime is a factor? And if you are a young person on the threshold of adulthood, you will not do much for your future prospects if you get caught up in criminality, and that will be a real danger for some living in areas where gangs are operating.

So, one of the points I made to the prime minister was that if we are to steer certain young people away from the organized gangs as well as the economic leveling up—the provision of jobs and opportunities, we also need to see restored the youth services that once existed but were casualties of the years of austerity. Youth clubs, youth centers, and youth workers are not directly a police matter. I try to give funding whenever I can to projects that help to keep young people occupied in the evenings and in the long summer holidays; but the people needed to run them have to exist for me to do that. And what I can't do is fund a proper youth service. That is the responsibility of the local authorities; but their grants have been more savagely cut than any other part of the public sector.

If we want young people to come under the influence of adults who will be good role models for them and help them make sensible choices in their lives, we need those youth workers again who were once so active in youth centers and in communities. Not every young person is fortunate enough to have family members who will play that role. As long as those youth leaders are missing, the gangs stand waiting to take their place.

The prime minister listened; but I don't think he was persuaded.

Lived Experience Is Not Enough

I was stopped in the street by someone who was very aggrieved because an organization he had started had been turned down for a grant. This had been quite some time ago, but it still rankled. He wanted funding to go into schools and run programs about knife crime and its dangers. When I said there were already such programs, he said that his was different because he would be bringing lived experience. By this, he meant that he had once carried a knife, had been involved in fights, had been badly cut, and spent time in prison. But now, he had turned his life around and wanted to give something back.

From time to time, we have applications for funding where a principal selling point of a project is that those running it have lived experience. What are we to make of that?

In some instances, it can certainly add something of value. When I first became PCC in the wake of the child sexual exploitation scandals in Rotherham, I set up a panel of victims and survivors so that we could learn directly from these young women how grooming worked and why the various authorities had failed to help them. This was using their lived experience. But it does not follow that someone with lived experience, say of serious violence, by virtue of that experience alone, knows what needs to be done to prevent others being drawn into it. Sometimes, what the person with lived experience proposes is not helpful at all.

The man who stopped me wanted to show young people some of the blades he used to carry when he was a teenager and talk about how, on one occasion, his own knife had been seized by another gang member and used against him. He was convinced this would be enough to cause young people not to carry knives themselves. Yet, all the evidence I have seen suggests otherwise. Some young people may be frightened into thinking that others are routinely carrying knives when they are not. Others may decide they need to arm themselves if that is what is happening. There is little evidence that these attempts to scare young people into behaving in a particular way actually work.

Lived experience has its place. It helps our understanding of what it feels like to be a victim or an offender. But being a victim or an offender does not in and of itself give insights into what does or does not work. For that, we need other kinds of evidence. Lived experience does not trump everything.

August 23, 2021

Mental Health

Last month, over one hundred people were detained by the police in South Yorkshire using powers under the Mental Health Act. Section 136 allows officers to detain people who are in immediate need of care and control, and to take them to a place of safety. The use of this power went up at the start of the pandemic and has remained high ever since. Looking back over last year (April 2020 to March 2021), the monthly figures mainly hovered around 100 to 116, but in May, there were 145 detentions. This was an overall increase of 21 percent on the year before.[4] Mental health has become a major issue for the police.

Of course, police officers are not medically qualified and, as with many police decisions, we have to rely on the good judgment of individual officers if they invoke Section 136 powers. If people are facing a mental health crisis, they should be conveyed to a place of safety, not by police officers in a police vehicle but by people who are medically trained in an ambulance, who know what to do if the person's condition becomes more acute. That is the ideal. But the ambulance service is also stretched, and it may be some time before a crew can reach the person with the health issue. So again, a judgment has to be made: Does the police officer wait or take the person in a police car? And that raises another matter. Supplying a place of safety is the responsibility of the local authority, and they, too, are under great pressure. If no place is available, the only resort the police officer may have is to take someone to a custody suite, which is not good. People with mental health issues should not be in police cells.

At the start of last year, 70 percent of Section 136 detainees were taken by police vehicle to a place of safety, and that concerned me greatly: this was not good for the person with the mental health issue or the police officers who had to take on this responsibility. I am pleased to say that by

4. My analyst provided me with this data from police briefings.

March 2021, those transported in police vehicles had fallen to 50 percent, and throughout the year, no one was detained in a police cell.

All this is just one more example of what we ask of the modern police force. Yet mental health does not figure in the Home Office list of key requirements for police forces. And the danger with that is that if it is not seen as a top priority nationally, it will slip from being a priority locally.

August 30, 2021

Cricket and Football: The Difference

What's the difference between cricket and football? One answer has got to be police overtime. We don't have test match cricket in South Yorkshire, and so I may be quite wrong about this, but I imagine the call on police resources in Leeds, Manchester, or Birmingham to maintain order for one afternoon of football far exceeds anything a cricket match requires, even over several days. What I note, as an outside observer, is the difference in crowd culture between football fans and cricket supporters. They can both be very partisan and equally passionate and vocal, though, if anything these days, the crowd at cricket matches can be more colorful. (All very different from when I went to Grace Road and Filbert Street in my youth.) But what you cannot do at a football match is have supporters from opposing sides sitting together, intermingling.

I have many good friends who are normally quite sane, calm, and rational. Some of them are even MPs. Until they come within a few yards of a football stadium. Then raucousness, excitability, and irrationality take over.

At the test match (I am writing this on day two, confidently expecting an England victory), emotions are running high, yet people are not segregated, and no one is behaving badly towards supporters of the other side. Passion is defused through shared good humor.

How do we get cricket culture into football grounds? That could be the greatest contribution football could make towards the overtime bills of the police service.

Making a Difference

There is no doubt, however, that sport can play a really significant role both in keeping some of our young people out of trouble and, more importantly, in teaching how to behave well by learning self-control and respect for others.

Last week, I visited the Firth Park Boxing Academy in one of the more deprived parts of Sheffield. We had given them some funding and I wanted to see how they had spent it and what they did in their sessions. By chance, the former sports minister, Richard Caborn, was also visiting. He maintains a keen interest in amateur boxing.

The club is housed in a room that was at one time part of a pub, now closed and turned into flats. I met the developer and former owner. She has very kindly given the club a long lease at a peppercorn rent so their future is secure. It is open seven days a week with a session for younger ones in the first part of the evening, then the older ones later. There were dozens of children and young people, mainly boys but some girls as well, and from all the different ethnic groups who live locally. They were all energetic and active and there was a really friendly buzz in the hall.

The parents I spoke to said the club was a godsend and a lifeline, somewhere safe that they could send their children to. They had no doubt that their young people were better behaved, more responsible, and more focused because of the values of the club.

As with many such clubs, Firth Park Boxing Academy is only possible because of the devotion and determination over many years of the head coach, Nasser Hussain, and his five voluntary helpers. He started the club when he worked on the railways and is there every day. And in this case, the club was also indebted to the landlord for her sheer generosity.

One of the privileges of this job is being able to meet such people who make the lives of many of our young people richer and worthwhile, while keeping some away from potential criminality.

September 6, 2021

So, What Works?

This is one of the most important questions I ever ask the police in my holding to account role. I don't, of course, put it as impertinently or inelegantly as that; but I have to ask it. Understanding what works is crucial if policing is to be effective.

When, for example, at the Public Accountability Board, the district commanders give their reports on policing activity over the previous quarter, I always get good presentations. A great deal of work is described and there are often impressive statistics to back up the narrative. But sometimes, I am left wondering what some of this activity has amounted to. I need to know not only what has been done but also what the outcome was. Did all this activity actually result in crime or antisocial behavior going down? Do you have a way of measuring your effectiveness? In other words, what works?

Sometimes, we discover what works from academic research, and sometimes, the results of that research are not what you might think. So, for instance, when I ask community groups what they most want from their police, they often say greater visibility. This, they believe, is the deterrent that makes all the difference to crime and ASB going down, which prompts the question, is it true? Does it work? It's an important question because, with resources being finite, we know there is no way a police officer can be in every street every minute of the day. We also know that some areas have little or no crime or ASB, so what impact would a patrol have there?

When I point this out, people understand the situation very well; but they are sure that some high visibility patrolling would make a difference. But where and how much? This is where academic research comes in.

The Violence Reduction Unit (VRU) recently considered some research that shows that high visibility patrolling can make a difference in specific circumstances, namely, in hot spot areas. Patrols should not be everywhere or anywhere but tightly focused on those places that are most blighted by crime. Fortunately, we now know in some detail where these hot spots are, thanks to the work of the VRU, which has been mapping them.

The research suggests that high visibility patrols in daylight hours over a number of days for no more than fifteen minutes are very effective. This reduces crime and ASB. However, and counterintuitively, patrolling for a longer period or in non-hot spot areas does not have the same effect. I suppose this is not as mysterious as it might seem. A patrol at, say, 4:00 p.m. will be seen by many people, and the word quickly spreads that the police are about. And the fact that officers are not hanging about gives the impression that they are patrolling purposefully and might suddenly appear anywhere. I asked whether it really did suppress crime or merely cause it to be displaced elsewhere. The research suggests that it is not displaced.

All of which points to the need for us to go on asking what works and for the police to continue getting smarter by using the best research.

Changing Offender Behavior

And that research includes insights into how we can change offender behavior. For example, over the years, there have been times when we have become very concerned about increased levels of violence in prisons, not least the four in Doncaster. This affects all who work in them and also impacts on police resources because they have to investigate crimes that take place there. How can we reduce this?

One interesting answer, from research, is through changes in diet. It seems that the food prisoners eat can make a significant difference to their behavior.

At Aylesbury Prison and Young Offender Institution, the charity Think Through Nutrition reduced violent incidents by 26 percent and seriously violent incidents by 37 percent through dietary changes.[5] These incidents included attacks on other prisoners, on prison officers, and self-harming, all of which affected the health and well-being of individual prisoners as well as having financial implications for the prison, the NHS, and the police. More recently, at HMP Eastwood Park, trials have shown that particular diets can improve cognitive functions, such as concentration, as well as make prisoners more willing to join in activities and so reduce tensions.

These are important and positive conclusions, and one wonders why what has been discovered is not being rolled out universally. One answer might be, and I am only guessing, the cost of any change. My wife and I live fairly frugally, but I reckon that even for us, our food bill works out at about £4 per day. Those who run prisons have to do it for around £2. That does not give much scope for innovation.

September 20, 2021

Project EDWARD

On Friday last week, I was out and about with Dame Sarah Storey. Well, I was more out than about in that I didn't take a bicycle along as she did. She had come to support South Yorkshire police as they contributed

5. Gesch et al., "Aylesbury Study."

to Project EDWARD. This is a national attempt to raise consciousness around road safety and to try to move us to the point where we might have days without fatalities on our roads: "Every Day Without A Road Death." In September, they have days of action.

The police operation that Dame Sarah took part in centered on the A57, a major route from Sheffield to Manchester. Sarah and two police officers in ordinary clothes cycled a few miles from Rivelin Valley Road, recording the behavior of passing motorists on cameras mounted on their bikes. Those who passed very close or drove dangerously were reported ahead and pulled in by police officers. The officers explained why they had been stopped and how they needed to improve their driving when approaching or overtaking cyclists. It was educational rather than enforcement action, though vehicles were checked for tax, insurance, and general roadworthiness.

In the morning, I had watched a similar exercise towards Bradfield in the Loxley valley, though this time, the issue was motorist behavior when passing horses. Two mounted officers in civilian clothes took part.

What was noticeable in both instances was the very different attitudes drivers adopted. Some immediately accepted that they had been rather thoughtless and readily took instruction and advice. They were kept for little more than ten minutes. But others started to argue and posture, which probably doubled the time they were detained.

So, many thanks to Dame Sarah, who, despite an extraordinarily busy schedule since her astonishing wins at the Tokyo Paralympics, still found time to support the EDWARD initiative in South Yorkshire. For the motorists who were told they had just carelessly passed Sarah Storey, it was a lesson about the safety of other road users they are unlikely to forget.

Unmanned Aerial Vehicles

In the year I became PCC (2014), I published a paperback on the two-thousand-year history of Christian attitudes to war (*The Dove, the Fig Leaf, and the Sword: Why Christianity Changes Its Mind About War*). In the final chapter, I speculated on the way Unmanned Aerial Vehicles (UAVs), now universally known as drones, might alter the nature of warfare. I assumed that drones would be used increasingly by the military, and so, we needed to think through the ethical issues they posed. These were around the extraordinary degree of unobserved surveillance capability drones opened up and the ability they gave to strike targets without putting your own soldiers at risk. Fighting could become a desk job. Did this make it easier for politicians to see force rather than nego- tiation as the preferred option in situations of conflict? What I did not anticipate was that some of the same ethical issues would be posed for police forces, though not around lethal force!

Over these past few years, the use of drones by the police has in- creased exponentially. I am not sure when the first drone was acquired by South Yorkshire police, but I do recall an early discussion about sharing one with the fire and rescue service, who were using a drone to get an aerial view of burning buildings.

South Yorkshire police currently have thirty-six qualified Civil Aviation Authority (CAA) approved drone pilots. They are a mix of offi- cers and staff, and they all have other roles. There are eleven operational aircraft and four training aircraft. Each of these has different capabilities and flying times, giving the police a range of options when it comes to deployment. In 2019–2020, there were 1,000 operational flights, but in 2020–2021, this had increased by 40 percent to 1,400; and this year, there is already 30 percent growth.

The type of incidents when a drone is deployed varies considerably, from area searches, when people go missing, to the management of a serious road traffic collision. A scene can be relayed to senior managers in the police and other emergency services and viewed in real time.

Most people would probably accept that this use of drones poses no particular ethical issues for us. But as with much new technology, it raises other possibilities, especially around surveillance, and they do need careful thought. For instance, a drone has tremendous capability to observe and watch citizens without their being aware of it. Individu- als may be captured not only unawares but also by chance. There could be operational creep, going beyond what might be considered ethical and reasonable. And without good management, operators could cor- ruptly use a drone for their own purposes.

When I was looking at drones in a military context, people were already talking about semi-autonomous or "thinking" UAVs, drones that would make autonomous decisions about whether to use lethal force or not: the UAV would decide whether the target it was seeing was a com- batant or a civilian; tricky decisions in the context of urban conflicts.

I am glad to say we have in South Yorkshire an ethics panel who consider for us such matters in a policing context, and one member who specializes in these issues in her professional life. But drones are just one example of the way technology moves on and we have to keep alert to any ethical implications.

September 27, 2021

Test Pilots

No pilot scheme ever fails. At any rate, if they do, we don't hear anything about them. And we can see why they always succeed. (A pilot is a small-scale project or limited trial to see whether something should be done more widely. One or two police forces, for instance, might pilot something on behalf of all others.)

Pilots succeed because the original conviction that something will work will be based on some insight, it's not a total stab in the dark, and those undertaking the pilot will be enthusiastic and committed, going the extra mile, and so on. But whether something should then be rolled out more generally needs a further test. It is not whether the pilot works but whether it works when undertaken by those who are not the initial enthusiasts—those for whom this will just be part of their daily work, business as usual. Pilots always work; but it doesn't follow that the general rollout will.

Over my time as PCC, I have heard about many pilots. Some have indeed been rolled out more widely and proven successful. But others have seemingly vanished. Often, this is because resources were not available for them to be replicated more generally. Pilots are usually funded by one-off grants, but for other forces to adopt them may well mean having to identify money from within an existing budget, and that means taking resources from something else. It is not enough for an innovation to work; it has also got to be recognized as a better use of scarce resources than some existing commitment, a point that MPs in particular don't seem to appreciate when they write to tell me about something that was trialed in some other force and had good results; so, why aren't you doing this in South Yorkshire?

But I now realize that what is piloted can disappear for that other reason: introducing new practices into any organization also needs committed people, enthusiasts, believers, to make them work and have them accepted. Every innovation needs a bit of passion around it, even as it is rolled out. Perhaps, especially as it is rolled out.

October 4, 2021

Victims of Crime

There was an extraordinary paradox at the sentencing of the man who murdered Sarah Everard. On the one hand, we saw someone who betrayed everything a police officer is meant to be. On the other, we saw police officers commended by the judge for the most impressive police investigation he had come across in his entire thirty-year career. The worst and the best.

The accused had abused his position as a police officer in order to persuade Sarah to get into his car. It is all very well now for people to say, wise after the event, that if a lone woman finds herself approached in similar circumstances, she should vigorously question the officer's authority. But the whole point of this shocking abduction, rape, and murder is that there was no reason to question. This man was a serving police officer, not an ex-police officer or a fake one. He had a warrant card and, it seems, arrested Sarah on the basis of his valid credentials and, no doubt, his authoritative and confident manner as an experienced police officer. And in any case, we all know that resisting arrest is in itself an offense. (One can see how this advice to people, when stopped by an officer, could have the perverse and unintended consequence of leading some who are legitimately stopped, getting themselves into further trouble by resisting.)

But what also struck me about this chilling crime was the way it created multiple victims. The primary victim was Sarah, and we do not forget that. But reading the extraordinarily powerful impact statements that her family made revealed in terrifying detail how they, too, were victims of this man's brutality. We also learned that he had a family of his own, including two children. He has devastated their lives as well because the knowledge of who their father was will follow them all their days. Then, there were those in the emergency services, particularly the police, who had to recover Sarah's burnt body. And, as the ripples extend, every woman in the country has felt a little less safe and a little less trusting in the police service. A very long shadow has been cast.

October 11, 2021

A Week of Contrasts

Last week was fairly uncomfortable for the police service. It began with criticisms of the Met over its presumed failing to realize what a danger to women one of its officers posed, until it was all too late. There were calls for the commissioner, Dame Cressida Dick, to resign. There will be enquiries and the results may make painful reading. But it soon developed into a more general criticism around police officers abusing their positions of power to gain sexual favors, with accusations that forces were more interested in their reputations than dealing with those officers and safeguarding victims.

In South Yorkshire, we understand very well the importance of high standards and ethical behavior by the police, if trust and confidence is to be maintained, and without which, policing becomes so much more difficult.

So, the contrast could not have been greater when I went to the annual South Yorkshire Police Memorial Service in Sheffield Cathedral on Saturday. This year, a new memorial stone was dedicated to the memory of those who have been killed while on duty in our county, a poignant reminder that what motivates the overwhelming majority of our officers is the desire to keep us safe, yet knowing that some have made the greatest of sacrifices as they did so.

I found it very hard to read out the names of those killed on duty in front of their families and fellow officers gathered to remember them.

Women's Aid

Women's Aid is a small South Yorkshire charity, established in 1974, that provides housing for women and children who need a place of safety. Although the accommodation is local, the women, all victims of domestic abuse, can come from anywhere in the country. Sometimes, a woman needs to put some distance between herself and her abuser, and it is important that charities do not limit their service to those who live locally.

I visited one of their refuges. They have two in this area with sixteen and twenty self-contained flats. I was very moved to see how happy the children could be in such a welcoming house, even though many of them, if not all, had witnessed distressing scenes before arriving.

The women do not stay long here. This is temporary accommodation until something more permanent can be found.

I support the police in their work of rescuing women from abusive partners. But I am always acutely aware that without charities such as Women's Aid, the chances of some women getting away and finding the courage and the wherewithal to start afresh is so much more limited. In fact, for some, it is probably impossible. Yet, the funding of such charities is never secure.

October 18, 2021

MP Security

I am writing this following the shocking murder of the MP Sir David Amess at his constituency surgery in Southend. We are beginning to learn that the man suspected of attacking him may have had links to an Islamic extremist group and may, therefore, have been motivated by its ideology.

It raises again the question of MP security. There is nothing new about this. Throughout the time of the troubles in Northern Ireland, security was a constant concern. Airey Neave MP was blown up as he drove out of the House of Commons underground car park in 1979. The Irish National Liberation Army claimed responsibility. In 1984, a bomb exploded in the Grand Hotel, Brighton, during the Conservative Party conference. It had been planted by the Provisional IRA some weeks before but timed to go off during the conference. Sniffer dogs had failed to find it, probably because it had been wrapped in cling film. The prime minister Margaret Thatcher survived, but five died in the attack, including several MPs. Then, more recently, we had the murder in West Yorkshire of Jo Cox, MP for Batley and Spen.

Many have said, again and again, that lessons must be learned. But it is hard to know what lessons there are left to be learned. The Brighton bombing led to party conferences taking place in what one commentator called impregnable citadels. Spending on MPs' security shot up from £170,000 in 2015, before Jo Cox was killed, to over £4.5 million the following year.[6] Over the past weekend, police have contacted each MP, including here in South Yorkshire, to review their security.

6. *Yorkshire Evening Post,* "Cost of MPs Security Rises."

A range of common sense measures can be taken, such as only seeing people by appointment, which is what I do. Even so, Sir David's attacker may have made an appointment, and it is unrealistic to suppose that there can be police protection always and everywhere. MPs go to events and meetings almost every week. Jo Cox was not murdered at her surgery but in the street. Sometimes, I have joined South Yorkshire MPs at a street surgery, which is advertised on social media. We stand in the street and people walk up to us to have conversations. At moments like these, everyone is vulnerable.

Even secure buildings are never as secure as we would like. My office is in a secure police station, but a couple of years ago, someone managed to get through a security gate, then in through a door that requires a pass to open, and into my office. He was disturbed rather than dangerous, but it made my staff very nervous until two police officers arrived to take him away.

We shall have to await the review of security now underway. But whatever recommendations are made, the chances are that they will only serve to make our MPs seem more remote and less accessible, which is what neither we nor they want. We must do what we can, but at the end of the day, it will still be about relative risks and mitigations. There is only so much that can be done.

Reducing Violence

We all understand that if we are to reduce violence in our communities, we must try to prevent people being drawn to it in the first place. This starts with children. They learn by what they see and hear around them every day, and if, for example, abusive relationships are the norm in their household, it is hardly surprising if they exhibit the same patterns of behavior themselves. So, what can we do?

Worth Unlimited is a charity that works with schools across the Doncaster District. It provides early intervention for children who are displaying signs of anger, or who live in violent households, and whose behavior is such that they are likely to be excluded. And we know that excluded children become prey to violent, criminal gangs.

The school refers the child to Worth Unlimited and they assign a mentor to work with them. The service is free to the school, which provides a real incentive to schools in disadvantaged areas whose budgets are under pressure, especially for such a potentially costly provision. The mentor works one to one with the child, helping them to understand why their behavior causes them to get into trouble with their fellow students and teachers, and how they can learn to overcome their anger or disturbing behavior. Mentors can also help young people understand what is happening at home and how they can best cope.

I recently met with the founder of the charity, Ken Foden, and one of the mentors, Carol Parker-Cowan. They were both impressive people, dedicated and committed to make a difference to the lives and life chances of the young people they engage with. We met at one of the schools where they are working (Hatfield-Woodhouse Primary) with their equally committed head teacher, Helen Acton.

But does it work? The charity measures its success in two ways. First, if the child they are working with is not excluded. And second, if the number of incidents falls by at least 60 percent.

I was visiting the school in my capacity as chair of the Violence Reduction Executive Board along with Graham Jones, the VRU leader. We have just awarded the charity £25,000 to develop their activities. Working with these children is painstaking and requires a great deal of patience. But if we are serious about reducing violence, we have to start here: prevention at an early age.

October 25, 2021

Leaving Lockdowns

Emerging from one of Doncaster's prisons last week, I realized that many of us have probably just come as close as we ever could to being a released prisoner. When the anti-coronavirus lockdowns finally ended, we took tentative steps to return to normal life and sometimes found it quite disorientating. Going out again made many of us feel uncertain, and a few were quite disturbed. One of my neighbors says that even now, she finds going into a supermarket difficult. We had to retune our minds and it wasn't always easy.

When a prisoner leaves, he (they are mainly males) comes out through the main gate and enters what is now the half-remembered, half-forgotten world of freedom. The longer the sentence, the more difficult the adjustment, because the world of freedom demands a different mindset from the world of incarceration, where every minute of every day has been determined for you. But you have to adapt quickly. A range of practical matters can seem overwhelming. Where are you going to stay? How can you get a bank account set up? What about benefits? You leave with the clothes you came in with, but it was summer then and it's winter now. How are friends and family going to react? It is hardly surprising that so many ex-offenders find themselves back inside in a relatively short period of time. And that is not in any of our interests.

Part of the point of my visit was to see what the Serco-run prison at Marshgate has done to make this leaving work better. They have a project they call the Departure Lounge. The Departure Lounge has been created in the visitor center just outside the main gate. No one is obliged to go there because once the men are through the gate, they are free to do whatever they want, and some simply pass on. But for those who call in, there are helpful people from the prison and from charities to help them make the return to the world they had lost.

In the Departure Lounge, they can get a cup of coffee and pick up a packed lunch. Workers from the National Association for the Care and Resettlement of Offenders, as well as prison staff, are on hand to help ex-offenders negotiate everything from accommodation to a bank account, and a local charity assists with clothing. If families have come to meet them, they can do that in the Departure Lounge as well.

One major obstacle to successful resettlement, and one that is often overlooked, will always be not just the material needs but the sheer difficulty of changing a mindset—from being incarcerated to being free. And because of coronavirus, those being released now will have spent a large part of the last eighteen months locked in a cell for twenty-three out of twenty-four hours each day. There is nothing easy about resettlement, but the Departure Lounge makes a significant contribution in these most difficult of times.

November 1, 2021

The Budget

Last week's budget was quite a surprise, even though most of the big announcements had been well trailed. The surprise was realizing just how much spending and how much taxing it all implied, record amounts of both. Policing is a case in point.

The chancellor was first able to announce that the Spending Review (SR) was for the next three years. In other words, we now know the overall amount of funding that policing can expect over that period of time, and this allows for more sensible financial planning. We are grateful for that. It means that we can take, say, a decision to fund an expensive project in year one, knowing that we can pay for it over a number of years because the funding in those later years is secure and won't suddenly reduce.

We also know that the policing minister has secured more money overall than many of us expected a few months ago. We had assumed that the chancellor would now be anxious to start to pay off the huge debts that have been run up over the past eighteen months, largely as a result of the pandemic. We were wrong. Spending continues.

But there was a sting in the tail. More will be spent on policing in the coming years, but this will not all come from government. Police and crime commissioners are being given the flexibility to raise council tax (precept) by up to £10 per annum on a Band D property, and government figures assume that PCCs will exercise this freedom to the maximum. (In South Yorkshire, this would be more than 4 percent for each year of the SR period.) If we fail to do that, we should not be surprised if any requests for more funding in the future were met with a frosty reception: we had the chance to raise more from council tax, in our case, perhaps as much as £17 million over three years, and we didn't do it. (In our case, some of those extra asks include wanting help paying the civil claims arising out of the Hillsborough football disaster and child sexual exploitation in Rotherham. We have made a lot of progress with both but big sums of money remain to be paid out. I shall have to continue asking the home secretary for help.)

The question of the precept is a real dilemma for those PCCs—I would see myself as one—whose police force areas have within them many people living in relative poverty, who can ill afford any increase in council tax. These parts of the country, often the most urban, are also places with some of the most serious crimes. I will feel pressure from the force, therefore, for extra resources to combat serious crime while also recognizing how hard up many of our residents are—the very poverty that lies behind some of our young people being drawn into crime in the first place.

The police precept may not be large in cash terms, but it is a few more pence per week that someone has to find at a time when other parts of the council tax bill are going to go up as well, to pay for services and social care, and the cost of living is rising fast. The point about council tax, and one reason why people can be so angry about it, is that unlike many other costs that they can control, such as the cost of heating and eating, council tax is beyond our power to reduce; and we have to pay up. In December, we shall know what the share of government funding is per force. By then, I shall have asked people in an online survey what they want from their police and what they might be prepared to pay. Then, the hard choices will have to be made.

November 8, 2021

Chief's Log

Each morning for the last seven years, I have read something called the "Chief Constable's Log." This is a brief summary of some of the more serious crimes and other incidents that have concerned the police in the previous twenty-four hours. It can be a depressing list, from domestic abuse to commercial burglary, drug dealing to homicide, across all districts. The "Log" is a window into some of the darker aspects of human nature and, as a result, I am not easily shocked when I hear or read about others. But last week was an exception.

I read about some research into the sexual attitudes and behaviors of heterosexual male university students, undertaken by the University of Kent's Centre of Research and Education in Forensic Psychology. The research consisted of two online surveys. The first was completed by 295 students from 100 universities across the UK, the second by 259 students at one university in the south east of England.[7]

The results were shocking. Of the 554 participants, 63 admitted to committing 251 sexual offenses in the previous two years: sexually aggressive acts, attempted rapes, rapes, and other coercive and unwanted acts. The perpetrators of these offenses had pronounced misogynistic views and the researchers found a strong correlation between this type of toxic masculinity and sexual violence. These offenders believed, for example, that women who get drunk have only themselves to blame if they are raped. And they revealed that they had sadistic sexual fantasies about raping or torturing women.

It was sobering to realize that some of the offenses would have been committed while the students were still at school. Yet, these were probably among the best performing students in their year and are on

---

7. Hales et al., "Understanding Sexual Aggression in UK."

the threshold of having careers in business, the public services, and the professions.

I read this research shortly after being asked by students at local universities to support an anti-spiking campaign, which I was happy to do. But whatever happens in our town or city centers on Friday nights, the students may also have to turn their attention to something a little closer to home: their fellow students.

Not all the males in the surveys were like this, but a significant minority were. And the strong association between sexual assaults and underlying negative attitudes towards women ought to concentrate all our minds.

The police are generally involved after the event. But if we are to reduce sexual violence against women, there is profoundly important work to be done around the attitudes and behaviors of young males. We need the 491 who did not have misogynistic attitudes to be supported, and we need to encourage them to make their views known to some of their fellow students. They have to be the role models.

November 15, 2021

Close E-Encounter

E-scooters had never entered my consciousness until a few days ago. Then, I had a close encounter with one in the town center. The rider came up behind me on a pedestrianized street and whooshed past, narrowly avoiding me and another person. A few days later, an MP wrote asking what the legal position was as some of his constituents were reporting similar incidents. I asked the police.

The legal position is clear. Electric-powered scooters fall within the legal definition of a motor vehicle, with the same rules applying to them. The driver must have a licence and the vehicle must be taxed and insured. At present, they can only be used on private land (with the landowner's permission) or rented for use on those public roads and cycle lanes where there is a government-approved trial going on. Otherwise, you will probably be committing an offense under the Road Traffic Act 1988 or, if you scoot on a pavement, under the Highway Act 1835. There are no trials taking place in South Yorkshire, so anyone riding them here is almost certainly breaking the law. They could be prosecuted.

Some scooters can reach speeds of up to 70 mph, which seems extraordinary. The person who went past me wasn't doing that, but when you are sauntering along Fargate on a Saturday morning, and one passes you from behind unexpectedly and closely, it certainly felt like that!

I am not sure whether this is a growing or emerging issue in the county, so if something similar happens to you, please let me know.

Shopping Criminals

Last week, I met with the National Federation of Independent Retailers (NFIR), the body that speaks for small shopkeepers, of whom we have many hundreds in South Yorkshire. We talked about retail crime: shoplifting, thefts, burglaries, assaults, and so on. I was accompanied by Inspector Danielle Spencer, who is part of the Sheffield city center team, and PC Tony Nicholls, a SPOC (Single Point of Contact) for retail crime. The force has also just appointed a lead officer, Chief Inspector Gareth Thomas. There is a new determination by the police to be more proactive around retail crime.

Adrian Roper from the NFIR pointed out how vulnerable the independent retailer can be. They cannot afford the security that the bigger store may have, and they will not have a police station and police officers on site, like Meadowhall. So, they need an efficient way of reporting. But it is almost impossible to mind the shop while dialing 101 or filling in a long report online. As a result, there is considerable under-reporting of retail crime. Yet, as the police pointed out, if there is under-reporting, intelligence is lost and patterns of crime may be missed. Then, when someone is caught and goes to court, the full extent of their crimes could be unknown with the result that they receive a lesser sentence. So, we discussed how reporting could be made easier.

One of our district councils, for example, has new software that enables shopkeepers to upload CCTV onto the council's systems without an officer having to call, something that both saves police time and speeds the process of getting critical information to the authorities.

We also discussed the need for shopkeepers, who are the victims of crime, to complete victim and business impact statements. And where the shop plays a vital role in a local community, making a community impact statement as well, all of which could play a significant part in sentencing.

We have agreed to meet again, this time with shopkeepers them-selves, and I have said that I will ensure that retail crime is referenced in the new Police and Crime Plan.

Remember Them

Last week on Remembrance Day at 11:00 a.m., officers from my neigh-borhood police team went to each of the war memorials in our area and remembered the fallen in two world wars and other conflicts. It was very well received locally.

I went to a school a couple of years ago in November wearing a poppy. One of the pupils said he thought it was wrong to wear one and glorify war. I said I thought he was mistaken. This is not what we are doing. When we as a nation came to remember the first and then the second world wars, we could have called to mind victories, but chose not to. Our commemorations do not recall battles won and enemies defeated. They don't happen at an Arc de Triomphe but at a cenotaph, where we remember the dead and the cost of war.

November 22, 2021

Emotional Intelligence

The reason restorative justice (RJ) works is because most human beings, even offenders, have some degree of emotional intelligence (EI). In other words, they can put themselves in the shoes of another person and feel what it is like to be them. What I think happens in a successful RJ en-counter is that both parties are able to draw on that EI and grow their ca-pacity to feel as the other person feels. So, when a victim speaks honestly and spells out just how they felt when their small corner shop was broken into or their grannie's wedding ring was stolen, an emotional connection can be made. This must be one of the most powerful means we have for changing the behavior of another person.

I see now why, when I was burgled in Birmingham many years ago, the burglar turned all the photographs of my family face down on a side table. He didn't want to think about the human beings that lived there. He wanted his burglary to be an unemotional and purely mechanical affair. He had a smidgen of EI.

November 29, 2021

Reflections on Women and Male Violence

Both of my parents worked full-time in factories. But my mother also did all the washing, cooking, cleaning, and child care. I never thought about this growing up because that was the norm for every household around. It was only later that my understanding was changed. First by Charlotte Perkins Gilman's short story *The Yellow Wallpaper*.[8] I read this as a student. It paints a harrowing portrait of an intelligent but unnamed woman driven to despair and madness by an oppressive domesticity and enforced confinement after the birth of her child. She struggled to find a publisher.

Then I recognized my mother, albeit my mother was not middle class, in Virginia Woolf's description of the kind of selflessness that was demanded of women in pre and post-war society: she sacrificed herself daily. If there was chicken, she took the leg; if there was a draught, she sat in it. In short, she was so constituted that she never had a mind or a wish of her own but preferred to sympathize always with the minds and wishes of others. Woolf's fervent desire as a woman writer was to kill this idea of the woman as the angel in the house.[9]

So, we have come a long way in a comparatively short period of time. Or have we? Given how our eyes were opened by Perkins Gilman, Woolf, and others, who could have predicted what we are now witnessing, an apparent epidemic of violence by men against women?

Or is this what we should have expected after centuries of patriarchy, some sort of unconscious male reaction to, or even rejection of, a more equal society? Is this about the erosion of male imperialism, the potential loss of control, and the frustration and anger that brings?

I have no idea. All I do know is that we seem to be living through a time when women are facing a great deal of violence from men. We hope we can have a more coordinated response to violence against women and girls across the county. And all this will inform the priorities for my new Police and Crime Plan when it is published early next year.

Violence against women and girls is a national scandal and we must give it our urgent attention.

8. Gilman, *Yellow Wallpaper*.
9. Woolf, *Killing the Angel*.

Where Thieves Break in and Steal

Churches, synagogues, mosques, gurdwaras, and temples are no more exempt from crimes than any other buildings, not least, it seems, in South Yorkshire. Data obtained from thirty-eight of the forty-five UK police force areas by the Countryside Alliance shows that last year, over four thousand crimes were committed in them.[10] These ranged from theft and vandalism to assault and burglary. This was despite the restrictions and lockdowns brought about by the coronavirus.

Among the reported crimes, 1,336 were for theft, of which 115 were for lead, and there were 1,688 acts of criminal damage, including arson. The worst affected areas were in the South East, with Sussex recording 367, Kent 209, and the Met 575, though City of London police had nothing to report. The figures for Sussex include six sexual assaults and a rape in churchyards. In Caldecote, Hertfordshire, the windows of the fifteenth century church of St. Mary Magdalene were smashed shortly after the church had reopened after spending £150,000 to repair previous acts of criminal damage.

But South Yorkshire figures for churches and graveyards were also high at 227. (West Yorkshire was 189 and North Yorkshire 53.) South Yorkshire included 81 cases of theft, 65 of criminal damage, and 43 of violence. There were incidents of kidnapping, stalking, drug trafficking, possession of weapons, and sexual assault.

Each year, the police hold a national week when they focus intensively on metal crime, some of which is stolen from places of worship. Metal is recovered and there have been many prosecutions. Overall, the number of metal theft crimes has decreased, which is good news. But as far as theft and burglary is concerned, there is probably much more that church leaders could do. Isolated churches with lead on easily reachable porch roofs are particularly targeted. And no one should repeat the mistake of the church that conveniently had a wheelie bin standing by for thieves to load the lead into and take away.

Perhaps, church leaders in South Yorkshire could undertake an annual check of their buildings with a view to prevention.

---

10. Countryside Alliance, "Rural Charter."

December 6, 2021

What Are the Police For?

People often tell me what, in their view, the police are for. They do this directly: we want the police to catch the bad guys and lock them up. They also do it indirectly: we want to see more high-visibility jackets in our streets. I hear this wherever I go, in towns and villages, in the inner city and in the suburbs. This is what the public believe the police are for. It's about crime and antisocial behavior. Sometimes, as people say this, I compare it mentally with what the police actually do. I don't mean to suggest that they don't catch the bad guys or realize the importance of being seen in a variety of settings. But there is often a mismatch between the public's idea of what the police are for and what the police have to do, day to day.

One way of thinking about this is to envisage two concentric circles, a big one and, within that, a smaller one. The big circle represents the totality of what the police do and the smaller what many of the public think the police should do, what they are for, which is only part of what they do.

The bigger circle includes such things as finding missing children and bringing them back to a children's home, helping someone who is having a mental health episode in the town center, maintaining law and order in the streets around a football ground, talking to pensioner groups about protecting themselves from cyber fraud, going into schools and speaking to children about the dangers of carrying knives, and so on.

When I explain to groups how much time these non-crime matters or incidents probably take up, some people can become quite agitated and even angry. "We don't pay the police to be social workers" is a common reaction.

There may be some unreality behind these remarks; the police could not refuse to find an elderly dementia sufferer who has not come home. But there is also a sober recognition that resources are limited, and therefore, every hour that an officer spends dealing with incidents and non-crime matters is an hour that is not being given to investigating crime.

All of this matters for two reasons. First, the demand that is not crime is growing, and there is no way the police can refuse to respond. The teenager who has missed an 11:00 p.m. deadline will have to be found and brought back safely, however time-consuming and resource-intensive it will be. But also, each year, I have to determine what the precept (council tax) should be for policing. If I raise it, I have to give good reasons, and for many people, spending more time on non-crime matters is not a good reason.

There has to be an expansion of the public understanding of what the police do and a greater willingness to see this as what the modern police force is for. Otherwise, we are on a journey to endless frustration, however many new officers we have.

Cannabis Cultivation and Power Cuts

You may not see the connection between cannabis growing and the lights going out, but for people living in Hexthorpe, Doncaster, they have understood this very well in recent months. I'll explain.

Last week, I was walking in the area with Mayor Ros Jones, the local councilors Sophie Liu and Glyn Jones, the police, and local authority officers. We were looking at some recently installed CCTV that we had funded from a Safer Streets grant.

Then, by chance, we suddenly found ourselves in the middle of an unscheduled police operation. They were knocking in the front doors of several houses in one street and finding cannabis being grown in various rooms in each property. It started with one house, but intelligence gained from the occupant in one had soon led to three houses being discovered.

The rooms looked like industrial workshops with overhead cables, extractor fans, and lamps projecting heat and light down towards pots of cannabis plants in every room, twenty or so pots per room, with street values of about £1,000 per plant. The electricity by-passed meters and was taken directly from the main supply cables. It was very sophisticated, the engineer from Northern Power said. They knew what they were doing. But very dangerous. And that was the link between the cannabis growing and the lights going out, because what had alerted the police to the area in the first place were the power cuts triggered by this intensive cannabis cultivation and the overloading of the electricity supply.

Residents are often scared to report what they suspect may be happening in their street. If they don't report, however, the price may be an inconvenient power cut. But it could easily be worse. The risk of a fire and the risk of other gangs, looking for cannabis plants, breaking into the wrong address is considerable and has happened.

This was a good result and the installation now of more sophisticated CCTV may make it easier in the future to capture the evidence needed to identify, catch, prosecute, and convict those who are blighting parts of our towns. I think the mayor, who quite rightly gives me a hard time if she thinks that Doncaster is not getting its fair share of police resources, was probably impressed on this occasion.

And Finally

One of my PCC colleagues said in an interview last week that his greatest asset was his sense of humor. I think that was the funniest thing I ever remembering him saying. But perhaps irony is his really strong point.

December 13, 2021

Child Murder

(In early December, the stepmother of six-year-old Arthur Labinjo-Hughes was convicted of his abuse and murder and his father of his abuse and manslaughter. They were given long prison sentences. The crime caused widespread public revulsion.)

The murder of Arthur Labinjo-Hughes by his stepmother was so shocking, it was hard to take in. After seven years as a police and crime commissioner, I have become used to reading about the appalling things human beings are capable of doing to one another. Even so, this still made me shudder with disbelief. How could those who had the care of this little boy do anything so cruel?

Inevitably, it will raise, and in the most acute form, something I wrote about last week: the scope of what the modern police service is asked to do. Safeguarding children who may be at risk of harm is on that list, and what the police, along with other agencies, knew and did or didn't do in this case will now be scrutinized intensively. We will have to wait for some time before the full facts become clear and we see what role the various agencies played and how much information they shared. Whatever the outcome, we should not forget that the ones who were intent on causing this little boy harm were the ones who are now behind bars.

But following this terrible crime, I was pleased to hear last week about an initiative that South Yorkshire police have taken to help officers understand how children might need protection, even from those who we assume are looking after them. After all, police officers often find themselves in people's homes, not least as a result of being called to a domestic incident.

Assistant Chief Constable Dan Thorpe told us at a meeting of the Public Accountability Board that the force is developing an innovative form of in-house training for all who might come across issues of child protection, safeguarding, or neglect. It is a day of intensive training called "Child Matters." (The force had a similar day on "Domestic Abuse Matters.") Officers will be trained to be professionally curious, to recognize when a child might be at risk, to spot the signs of neglect, and to understand the need to act on what they are finding. The initiative shows clearly that today's force is in a very different place from where it was at the time of the Jay Report in 2014.

In addition, each district has a bespoke Child Protection Team. In all this, the force is working with the National Society for the Prevention of Cruelty to Children (NSPCC).

We don't know to what extent there will be criticism of any of the agencies that had dealings with the father and stepmother of Arthur Labinjo-Hughes. They were clearly sly and highly manipulative people. But we cannot let the neglect of that little boy and the cruelty he was shown pass us by. Child Matters training is the appropriate response.

Diary for 2022

The New Normal?

January 3, 2022

A Hierarchy of Wounding

I read an account of a young black man in South London reflecting on his former life as a gang member. It was a graphic picture he painted. The key question was, what actually caused you to turn your life around? But this seemed to be the only one he couldn't answer. He mentioned a role model and a charity; but he could not say what had made the critical difference and shifted his perspective on life so that he turned away from violence.

I have heard his story, or something like it, many times. He grew up in a family where violence was normal and mixed with people who also knew little else. He had carried a knife since he was fifteen. He was now in his late-twenties. This was not some lifestyle choice but a matter of survival on the streets where he lived. (I don't mean he was homeless. He shared a house with his mother, but he lived on the streets.) All this was wearyingly familiar. Whenever people tell me to listen to those with the lived experience of once carrying a knife, I hear something like this every time, and there is rarely anything new or revealing. What I really want to understand is what they can never articulate: what caused your radical change of mindset? However, this particular young man did say something I had not heard said before, at least not quite in this way.

People who have renounced violence often say that they carried a knife because it got them respect. This young person put that a little differently. He said he carried a knife to avoid humiliation. In his circle, to be stabbed is to be humiliated and that is something almost impossible to bear. So you have a knife to make others think twice before attacking you, to get respect; but if they do attack, you can retaliate in kind, though more violently, to wipe out the stain of humiliation. If they cut you on the leg, you will aim to stab them in the chest or neck. There is a hierarchy of wounding.

This is why most of the campaigns aimed at stopping knife crime by pointing out the risks and dangers fail. Those who are drawn into violence are not lacking in understanding of what the consequences for them could be. They know the risks very well; but they balance the risk of being attacked for carrying a knife against the risk of not being able to defend themselves or being humiliated.

Last year, we had more fatal stabbings on the streets of South Yorkshire. As the new year begins, we have little reason to suppose the situation will change any time soon. Violence will continue, and perhaps, the young man whose story I read gives further insight into why this will be. Depending on the mindset by which we each live, our lives are held by powerful psychological and emotional forces that drive our behavior and are not always easy to manage or overcome. For those whose mindset is that of those who live on the streets, the fear of humiliation must be one of the strongest drivers of behavior.

Nevertheless, people do change, and we must keep the exits in place for any that want to escape a life of violence, often associated with drugs and gangs. But what causes the change of mindset, the shift in perspective, and whether it is the same for all, remains as mysterious as ever.

The Good Gang

Continuing with the theme of violence, and especially its prevention, we are often asked to fund projects at a sports or martial arts center, a gym or boxing club. Those who run these organizations tell us, correctly, that they help to steer young males away from the gangs and their drug-related criminality. I am given all sorts of reasons why they succeed in doing this, but the most convincing is surely the most obvious. What the clubs offer is something that the criminal gangs offer and use as a powerful recruiting tool: they offer friendship.

Whenever I visit these clubs, I am always acutely aware of the crucial role played by the leaders. All through the time of my visit, I notice the way various young people will come over and have a chat with the leaders about all sorts of things; and the leaders listen patiently, without interrupting, and respond. They give the boys (and increasingly, girls, too) their full attention. Sometimes, they will notice a boy or girl who is a little aloof, and they will go across and chat with them. If you come from a household where your father is absent, your mother is worn down with domestic chores and other children as well as a job, having an adult devote time to you is a rarity. The greatest gift the club and its leaders give is this quality time. If I could wish for one thing this year, for all our young people at risk of being drawn into criminal gangs, it would be this: that they might find one of these good gangs to belong to.

January 24, 2022

Canine Comfort

At one time, I had three dogs in my life. They varied in size. Daisy was a dachshund, Murphy was part-German shepherd, and Magnus was a Weimaraner. It was only when they had gone that I fully appreciated the part they played in my life, and that of my children, over many years. They rejoiced when we did, and when I was fed up, they listened to my outpourings of frustration with great fortitude. They curled up at or on my feet (the dachshund), offering sympathy and understanding. They never complained. So, I am not surprised by the latest initiative of South Yorkshire police to help the well-being of staff and officers by using Well-being and Trauma Support Dogs from an organization called OK9.

There has been a growing realization in recent years that the well-being of officers and staff must be taken far more seriously. Those who work for the police can be faced with significant trauma on both a regular and an occasional basis. And it is not only those officers who have to go to the scene of some horrific road accident or homicide. It can also be those who, for example, spend many hours having to look at images of child abuse. In addition, the period of the lockdowns and working entirely from home meant that everyone's mental health and well-being might have been affected. (None of this, of course, is to suggest that people in other occupations cannot also be affected in similar ways.)

The Oscar Kilo (OK9) dogs and their handlers (who are mental health first-aiders) are brought into the workplace to help people's well-being. There is a scientific basis to what the dogs trigger when introduced for a session. Humans and animals share a hormone that engenders affection and trust and a sense of security. In doing so, cortisone levels are lowered and stress and anxiety are reduced.

At the time of writing, some thirty police forces (and some fire and rescue services) across the country are part of the OK9 network of Wellbeing and Trauma Support Dogs. It is surely one of those simple ideas that can help make a significant difference.

January 31, 2022

Who Does What?

There are so many agencies involved with roads, speed limits, and road safety that none of us know who to turn to if we have a problem.

Try these simple tests. Who is responsible for speed limits on major A roads, like the A629 or A616? Which agencies carry out speed checks, decide speed limits, paint white lines, maintain signage, or take responsibility for cars badly parked outside schools? What are the criteria that could lead to a change in speed restrictions or would enable a speed-watch scheme?

During the period of the lockdowns, the issues that people most wanted to talk to me about in rural areas were those of road safety and speeding. It was as if, tied to home, we became more conscious of the places where we lived and any passing traffic. But few knew what to do next.

Rebuked by the Chief Constable

Recently, I sent an email to the chief constable about Violence Against Women and Girls. In her reply, she changed the acronym VAWG to MVAWG, the M standing for Male. It was a way of reminding me that the violence we are talking about is male violence, ways of behaving that for too many men are normalized and routine. I felt suitable rebuked, but take the point. If we can't do something about male attitudes and behavior, we shall not make the world safer for women and girls.

February 7, 2022

Leveling Up at Every Level

I had not heard of the Broomhall Homework Club until last week. But when a BBC reporter began to talk about it on *Look North* last Friday, I stopped what I was doing and took notice. Broomhall is an area of Sheffield that I know well. I once lived there for five years as the local vicar, though my vicarage is now an Islamic center and the church has been converted into flats. It is probably one of the most deprived parts of the city. The homework club meets in what was once the church hall but is now a locally run community center. Their website tells me that they bring together volunteers and up to fifty students, aged eight to eighteen, mainly from ethnic minority groups, to do homework.[1] Seeing and hearing them on television conveyed an atmosphere in the club that was a mix of excitement and fun but also of real purposive learning. Yet, they struggle to find the £6,000 they need to keep going this year. And quite small sums make a big difference: £11 provides staff time for an hour; £60 would cover room hire for a week.

One reason this is of interest to me, from a policing and crime point of view, is because this is one of the hot spot areas of the city as far as drug dealing and crime goes. If we are to keep young people away from the gangs, we need clubs like this one, where students are not only helped to do well with their academic work but can also find sympathetic adults they can talk to, and, for some, good adult role models that may otherwise be missing from their lives. If we are serious about leveling up, closing the gap between the richer and poorer parts of the country, we are going to need not only the big projects for renewal and regeneration but many small local groups like the Homework Club.

February 14, 2022

Met Matters

The troubles with policing in the capital took a dramatic turn last week with the resignation of the commissioner, Dame Cressida Dick. We should all be concerned. The Met is the biggest police force in the country, with over 45,000 officers and staff, seven times the size of South Yorkshire police. So it consumes a lot of resources. The Met also has

1. Sheffield's Student Union, "Homework Club Action Group."

national responsibilities, such as counterterrorism. And it ensures the security of some of our most important national institutions, such as parliament. If confidence in the Met is shaken and if morale within the force is damaged, that is bad news for us all.

At one point, my path and the former commissioner's crossed for a short time. After the urban riots of 2001, we served together on a community cohesion panel set up by the home secretary to advise him on how we might bring about more integrated communities in those urban centers where there had been rioting, particularly Bradford, Oldham, and Burnley. She was much more junior then, of course.

The panel was chaired by Professor Ted Cantle. He had produced a report following the disturbances. This concluded that although the different ethnic groups in those places lived side by side, there was little or no interaction. People lived parallel lives. Hence, the need for community cohesion. (I remember reading Benjamin Disraeli's *Sybil, or The Two Nations* on the train journeys down to London, a novel about the social divide in Victorian Britain, though that was about class rather than ethnicity. The basic theme of the novel was also the inspiration for the One Nation group of Conservative MPs.)

As a result of the report and the work of the panel, community cohesion became a huge agenda for towns and cities across the country, bringing together people in the public, private, voluntary, and faith sectors to work for more integrated communities. Cressida Dick's contributions to the discussions were always among the most perceptive, so I was pleased when she became commissioner.

I am sorry and concerned that the Met now finds itself where it does. But for me, it raises different questions from those that have largely dominated the public debate so far. I would ask, is this police force simply too big and unwieldy for anyone to affect cultural change in all its parts with the urgency needed? Should the national responsibilities be given to a national body, such as the National Crime Agency? Does it make sense to have the mayor as the police and crime commissioner? How can he find the time to do all that being mayor involves and get to grips with the issues facing this huge force as well? After all, in South Yorkshire as PCC, I work a full week, often with evening and weekend engagements, yet I am PCC for a police force and population only a fraction of London's. How can the mayor, any mayor, give policing the time and attention needed? How can they properly hold the chief of police to account if they don't have the time to do it? This may not be the time to ask these questions. But unless they are asked, we may be here again with another commissioner, another set of issues, and another unhappy ending.

February 21, 2022

Criminals Prey on the Vulnerable

Sometimes, we advertise vulnerability without realizing it. I was speaking to the Barnby Dun and Kirk Sandall parish council last week about a spate of burglaries they had been experiencing. The local inspector Alison Carr came with me to reassure the meeting by outlining what the police knew, what suspects had been identified, and how their investigations were progressing. But during the conversation, the issue of burglaries from bungalows, where some older and more frail members of the community lived, came up. They receive care during the day and carers accessed their homes with keys kept in a key safe on the outside wall. These are a familiar sight, often positioned beside the front door. The carer knows the code to open the key safe. But to a thief, this is the equivalent of announcing that a frail, elderly, or vulnerable person lives here, and the key to the door is in this key safe.

However, some of these key safes are anything but safe. It's almost like putting the key under a plant pot. One blow knocks them off the wall and the thief gets them open, takes the key, and enters the property through the front door, as the carer would, which must be a great shock to the resident. The answer seems to be to ensure that those who have a key safe have one that is very robust and securely fixed, which probably means paying something in the region of £50 or £60. This is a lot of money for many in our communities, but for peace of mind, it should be done. We need to check on our relatives.

February 28, 2022

Ukraine

In the 1980s, I was deputy leader of Sheffield City Council when the city was twinned with Donetsk in Ukraine. At that time, the country was still part of the Soviet Union, and the idea of twinning was to try to play some small part in breaking down the walls of suspicion between the communist east and the democratic west. Ordinary citizens from community groups and organizations went from Sheffield to Donetsk and vice versa. (I remember how delighted visitors were to discover John Lewis in Barkers Pool.) I was part of a civic delegation, guests of the Donetsk city council. The communist party controlled everything, which is why the police were instructed to stop the traffic to allow our Zil cars to go from the airport to the hotel, the Shakhtar (Miner), unimpeded.

Donetsk had been chosen because it was a mining and steel town. We were taken down the deepest mines in Europe and visited a mill with its praise and blame boards, on which individual workers were named or shamed for their previous week's productivity or lack of it.

The civic leadership, before Ukraine became a democracy, was communist and looked to Moscow. They were mainly ethnically Russian, speaking Russian rather than Ukrainian, and had Russian names. It was a sign of things to come in parts of the Donbas.

What we are seeing now in Ukraine is heartbreakingly depressing but a sharp reminder of how fragile are the freedoms we take for granted and how easily they can be lost. Respect for the law, whether international or national, is the bedrock on which our security and well-being always depends.

March 7, 2022

Preventing Violence

How do we help upcoming generations to live without violence? This is one of the objectives of our Violence Reduction Unit, and last week, one of the projects it supports was on *BBC Breakfast*. The project is called Mentors in Violence Prevention (MVP) and it is currently operating in eight schools in South Yorkshire. The BBC featured Brinsworth Academy, Rotherham.

It works like this. For a few weeks, between four and six members of staff at the schools are trained in the methods of MVP. In turn, they identify a small team of pupils who have volunteered to help their peers recognize potentially poor behavior and call it out. The teams go into classrooms and lead sessions on what makes for healthy relationships. They encourage their colleagues to be what they call "up-standers" and not bystanders. Bystanders, for example, see their friend behaving in a bullying fashion and say nothing, whereas up-standers pluck up courage, take their friend to one side, and say they think this is not right.

The teams may also take sessions on how to recognize other examples of poor behavior, such as misogynistic language or harassment. On one occasion, when I saw the program in action in a Glasgow school, two pupils took a class of year 10s for an hour and spoke about how to recognize domestic abuse and what to do about it. They were very knowledgeable: they had obviously prepared very well and led the class in a challenging and thoughtful interactive session. Young people broke into groups for intense conversations on themes around healthy relationships that their peer mentors had suggested.

The theory behind the program is that young people are more likely to listen to their peers than to adults, and there is a good deal of academic research to support this, from Scotland, Sweden, and the USA. The researchers found that the attitudes of the young people improved, fewer pupils were being excluded from school, and pupils said they felt safer. They also found that academic results improved as well, though this was not an aim of the program.

Mentors in Violence Prevention is a good example of how the Violence Reduction Unit is helping to influence the present generation of young people. My guess is that they will also influence the attitudes and behaviors of some of the generations above them as well. They will not be bystanders in the home either.

Future Remembering

Last week I visited Bramley Parish Council in the Rotherham District. We had a good, frank, wide-ranging discussion. I really value these occasions because I often learn more than I think I am going to do when I look at the agenda. Although we spoke about the reasons for the visit, which was residential burglaries, speeding issues, and how contact with the neighborhood police can be made better, we also touched on other matters and one in particular: Remembrance Day.

The councilors told me about the extensive commemorations that happen in Bramley. In particular, they spoke about a march and gathering on Remembrance Sunday that attracts as many as one thousand people, which is a big event. The MP John Healey has been very supportive.

They pointed out how these numbers had grown in recent years. This is true across the county and I imagine across the country. Yet, I can recall debates and discussions not so very long ago when it was being suggested that Remembrance commemorations were falling away and would not continue beyond the lives of those who had seen active service in either of the world wars. Yet the opposite happened. It is almost as if the realization that these veterans were becoming so few that we determined to rouse ourselves and ensure that their sacrifices really were not forgotten.

The reason Bramley Parish council raised the matter was because in the past, they had been well supported on the day by police officers who helped the procession cross busy roads. But this support had been withdrawn in recent years (and this is county-wide), and they were bewildered by that. And so am I.

I realize that the parish councils will have to apply to the district council to get roads closed. That is not a matter for the police. And I realize there is a cost to the police, financial and organizational. But there is another cost that needs to be considered: public goodwill towards the police. If the police want to find occasions when they can be highly visible, when they can do something for their communities that is much appreciated, and build relationships and trust, there are few better ones than this. So, I will be speaking to the chief constable about it. If we start now, we can have things in place for Remembrance commemorations in every part of South Yorkshire in good time. The police may not be able to do as much as they once did. But we need to be clear about what can be done well in advance. This will be time and money well spent.

Smart Motorways, Law, and the Layperson

As I understand it, the Crown Prosecution Service has told the police that there is no legal basis for bringing a charge of corporate manslaughter against National Highways (formerly Highways England) for the deaths of some of those killed on smart motorways because the agency has no duty of care towards them.

I am not a lawyer so I cannot comment on whether this is a correct understanding of the law. But as a layperson, it does not seem right. I can understand why such a duty might not apply to the existing motorway, but I cannot understand why there is no duty of care when the agency makes substantial, material changes to a motorway that introduce a danger that was not there before. It seems to me that this would be in some ways analogous to saying that, when undertaking repairs, the agency had no duty of care to the workers on the site or the motorists who were passing by or those who subsequently drove there. I can't believe this is the case.

If the review of smart motorway safety currently being undertaken by the government shows that safety has been compromised rather than improved by reconfiguring the motorways in this way, I have a feeling that the issue of duty of care will be revisited. In the meantime, what do the academic lawyers, as opposed to the armchair lawyers like me, make of this?

March 14, 2022

To Frack or Not to Frack

The possibility that there might be fracking either in South Yorkshire or close to our boundaries was never good news for policing. Fracking (to release shale gas) is controversial. It is generally opposed by those who live near to the fracking sites, and it attracts environmental protestors from far and near. We saw this happen at Kirby Misperton in North Yorkshire and over the hills in Lancashire. I remember spending some time a few years ago looking at sites near to Misson in North Nottinghamshire, which would impact our side of the county line. I also spoke with residents in Woodsetts, another site but in South Yorkshire. People knew they would be affected by daily convoys of lorries both while the site was being pre- pared and also afterwards, taking away the water used in the process for decontamination at Blackburn Meadows in Sheffield. But they also feared having their drinking water affected or properties disturbed by minor tremors. Yes, they told me, we are united in our opposition.

These protests are not easy to police. Sites are often in open coun- tryside, giving many points of access. It is difficult to remove determined protestors from trees or underneath vehicles. The police face the usual dilemma: they must enable peaceful protest but also make it possible for people to go about their lawful business. This is potentially a huge demand on officer numbers and quickly runs up big bills in overtime, as the Lancashire constabulary found.

In the end, fracking turned out to be financially more risky than first thought. Perhaps, it was not surprising, therefore, when the government declared a moratorium.

But now, the war in Ukraine and the sanctions imposed on Russia, including its lucrative business of supplying the west with natural gas, is seeing energy costs soar and a rising demand for alternative sources of energy. The possibility of fracking is returning, even though, in a recent poll, only 17 percent of the population supported it. I am not sure what our most recently elected MPs will do if the government says it will lift the moratorium.

I had a policing protests panel the last time fracking looked as though it might happen. Panel members are briefed by South Yorkshire police (SYP) and then observe how the protest is managed. This is how I satisfy myself that SYP are walking that very difficult tightrope of enabling protestors to protest and workers to work. I will revive the panel if needed, but I would much prefer none of this to happen at all.

March 21, 2022

Spring Cleaning in Maltby

As I walked with the neighborhood police team down Morrell Street in Maltby and entered Coronation Park from the lower side, I was appalled by the sheer amount of litter in the street and in the park. This is not a police matter, of course, but because of the partnerships we have on the Local Criminal Justice Board (LCJB) and the Violence Reduction Unit (VRU), both of which I chair, I think we can help spruce up this part of Maltby.

The Probation Service, who are partners on both the LCJB and the VRU, run a scheme for offenders who have to do so many hours of service in the community as part of their rehabilitation. So, I have asked the VRU officer who deals with Rotherham matters, Rachel Fletcher, to find a way of bringing a team to Maltby. This will help the Probation Service find unpaid work for the offenders; it will help the offenders complete what is required of them; and it will help tidy up this part of Maltby—three good outcomes.

I think it helps policing, too, because the failure to deal quickly with things like litter and graffiti creates a sense that other antisocial acts are also acceptable. It leads to further run down and these are the conditions in which antisocial behavior and crime start to flourish. (The academics know this as the "broken window effect.") So, I hope Maltby notices a difference soon and the town council can think about how it might prevent this happening in the future.

March 28, 2022

Reaching the Young

If we are to keep young people safe, we need to help them understand life's dangers from an early age. For many years now, South Yorkshire Police (SYP) and South Yorkshire Fire and Rescue Service (SYFRS) have jointly supported the Lifewise Centre at Hellaby in Rotherham district.[2] This is a building on a small industrial estate that has been turned into an educational center. A large part of it consists of a series of "sets" (rather like a film or television studio) of a cafe, a shop, a kitchen, a sitting room, a garden, a road layout, and so on. Each set is designed to illustrate potential hazards or dangers that people might face in daily life. Children from primary schools across the county visit and SYP and SYFRS staff help them to appreciate the risks.

During the pandemic, visits were severely curtailed; but when I look at the figures for last year, the results are impressive. The number of schools that brought children were 84 of 86 from Rotherham; 73 of 78 from Barnsley; 88 of 91 from Doncaster; and 119 from 124 from Sheffield. In total, 5,921 pupils came from 158 schools.

In addition, twenty-eight sessions were delivered by staff to 4,960 older students on guns and knives programs. And a new program called Your Life, Your Choice, about how gangs can draw young people into criminality, has been trialed in two schools for those in year 9.

All this is work that continues on a regular basis, about which we probably hear little. But we should thank those at the Lifewise Centre who seek to keep our young people safe in this way.

April 4, 2022

Custody Visitors

When someone is arrested, they are taken to a custody suite. We have three in South Yorkshire: at the central police stations in Doncaster and Barnsley, and at Shepcote Lane near the M1, for Sheffield and Rotherham. As police and crime commissioner, one of my responsibilities is to ensure that those who are detained are properly treated. It is, after all, a serious matter to take away someone's liberty. So, how do I monitor what happens in the custody suites?

2. www.lifewise999.co.uk.

Before the pandemic, I relied on a group of volunteers called Independent Custody Visitors (ICVs). They went into custody suites to observe and check. But when visits were for a while suspended, we had to do things differently, remotely. So, a member of my staff scrutinized on a regular basis a sample of the records that have to be kept on each person detained. It has turned out to be a very useful way of checking. We can see whether there is consistent recording. We can see whether everything that should be done has been done, or at least we can see whether it has been recorded as being done; and if there is no record, we can follow up by asking.

While we will probably continue to do this, it could never wholly replace the vital work of having people visit because the ICVs need to look into the cells and speak to the detainees, the police, and detention officers. So, last Friday, Sally Parkin from my office, who organizes the ICVs, brought them together for the first time since the pandemic and I was able to meet them.

As well as our experienced ICVs, we now have some new volunteers. And they are a most interesting mix of people: male and female, mainly relatively young, from all walks of life, and from various parts of the county, though we remain a little light on volunteers from Barnsley.

They were introduced to the new head of custody, Chief Inspector Lee Dowswell, who told the ICVs that they were the conscience on his shoulder.

They also met others whom they might come across when they visit: the liaison and diversion teams and Plan B Navigators.

Liaison and diversion staff pick up those detainees who have very particular or complex needs to see whether they can be helped. Those, for instance, who have issues with accommodation, drugs, alcohol, or with their mental health. The Navigators work with those who are involved in serious violence, principally, knife incidents. They offer to help them break with the habits of violent behavior and turn their life round. The Navigators have found that this time of enforced reflection in a custody suite cell does sometimes lead people to being open to other possibilities; it is what the Navigators call a "reachable or teachable moment." As one such person once told me, he realized that he didn't want his children to spend the rest of their lives visiting him in prison.

Our teams of independent custody visitors are beginning their work anew, some for the first time. They will go in pairs to the custody suites, unannounced and at a time of day or night that suits them, to ensure that all who are detained there, whether adult or child, are being treated well.

This Digital World

I was interviewed this week by two of Her Majesty's Inspectors of Constabulary. They are looking at how prepared forces are across for dealing with digital forensic work. Digital forensics can embrace everything from DNA to the internet, some of which is dealt with at a regional level and some locally. This is a hugely important matter because the world we are now in is a digital world. This is not the future but the present; and there will be no turning back. Criminals, for instance, are increasingly pursuing their activities online, and 54 percent of all crime is already cyber-related.[3] Criminals are even building up their assets and hiding them this way, through cryptocurrency.

I wanted to assure the inspectors that in South Yorkshire, we understand the need for a digital police force and the necessity of investing in it. In one sense, all policing is now digital anyway. Every police officer depends on a mobile device of some kind for both recording and receiving information. Every police force has to get better and quicker at receiving information digitally, such as CCTV, data on mobile phones, or clips from body worn cameras, assessing its relevance and presenting it in court. Every force needs analysts who can trawl through acres of data and help officers to understand types or patterns of crime in their area, to identify trends and predict developments.

Digital policing is not some discrete area of police work but the water in which everyone swims. As I look to the future, I see a hopeful sign and some danger. The hopeful sign is the fact that the force is changing very rapidly, because we are having to recruit so many new officers. They may lack experience but they are not intimidated by technology. This is their world. Experience will come over time, but I have no doubt that they will adapt to changing technology with an ease that other generations find a constant struggle. The modern detective in particular will need to be both confident around technology while having the attention to detail and professional curiosity that makes for a good investigator. (I'm afraid Inspector Morse would fall at the first hurdle.)

The danger is being able to retain in the police service those, mainly staff, who spend their days digitally, interrogating and analyzing

3. My analyst provided me with this data from police briefings.

data. They are highly skilled and those skills are valued beyond policing, not least in the private sector. We need to encourage in them pride and satisfaction in working for the public good. Police staff are rarely seen by the general public, but their work is every bit as crucial for keeping us safe as a high-visibility jacket on main street.

April 25, 2022

Sentences and Perceptions

Crime and the public perception of crime are often quite different. So also are they about other aspects of crime and criminal justice. Take sentencing. What do we think the trends have been in sentencing over, say, the past twenty-five years? A national charity ran a survey.[4] Below is what the public think has happened over this period (expressed as a percentage, but excluding "don't knows" and "prefer not to says"). You can test your own perception against the general public, and at the end, I'll reveal the facts. So, over the past twenty-five years:

1. Has the average prison sentence become longer, or shorter or stayed the same?

   Much longer: 2 percent*

   Longer: 6 percent

   Stayed about the same: 11 percent

   Shorter: 37 percent

   Much shorter: 19 per cent

2. Have sentences for those convicted of murder (before release on licence) become longer or shorter or stayed the same?

   Much longer: 2 percent*

   Longer: 4 percent

   Stayed about the same: 13 percent

   Shorter: 31 percent

   Much shorter: 26 percent

---

4. I took these statistics from research by the Prison Reform Trust: prisonreform-trust.org.uk.

3. What was the average prison sentence for rape?

   Two years or less: 23 percent

   Three to four years: 22 percent

   Five to six years: 27 percent

   Seven to eight years: 9 percent

   Nine to ten years: 6 percent*

   More than ten years: 5 percent

4. What was the average prison sentence for burglars?

   Six months or less: 35 percent

   Seven to twelve months: 25 percent

   Thirteen to twenty-four months: 20 percent

   Twenty-five to thirty-six months: 5 percent*

   More than thirty-six months: 4 percent

In each case, the correct answer has an asterisk against it. How can we have a sensible debate around sentencing when public perception is already so wide of the mark?

May 2, 2022

Funding Figures

The more I get involved in national issues around the funding of police forces, the more perplexed I become. One way of looking at this is to ask how much a force is able to spend for each person in its force area. To find this out, you need to add together what each force gets by way of government grant and through council tax (the precept) and divide by the population statistics. The amounts of funding can be very different.

Some of these differences are not surprising. We would probably all agree that there are some police forces that need more funding than others because of the complexity of their context or the seriousness of the crime and non-crime activities in their area. It would seem right that our neighbors in rural Lincolnshire receive £190 per head, at the lower end of the scale, and the Metropolitan police should have £360 per head at the other. South Yorkshire sits in twenty-sixth place out of forty-three England and Wales force areas with £222.

But when I look at some of the forces that receive more funding than South Yorkshire, it is puzzling. Surrey police, for instance, have £228 per head. Surrey? I struggle to think what the complex urban areas of high crime might be. Even Durham at £231 does not seem right. Durham, Darlington, and Hartlepool are not big places, much of the county is rural, and its total population is little more than Sheffield. Cumbria? £258 per head. There are a lot of sheep in Cumbria, I used to live among them, but less than half a million people altogether. The biggest city, Carlisle, is a third the size of Barnsley. And so on.

What causes these differences in funding? It is partly the way government grant is divided up, the funding formula, but more particularly, it's about the ability of police and crime commissioners to raise money through local tax. Although I raised tax by the maximum permitted this year, the total tax South Yorkshire police get from precept is £57 per head because we have so few properties that are in the higher bands for council tax purposes. But Surrey police will receive £125 per head by way of precept because they have many properties in higher tax bands. If we are serious about leveling up, this is also an area that cannot be ignored. Businesses will locate themselves in those parts of the country where crime is being well-managed by the local force; and that does require fair funding.

What Are We Doing to Young People?

A young person told me about a presentation they'd had at school about knives and crime. I asked how it went. She said it upset her. She had never thought about people her age, or at her school, or in her class carrying knives before. And some of the photographs of the knives were pretty scary. She went on to say they now had lessons about the way we were destroying the world through climate change, about COVID persisting for the rest of her life, and whether the war in Ukraine might eventually lead to war across Europe. "My whole adult life seems ruined before I start."

We sometimes worry about criminalizing young people. Perhaps, we should worry about traumatizing them as well.

May 9, 2022

Boxing and Fighting Are Different Things

Last week, I dropped in on the Sheffield City Boxing Club in Sharow, Sheffield, run by Brendan Warburton MBE. I went with staff from the Violence Reduction Unit (VRU). The club is one of a number that receives a grant from the VRU to run sessions for young people. Generally, these grants are for teenage boys and girls navigating those critical years between childhood and adult life. We want to provide them with meaningful activities outside school and influence their behavior, a contribution towards preventing them being drawn into antisocial behavior or crime. But the session I went to see was for children from a primary school during school hours.

The teacher who came with them told me how the school and the community had become troubled by some aspects of the children's behavior. They seemed to have little respect for adults, parents, teachers, or one another. They didn't seem to have much respect for themselves either, poor estimations of their own worth. They also scrapped a lot. But since coming to the club, there had been improvements.

It was noticeable how respectful they were to one another and to the adults who were leading the activities, young professional boxers and two students on placement from Sheffield Hallam University. They sat still. They listened to instructions. They were focused. They joined in the activities with enthusiasm. They enjoyed it. And afterwards, they put away the equipment they used tidily. The coaches tell the young people that there is a world of difference between fighting and boxing. Boxing is about discipline and focus and learning to respect the people you train with and those you spar with.

Three things I reflected on. First, helping rising generations seems to require earlier and earlier interventions. Second, while adult role models are important, we don't always realize that the young people become role models to one another. They imitate the behavior of their peers. The club is able to set a standard. And third, as a result, we are very dependent on having clubs like the Sheffield City Boxing Club. They are able to engage the young people in activities that they really enjoy, but they are also willing to use that as the teachable moment when a difference can be made.

May 16, 2022

A Text of Terror

I briefly reverted to my previous occupation on Sunday when I went to preach at evensong at The Queen's College, Oxford. The chaplain asked me to speak about violence against women and girls and my role as police and crime commissioner in the light of one of the lessons being read. (If you want to look it up, it was 2 Sam 13:1–20.) This was a story of domestic abuse, the rape of a beautiful young woman by her half-brother. Although she was a royal princess, this did not stop the violence against her; and afterwards, she faced shame and ruin, living a desolate life. It is a terrifying story and as you may imagine, not one that is often read.

However, it gave me a chance to point out two things to the students and staff of the college. First, that most violence against women and girls is not from strangers but from within the household. And second, domestic abuse is a crime that involves people from all social classes. We all, therefore, especially men, need to have our underlying attitudes and behaviors challenged.

Many of the young people in that relatively privileged congregation are on the brink of having influential careers in business, the professions, the armed forces, parliament, and, yes, the police. If domestic violence is to be rooted out, there is no social group that is exempt, as the lesson reminded us. Given how long ago that royal rape took place, about 900 BCE, it also suggests that misogynistic attitudes are likely to be deeply and unconsciously embedded in all of us. We should not underestimate the task of making a difference.

May 23, 2022

An Attestation

It was quite moving to go to Robert Dyson House, the police training center near Wath on Dearne, to be part of a swearing-in ceremony for the latest group of new recruits. This was the first time the police had been able to hold an in-person ceremony with parents present since the coronavirus interrupted everything.

Proud parents watched as forty young women and men, neatly turned out in their new uniforms, marched in and took their seats. They faced one another, twenty on one side and twenty on the other, like an Oxbridge chapel. This was their second day.

The inspector welcomed recruits and parents. We watched a brief video showing some of the many and varied roles that South Yorkshire police undertake. The chief constable reminded them that policing is based on values. I said that while the public might have their criticisms, everyone wanted to see more police in South Yorkshire, and they were the more police.

They have to swear an oath in the presence of a magistrate and then receive their warrant cards. The heart of the ceremony was the declaration, which is called an attestation. Each new officer called out their name and then, collectively, they said this:

> I do solemnly and sincerely declare and affirm that I will well and truly serve the Queen in the office of constable, with fairness, integrity, diligence and impartiality, upholding fundamental human rights and according equal respect to all people; and that I will, to the best of my power, cause the peace to be kept and preserved and prevent all offences against people and property; and that while I continue to hold the said office I will to the best of my skill and knowledge discharge all the duties thereof faithfully according to law.

There are many things of interest about this declaration. There is a strong emphasis on values, such as fairness, integrity, diligence, impartiality, and respect. I am not sure that all members of the public would be aware of the commitment to uphold human rights or to prevent crimes and not just enforce the law. And the attestation also makes clear that the police have operational independence. They serve the Queen and not politicians. That includes police and crime commissioners. And government ministers.

I spoke to some of the new officers and their parents at a buffet afterwards. As we talked, I was struck by the number of times the parents and the officers themselves said that they had always wanted to join the police, as far back as they could remember. This is challenging for future recruitment campaigns. I am not sure what a campaign for the newly born looks like. However, it's an indication that being a police officer is a vocation and not just a job.

May 30, 2022

The Crooked Path

From time to time, someone is quoted in our local media saying, "Lock them up and throw away the key," or something similar. I understand the sentiment. Let's stop the career criminal from re-offending by taking them permanently off the streets. But there is a flaw in the thinking. The flaw, quite simply, is believing that criminals stop their activities once inside. This is far from the truth. This was brought home last week in a report to the Countywide Community Safety Forum, which I chair.

The forum brings together representatives from each of the statutory district community safety partnerships, whose task is to convene local organizations in each local government area to reduce and prevent crime, and the fear of crime, and keep people safe. One partnership report reminded us that the city of Doncaster is unique in South Yorkshire in having a prison. In fact, not one prison but four.

These four prisons hold offenders from every part of the country, and many of them are members of organized crime gangs in the places from which they came. The report estimated that each prison could hold, on average, men from forty-eight separate gangs.[5] In prison, they continue their offending behavior. They may be violent towards other prisoners or staff. They seek to corrupt prison officers. Some seek to run their gangs at a distance, smuggling small, not easily detectable, plastic mobile phones into the prison.

South Yorkshire police work with prison officers in the prison to tackle these crimes, disrupting the activities of the criminals. This Prison Crime Unit handles an average of one hundred-fifty live investigations. So, the mantra "Lock them up and throw away the key" betrays a woeful ignorance about the realities of criminality and incarceration. It is no solution but indicates that someone would sooner bury their head in the sands than think constructively about how to make us all safer. Unfortunately, crime does not stop at the prison gate.

---

5. Reports were regularly presented at closed meetings of the Countywide Community Safety Forum.

June 6, 2022

Numbers and Austerity

What happened to police numbers during the years of austerity? Until recently, I rather assumed that police forces across the country faced the same scale of cuts. Numbers would vary according to the size of the force, but the percentages of officers being lost would be about the same. I was wrong.

I should have realized why this would not be the case. As we know, police funding comes from two principal sources: government grant and precept (council tax). If police forces receive different amounts of government funding as a percentage of their total funding, then cuts to government grant will have a bigger impact on those forces that are more dependent on grant. In addition, those that are in areas with a more robust council tax base, because they have more higher value properties, will be able to offset some of those grant cuts through precept increases. This is probably what happened during the ten years of austerity. Some forces suffered less through grant cuts and were better able to make up for losses through council tax.

Some examples will show what I mean. If we look at the number of officers three particular forces had in March 2010, and compare that with the number they had by 2019, we can see the impact of cuts. Northumbria had 4,187 officers in 2010, but this had fallen by 29 percent to 3,081 by 2019. South Yorkshire went from 2,953 to 2,370, a drop of 19 percent in the same period. Surrey had 1,890 in 2010 and fell by 0.4 percent to 1,882 by 2019.

Being less dependent on grant, Surrey could maintain officer numbers at pre-austerity levels, whereas South Yorkshire and Northumbria took massive hits.

Now, as we start to come out of austerity, something equally dramatic happens. Surrey now has more officers in 2021 than it did in 2010 (a total of 2,086), while Northumbria and South Yorkshire are still well below the pre-austerity figures. (Northumbria has 3,416 and South Yorkshire now has 2,745.) Since 2010, Northumbria has lost 18 percent of its workforce and South Yorkshire has lost 7 percent. But Surrey has increased numbers to 2,086, an increase of 10 percent.

Yet, Surrey has no town the size of our two cities and two major towns. Its largest center of population is Guildford with 67,000. Despite the fact that it has no large urban areas and all the serious crimes associated with them, for ten years, it was able to maintain officer numbers, while places like South Yorkshire and Northumbria (Newcastle, Gateshead, Tyneside, Sunderland) had to cope with ever falling resources.

This had a significant impact on crime. It allowed the gangs to get embedded in some communities because, as fast as they were disrupted, there were insufficient police resources to stop others moving in to take their place. And this is one of the great lessons of this time. If the organized crime gangs are to be defeated, it is not just what you do in the first instance but whether you can follow through to help communities recover and regain their confidence in the police and their ability to tackle major crime.

June 13, 2022

Life Changing

Last week, I spoke at the launch of a significant, though modest, new project called Level Up. I am not sure whether there is anything equivalent to this anywhere else in the country, and I shall be interested to see in about a year's time what it has achieved.

Briefly, since the start of the pandemic, the Home Office have seen an increase in the number of parents and carers who are struggling with children and adolescents who are abusive and even violent towards them. Some 70 percent of social work practitioners, apparently, have reported an increase in referrals to them for this reason. We know that these attitudes and behaviors are likely to persist into adulthood and may even become more pronounced if they are not challenged. Yet, changing them is not easy. If children do not listen to their parents or respect them, who can help? When we look at the range of interventions we currently have in the county, there is a gap here.

The Home Office offered funding for programs that work with children, and we have secured funding for a one-year project. The organization that delivers our program to change the behavior of adults who perpetrate domestic abuse, Cranstoun, will also deliver the Level Up project. They will work on a one-to-one basis with those aged eleven to fifteen and seek to address their violence and aggression, their abuse of parents/carers or siblings in intimate settings.

It is a sad reflection of the times that such programs are even thought necessary. But for the sake of the children, the families, and eventually, wider society, we must try to find a way of changing their abusive behaviors now. Otherwise, we know, the police know, where their lives are headed.

June 20, 2022

Mini Aggressions

Last week, I attended the launch of a new police campaign that I have funded on the issue of violence against women and girls, now universally known as VAWG.

Each time I mention VAWG, I receive emails asking me about violence against males; and, of course, there is violence against males. But what we are trying to do with the VAWG campaign and other VAWG initiatives this year is to respond to a groundswell of public concern that has grown more intensively over the past eighteen months or so.

This campaign, called No More, highlights the many acts of mini-aggression that girls and women face every day, not least those who take themselves into town and city center bars, pubs, and clubs in the nighttime economy. All the unwanted sexual comments, so-called banter, suggestions, or touching. The campaign is designed to start a conversation among men as well as women, and between men and women in the eighteen to thirty-five age group about what is and is not acceptable behavior, and to say "No More" to what women should not have to put up with. We want to encourage women, and men, to have the courage to speak out. There are posters, leaflets, and digital advertising as well as a short, hard-hitting video that was previewed at the Curzon cinema in Sheffield.

Some of the models in the campaign were volunteers who also helped with getting the words right. Their authentic voices are captured, and this should resonate with those at whom the campaign is aimed.

One shocking detail was mentioned at the launch. When the models were being photographed at various locations for the posters and video, they experienced much of the sexualized and abusive behavior the campaign is seeking to call out.

June 27, 2022

Operation Linden: CSE in Rotherham

Last week, the Independent Office for Police Conduct (IOPC) published its long awaited and final report on the police response to child sexual exploitation (CSE) in Rotherham between 1997 and 2013, called Operation Linden.[6] The IOPC were asked in 2014 to look into allegations made against police officers who served in the force during that time. This was the period of time covered by Professor Alex Jay's report that laid bare for the first time the true extent of child abuse. Operation Linden has taken nearly eight years and cost £6 million. I was interested in the report and the reactions to it; but I was also left wondering whether this report now marks some significant milestone.

Of course, much of the Operation Linden report was about the experiences of individual victims from that time, not so much the appalling abuse they suffered as the different ways the authorities, principally, the police, failed them. Potentially, there are, according to Professor Jay, upwards of 1,400 such accounts. Each person has their own unique story to tell, though if we are to draw lessons, we must be able to find the common threads running through them all.

For much of the past eight years or so, we have been doing just that, finding out directly from the victims what happened to them, how the authorities got things so wrong, and how the work of the professionals can be made better; the common threads I listed above. But where do we go from here? Do we just keep hearing from time to time more stories? After this IOPC investigation, I wonder if we now need to start asking in earnest some different questions as well.

In 2014, shortly after I became PCC, I set up a panel of victims of CSE to learn firsthand about grooming. The group of young women who agreed to come on the panel and help said I should rename the panel the Victims, Survivors, and Their Families Panel, and include families, which we did. They pointed out that, as well as the primary victims, the girls themselves, there were secondary victims, including scared siblings and distressed parents. Moreover, those who had been abused were on a long journey: some still felt they were victims while others believed they had found the strength to be survivors. In later years, some even called themselves thrivers. The point they were making was that they could not spend

---

6. Independent Office for Police Conduct, "Operation Linden Report."

the rest of their lives defined by what had happened to them in their teen-age years. They could not be trapped in victimhood forever. They had to find the resilience to come through; they had survived.

So, just as there are stories to be told abut how they became victims, there are also stories to be told about how they became survivors, even thrivers. I only know a little of this, but for those on my panel, part of it lay in their meeting together as a group of women to give one another support. I met them once in a community room underneath a Rother-ham church where we talked about, well, everything under the sun. On another occasion, they organized a conference on CSE in Carlton Park Hotel, Rotherham, for professionals, social workers, police, and the like. They did all the administration, decided who they wanted to speak and the topics they wanted to cover, advertised it nationally, and found the funding. Several of them spoke, giving moving testimonies and chal-lenging the professional workers to reexamine their own practice. This, too, was an important part of their journey from victim to survivor, showing them that far from being something that forever blighted their lives or held them back, they could use their experiences, awful though they were, in this creative way.

And they were there for one another when their cases went to court and they had to be particularly strong as they confronted the men who had abused them. At this moment, for some, the support of an independent sexual violence adviser was critical, and for others, a sym-pathetic police officer.

I found Operation Linden disappointing. It cost a lot of money. It took a lot of time. It made recommendation to the police, which by and large were unsurprising. But if it marks a milestone, perhaps, what we now need are not more pieties for the authorities of the more must-be-done type but recommendations for helping victims become survivors, or even thrivers. What is the collective wisdom they need for navigating the rest of their lives? What are the common threads here?

July 4, 2022

From Anecdote to Evidence

From time to time, a politician or a community activist will tell me that I should condemn the police use of stop and search. "Our communities don't want it," was how one person put it to me last week. Yet three years ago, I met a group of women, mothers and grandmothers, from an ethnic minority community in Burngreave Vestry Hall, Sheffield, who said the opposite. "We don't want our children to carry weapons or take drugs," one mother said. "We want the police to stop and search." There was general nodding of agreement around the room, though all insisted it must be done respectfully, as one put it, because not everyone stopped and searched would turn out to be carrying drugs or knives.

So, while I have always known what these groups of women and girls thought about stop and search, I have always been a little reluctant about using these anecdotes, especially when the girls and women themselves would not be willing to say these things outside those private meetings. But now, my anecdotes have some empirical evidence to back them up.

New research by Datapoll, for the think tank Civitas, has found that 80 percent of black and minority ethnic families support the police using stop and search powers to help remove drugs from the streets.[7] Interestingly, this was higher than support from white families at 70 percent. More than 50 percent also supported schools routinely testing for drugs, which is not something I would have guessed.

I am not sure what the result would have been if this poll had been held, say, ten years ago. I would guess we might have had a different outcome. What I think has slowly registered with people is the link between drugs and serious violence. That has become much clearer in the last few years and families don't want their young men caught up in that.

July 11, 2022

Avoiding Blame Culture

How do our public institutions avoid having blame cultures? A blame culture at its most extreme is one where employees don't accept responsibility for their actions but constantly shift the blame for any mistakes onto colleagues. No one feels able to trust anyone else. People constantly write emails to cover their backs. And so on. All this means that the organization is incapable of learning because learning is a corporate and collegiate business. It requires everyone to take responsibility and play a part. But if responsibility is always shifted to someone else, the organization gets stuck and cannot move on. Once such a culture is established, it is hard to turn round.

7. Young and Bailey, "Parents Have Their Say."

Many years ago, the aircraft industry realized that if they were to improve safety, they had to enable those who made mistakes to fully admit them so that there could be learning. That is the opposite of a blame culture. Of course, if people made errors because they were drunk on the job or slapdash in their approach, that was another matter. But where mistakes were admitted, the situation that led up to the error being made could be examined: Was there something about the system or ways of working that had contributed to the mistake?

In a social services department, for example, people might make mistakes because their case load was simply too demanding, or they were working too many hours at a stretch, or there were flaws in the way records were kept, or because they had taken a parent's word about a child too easily, or whatever. The mistake needs to be acknowledged so that all can learn and a service improved.

A blame culture can be avoided if an organization promotes strong internal values, such as fairness, integrity, and trust. These three values are what South Yorkshire Police (SYP) are committing to. If everyone who works for SYP treats colleagues with fairness, acts with integrity (by which they mean doing the right thing), and builds trust, then a blame culture can be kept at bay. Mistakes can be admitted rather than covered up; responsibility can be accepted rather than shuffled elsewhere,

But this is not easy for a public body to bring about in a society that so often seems determined to turn our life together into one giant blame culture. Those who work in hospitals know how litigious people can be, even when doctors and nurses have done their best. A surgeon friend said to me that one of the hardest parts of the job was dealing with people's unrealistic expectations. If a really sick patient doesn't recover from surgery, the medical staff must have made a mistake. Then, the blame game starts.

Police officers can make mistakes in good faith and for many reasons, as people can in any walk of life. Where those mistakes are the result of some serious lapse of judgment or just bad behavior, that is one thing. But if we are to make progress and improve performance, we must resist creating a culture of blame. And that means embedding those values of fairness, integrity, and trust.

July 25, 2022

Flood and Fire

After the floods, the fire. It was only in November 2019 that we witnessed widespread flooding across parts of South Yorkshire, principally, around Doncaster. I remember being taken to see the devastation in a fire and rescue service jeep and gazing out over vast expanses of water, as far as the eye could see. I visited the village of Fishlake, which was all but cut off, and where the church had been turned into a food store. We talked to the churchwardens. There had been days of heavy rain and the fields were saturated. Everything was very cold and very wet. The meteorologists told us to expect more in the future.

If an excess of water was the problem then, lack of it was the issue last week, as whole swaths of the country were rendered so dry that they became like a tinder box. Then the fires started, and one of the places most affected was South Yorkshire. The meteorologists told us to expect more in the future.

In one day, South Yorkshire Fire and Rescue Service (SYFRS) received over 2,000 calls for service and responded to 228 incidents. As fast as operational crews dealt with one fire, they were sent to another. This continued all day and into the night, and for some fire fighters, it meant still being there the following morning as well. The police were similarly stretched and declared it a major incident.

I was struck by some remarks made by Dave Walton, the deputy chief fire officer for West Yorkshire, about his area, though they could just as easily be said here. He was interviewed by Channel 4 News in Leeds. Three things in particular lodged in my mind.

First, he pointed out that this was very different from previous fires caused by excessive heat. In Yorkshire, we are prepared for moorland fires and fires in rural areas and know how they have to be tackled. But these fires may have begun in a field or along a railway embankment, and they quickly spread to residential areas. We know, too, what the most likely causes of some of the moorland fires are: barbecues, discarded cigarettes, broken glass, and so on. We can ask the public to take precautions. The causes of these fires may be the same or they may not, and because fire crews were so busy going from one blaze to another, it may not be so easy determining all the causes. Someone suggested, for example, that compost heaps were catching fire because of the gases they generate. And the heat transferred so rapidly from ground to grass to buildings, with flames traveling as fast as people could run.

Then, second, Dave Walton suggested that if we are to see more days like this in the future, the way the emergency services plan for that future is going to have to change. What does policing and fire fighting look like if there are multiple incidents in residential as well as rural settings all at the same time? Our ever adaptive emergency services need different kinds of scenario planning. And that planning will affect people like call handlers as much as fire crews or frontline police officers. They had to decide what to do with call after call after call when all available fire tenders, fire officers, and police were already committed.

And that takes me to the third and very telling point the deputy chief fire officer made just as the interview was being concluded. He was asked how the emergency services were to match resources to demand in the future when demand looked like this. He said they couldn't. They could only match resources to risk, not demand. Call handlers, managers, and the police were having to make quick judgments as incidents were assessed and triaged. That sometimes meant that a fire would not be attended if there was no immediate danger to life or property. It sometimes meant that a fire, which might be property, had to be allowed to burn as long as it was contained.

These are the simple truths. Skills and resources will have to be matched to risk, not demand. This is not wholly new, but last Tuesday suddenly gave all this a much sharper dimension and focus.

August 8, 2022

Assisted Dying, the Law, and Hillsborough

In 1989, a seventeen-year-old football supporter, Anthony Bland, was caught up in the fatal crush at the Hillsborough football ground. He was not killed, but his lungs were crushed and he was starved of oxygen. This put him in what, at that time, was called a persistent vegetative state.

I thought of Tony Bland last week as I read about the contemporary and equally distressing story of twelve-year-old Archie Battersbee. Archie has been in a coma since he was found unconscious at home in April. Unlike Archie's parents, however, the family of Tony Bland applied to the courts not to have his treatment prolonged but to have it stopped. One of the judges in that case, Lord Justice Hoffmann, described his

condition in this way: "Anthony Bland has no consciousness at all. . . .
The darkness and oblivion which descended at Hillsborough will never
depart. His body is alive, but he has no life in the sense that even the
most pitifully handicapped but conscious human being has a life. But
the advances of modern medicine permit him to be kept in this state for
years, even perhaps for decades."[8]

Despite the fact that both the family and the medical staff treating
him were in agreement, they still had to go to court. This was because
the coroner in Sheffield was beginning to enquire into the deaths caused
by the Hillsborough disaster, and he was notified by the doctor treating
Tony Bland, Dr. J. G. Howe, about his condition and what the family and
the medical team wanted to do. The coroner accepted that maintaining
Tony Bland's life had no point but warned the doctor that he ran the risk
of the police pursuing criminal charges, possibly even a charge of murder,
if he intentionally ended Tony Bland's life.

And that has remained the position ever since. But we should note
how significant that moment was in February 1993 when the Law Lords
decided that doctors could intentionally end the life of their patient. We
had always accepted that a life might be lost if drugs, that were administered in order to reduce pain in the end, led to loss of life because the
intention of the doctor was not to end the life but to suppress the pain.
But this judgment allowed doctors to end a life.

An older Christian ethic about the sanctity of life for its own sake
was giving way to the idea that the value of a life turned on a judgment
about whether it was worthwhile or meaningful, issues about the quality
of life. The ethics of assisted dying have been debated more passionately
ever since, and the law has struggled to keep up. In the UK, at any rate, it
began with these decisions arising out of the Hillsborough disaster.

A Decade On

When I first became police and crime commissioner in 2014, the results
of the 2011 census were known, and we used them all the time to inform
our planning. Those figures are now more than ten years out of date,
but until recently, they were still forming the basis of a lot of thinking.
Gradually, however, we are beginning to receive the results of the 2021
census; and in some respects, they are starting to surprise us, and this
will have an impact on policing.

8. Global Health and Human Rights, "Airedale NHS Trust v Bland," 31.

Take population figures, which are one crucial factor in determining how much money we receive from the government for policing. Although our population in South Yorkshire has grown, it has not grown by as much as the average across the country as a whole. There are also significant differences within the four districts that may affect how police resources ought to be distributed here. So, while the England average population increase has been 6.6 percent; in Barnsley, it was 5.8 percent; in Rotherham, it was 3.3 percent; in Doncaster, 1.9 per cent; and in Sheffield, it hardly grew at all at 0.7 percent. In the decade 2011 to 2021, Sheffield's population stood still.[9]

Also, interesting are the figures for the various age groups. In Barnsley, the over-sixty-fives grew by a massive 19.2 percent. In Doncaster and Rotherham, this was also large at 16.9 percent and 16.4 percent, respectively, while in Sheffield, it was 10.6 percent. Those aged ninety-plus increased by 28 percent in Barnsley, by 18 percent in Doncaster, and 10 percent in Sheffield and Rotherham. At the other end of the age spectrum, while Barnsley's under-fifteen-years increased by 6 percent and Rotherham's by 2.3 percent, in Doncaster and Sheffield, there was a decrease of 0.2 percent.

Barnsley is perhaps the most intriguing: it is getting both older and younger, with smaller increases in the age groups between.

What it will all mean over the coming years is what we must now start to figure out.

Chinese Community

Last week, I was warmly welcomed at the Chinese Community Centre on London Road in Sheffield. I wanted to ask them about their relations with South Yorkshire police, which are good.

It is not often that members of this community draw themselves to my attention. They rarely figure in crime figures, either as perpetrators or victims, though the police were on the alert when coronavirus first began to spread. In America, President Trump referred to it as the "China disease," and there were fears that this might lead to assaults on Chinese people in the west.[10] At moments like these, we need to have already established good links between the police and a minority community.

9. UK Office for National Statistics, "Population and Household Estimates."
10. Reja, "Trump's 'Chinese Virus' Tweet."

The community did remind me, however, that tensions elsewhere in the world can have an impact in South Yorkshire unless they are carefully recognized and managed. There are, for instance, a number of very different Chinese communities now in our county who relate differently to each other in South East Asia.

The oldest Chinese community in Sheffield are those who came over from Hong Kong in the 1940s and 1950s when Hong Kong was a British colony. They speak Cantonese. Present in large numbers now are students from Hong Kong and mainland China, all of whom are under communist rule. Those from the mainland may be Mandarin speakers. There are also more recent arrivals: those Hong Kong Chinese who have settled here with British passports. And there are Taiwanese Chinese, whose relatives live in democratic Taiwan and are mainly hostile to communist China.

When there are tensions between these groups in the Far East, as there are currently between Taiwan and China, that is bound to concern people here. Part of the role of the community center is to bring people together and enable all Chinese to live peaceably together here, whatever is happening elsewhere.

We thank the community center for their hospitality. They sent Katie Dearnley, from my office, and me on our way with a box of dim sum, beautifully cooked for us. And before you ask, yes, we have declared them.

August 15, 2022

Negotiators

From time to time, I mention roles that police officers undertake that may not often, if ever, come to mind as far as most of the public is concerned. One such role is that of the negotiator.

Negotiators, or mediators, are skilled officers who are called upon when someone is threatening to take their own life. This is not an everyday occurrence, but over the years, I can recall instances in South Yorkshire where a negotiator has been involved. Of course, by the time the negotiator is sent for, other officers have also been doing what they can, sometimes for quite some time. The negotiator is the last attempt to bring about a nonviolent resolution.

In fact, we probably are aware of mediators because, from time to time, they feature in films or TV series about the police. In fiction, though, while the standoffs may be very intense, the mediator always succeeds and the woman on the bridge or the man with the can of petrol is talked out of what they were intending to do. But, as Superintendent Neil Thomas, the Doncaster officer who leads the small team of negotiators in South Yorkshire, points out, it is not always like that in reality. He retires later this year and was writing about his experiences in the force's well-being house magazine *SYP&Me.*

He recalls being the first negotiator at a domestic incident with an armed man. He talked to him for nine hours before he was replaced by other colleagues. But the siege went on for three days and, at the end of it, the man killed himself.

Reflecting on this, Superintendent Thomas acknowledges that dealing with these situations is highly stressful for officers. Even though they know it would be unrealistic to suppose every incident can have the outcome they want, they are inevitably under huge pressure to succeed; and afterwards, whatever the outcome, they take the emotions and the strains and stresses home with them. Part of the job as the head of the team, the force lead, is to be alert to this and to ensure that the right support is given to negotiators and their families.

There are some particular places in the county where, sadly, people are known to go in an attempt to take their life; motorway bridges are a well-known place. These places are patrolled from time to time in an attempt by the police to prevent suicide as far as they can.

I take this moment to thank Superintendent Thomas and the mediators for what they do and to wish Neil a good retirement. This work may be largely unseen, but that does not mean that it is not valued or not appreciated.

August 29, 2022

Why Rishi Sunak Gets My Vote

On Monday, I received as PCC for South Yorkshire a letter from National Highways, the body responsible for major roads, telling me that the latest data from our Smart Motorways Second Year Progress Report shows that, overall, in terms of serious or fatal casualties, smart motorways are our safest roads. Since I have written to them before about why I think their data is flawed, the letter seemed rather provocative. Then, shortly after-wards, one of the two candidates for the leadership of the Conservative Party, and so, prime minister, Rishi Sunak was telling the *Daily Mail* that smart motorways are unpopular because they are unsafe. Data shows, he said, that there were fifty-three deaths on smart motorways in the four years to 2019, with at least eighteen blamed on the roads. He went on to say that it was clear the British public has lost confidence driving on a motorway without a hard shoulder. He said further that it was time to put this experiment to bed and say no more new smart motorways.

It did leave me wondering at what point the former chancellor reached this conclusion. Was it while he was still a member of the cabi-net, and how many others shared his view? It also made me wonder why he finds the data for ending this type of motorway so compelling, but the transport secretary appears not to. At any rate, I welcome his conversion however late in the day.

So, he gets my vote. Well, he would if I had one.

September 5, 2022

Celebrating Twenty Years of PCSOs

On September 7, police community support officers (PCSOs) will have been in existence for twenty years. My good friend and colleague David Blunkett was the home secretary at the time. I can truthfully say that I have almost never found a community that did not rate their PCSO highly. The PCSO has often been the only stable police officer in many communities and valued accordingly.

PCSOs wear police uniforms, but they are police staff, not war-ranted officers. They form about 6.8 percent of all police employees, with about one quarter of all PCSOs in the Met.

They were not immediately accepted by everyone. Some police of-ficers thought it was a way of having more bodies on the ground without paying for trained, warranted officers. But they soon proved their worth, and within seven years, they had reached the peak of their numbers at 16,814. Then, austerity and the cuts came. Unlike warranted officers, however, they could be made redundant, and some were in order to save money and balance the books during the dark years of austerity. In South Yorkshire, their numbers were reduced, though the money saved was used to bolster warranted officer numbers.

PCSOs are part of a neighborhood team (at one time, called Safer Neighbourhood Teams). Over the years, they have performed a range of duties: high visibility patrols; tackling antisocial behavior; crowd control; directing traffic at public events; getting evidence; supporting frontline officers. One of their most important functions has been engagements with communities. This was especially important during the austerity years when neighborhood teams were subsumed into response teams (to save money), and the PCSO remained the only regular face of the force in communities. Now, the neighborhood teams are being rebuilt and PCSOs take their place in them.

I am sometimes asked why PCSOs are not given powers of arrest. But the consequence of doing this would be that every time they made an arrest, they would have to leave the neighborhood and go off to a custody suite to process those arrested. The whole point of the PCSO is that they are rooted in their neighborhood.

We thank the PCSOs for the last twenty years. We wonder what will be asked of this most resilient part of the force in the next twenty years as the world around us changes.

September 19, 2022

Queen Elizabeth II

I write these reflections the day before the state funeral of HM Queen Elizabeth II and the end of the period of mourning. This time began and ended for me with two formal occasions, bringing into play the mixed emotions that have run throughout the past ten days.

On Sunday, September 11, I went with the chief constable, the district commander for Sheffield, and my chief executive to hear the proclamation of the new King's accession. This had been done nationally at St. James's Palace in London, then repeated across the country. We gathered on the steps of the City Hall in Barker's Pool, Sheffield. This was the South Yorkshire Proclamation, read by the high sheriff. It recalled the death of the late Queen and proclaimed Prince Charles our only lawful and rightful liege Lord Charles the Third. The ceremony concluded with three cheers for the King, led by the lord mayor, and the singing of the national anthem, "God save the King." Similar ceremonies were held in other towns across the county.

Then this Sunday, September 18, the time of mourning came to a conclusion in South Yorkshire with a beautifully sung commemoration and thanksgiving for the life of Her late Majesty Queen Elizabeth II in Sheffield Cathedral. The gentle rhythms and simplicity of this evening service captured well the mood we were feeling on the night before what we knew would be the pomp and high ceremony of the state funeral the following day.

A Time to Say, "We Got This Wrong"

During the period of mourning, Nicola Mundy, a senior coroner for South Yorkshire, concluded the inquest into the death of Nargis Begum. Mrs. Begum died after the car her husband was driving broke down and stopped in a live lane on the M1, where there is no hard shoulder: the stretch of motorway in South Yorkshire known as "all-lane running" (ALR). She got out of the car and stood in front of it. A Mercedes smashed into their stationary, car causing it to hit and kill Mrs. Begum.

Many things have been said during this inquest about ALR, and I hope that both the government and National Highways, the agency that looks after major roads and motorways, will think carefully about them. For the moment, I note these.

First, the coroner concluded that the lack of a hard shoulder had contributed towards the death of Mrs. Begum. This is the second time, to my knowledge, that a coroner has said this about deaths on this part of the M1 in our county. In any other circumstances, we would expect the agency and the government to take note and remedy the safety hazard immediately; but the stakes here are so high. It would mean abandoning smart motorways. The building program is currently paused. It would mean reinstating installing hard shoulders, at some cost.

Second, it became clear during the course of the inquest that National Highways understands very well that ALRs are more dangerous than a conventional motorway for anyone whose vehicle stops in a live lane. But because the extra lane, the overhead gantries regulating speeds, and other technological solutions of the ALR increase safety in other respects, the increased risks to any stationary vehicle, a rare event, were, on balance, considered worth taking. The barrister representing Mrs. Begum's family asked whether, for those unfortunate enough to use an ALR motorway and come to a stop in a live lane because there is no hard shoulder, that particular risk has been sacrificed for the reduction of the other risks? The chief executive of National Highways replied yes and agreed that there is a balance of risks.

Third, it also transpired that 153 vehicles passed by Mrs. Begum's stranded car but didn't report it because, one witness said, they believed that ALR motorways are under constant camera surveillance, and the presence of the broken down vehicle would have been noticed, and the lane closure initiated. But it was sixteen minutes before the vehicle was detected. This also contributed towards Mrs. Begum's death.

But it's not just the fatalities that we should think about. While the inquest was taking place, someone wrote to me about a near-miss experience they had had on this part of the M1. She said she, too, had an incident that could have ended in serious injury, if not death. The reason was that she was driving in the nearside lane (what would be the hard shoulder on a conventional motorway) behind a transit van that effectively obscured her view ahead. The transit indicated that it was pulling out into the next lane. As it did so, she saw directly ahead another vehicle that, at first, she thought was indicating a left turn, but then realized all the hazard lights were on because the vehicle was stationary in the lane.

She was approaching at only 50 mph but too fast to stop. She made an evasive swerve into the next lane. Fortunately, there was no vehicle at close quarters in this lane, and so, she lived to tell this tale, which could have ended so differently. She is now fearful about traveling here. So, it's not only the number of fatalities that cause concern, it's the near misses as well and the fear this induces.

But if all these considerations are to be taken into account, the way relative safety is measured by National Highways and the government has to change. That involves saying, "We got this wrong"; and that is the biggest challenge of all.

September 26, 2022

New Home Secretary

Last Friday, the new home secretary Suella Braverman sent an open letter to police leaders of England and Wales. She began by thanking the police on behalf of the nation for the high standard of British policing that was shown during the period of national mourning. This had been an enormous operation in the face of an unprecedented security challenge.

The home secretary then goes on to talk about what she would like to see going forward. I would want to agree with much of what she says. We must have visible and responsive policing. The police must treat victims with respect and work to the priorities of the public, which is why police and crime commissioners draw up a local Police and Crime Plan. They must drive down antisocial behavior (falling across South Yorkshire) and neighborhood crime. For all these reasons, I hold a monthly Public Accountability Board, open to the public and viewable online, at which I ask the force to report district by district on these issues.

The home secretary also said that the public expect that an officer will visit them after a crime, such as burglary. This is true. This is the public expectation. I am often contacted by people who say they were burgled and no one came to see them. But the home secretary is wrong in suggesting that the reason for this is that the police have to spend too much time on symbolic gestures, such as initiatives on diversity and inclusion, which, she believes, may take precedence over common sense policing.

We are currently seeing two things happen that will not make the next few years any easier for policing. On the one hand, many experienced officers are retiring. On the other, many more new recruits are joining, but they will not achieve full operational competency for two or three more years. This increase in police numbers is to be welcomed, but public expectation has got to be managed around that, or that in itself will damage public confidence if people think the new officers will be fully trained as soon as they are recruited.

If the home secretary wants to free up more officer time for tackling neighborhood crimes and making calls, then we need help reducing other types of demand on the police, such as dealing with people in mental health crises. But that means strengthening other public services, such as mental health services. Without that, police resources will remain stretched.

October 10, 2022

A Fitting Memorial

On Saturday, I went to the annual South Yorkshire Police Memorial Service in Sheffield Cathedral. This is always a moving occasion. As well as reminding us of the dangers that all police officers face every day, there were many poignant moments as we remembered by name the nine police constables who have died while on duty since 1974.

I spoke with the parents of PC Sandra Edwards, who died in 1995. They live near Morpeth in Northumbria and have been making the journey to South Yorkshire every year to remember their loved one.

October 24, 2022

Suppressing Crime: What Works?

South Yorkshire is one of twenty police force areas (out of forty-three) that has a Violence Reduction Unit (VRU). The VRUs are mainly in the most urban areas of the country, where some of the most serious violence is found. This year, the VRU areas were given funding by the government to tackle serious violence more intensively. It's called GRIP funding and starts with the identification of those places where most violent crimes happen. In our county, force analysts have discovered that 50 percent of all (non-domestic) violent crime that takes place in a public space happens in fewer than 2 percent of places. From this, sixty violence hot spots have been singled out for particular focus.

One of the things the police have then been doing with GRIP funding is regular patrolling on foot in thirty different hot spots each day. Behind this lies a theory of patrolling that has been tried and tested elsewhere, so it is evidence-based. (It comes out of the work of Professor Larry Sherman and the Department of Criminology at Cambridge University.) What the evidence shows, and what the police are doing here, is to patrol regularly in high-visibility jackets for between fifteen and twenty minute periods at different times each day between 3:00 p.m. and 12:00 a.m. in the hot spots. The main point of the patrolling is to be seen.

It seems as if this fifteen to twenty-minute patrol is enough to send a powerful message around a community that the police are present and can suddenly appear at any time. That is the deterrent effect that leads to a suppression of crime and antisocial behavior (ASB). Interestingly, the evidence is that this fifteen to twenty-minute period is all that is needed. Patrolling for longer makes no additional difference. The patrolling leads to a fall in all crimes and in a wider area than the one being patrolled. So far, GRIP has enabled 750 hours of additional high visibility patrolling this year.

As the officers make their way round the identified area, they deal with any crime and ASB they come across, breaking up fights, arresting wanted people, stopping and searching, and so on. The fear I had was that while this might suppress crime and ASB in the area patrolled, it might simply displace it elsewhere. This does not seem to happen.

The reason the police analysts can be sure that falls in crime/ASB are the result of the patrols is because each officer is equipped with a GPS tracker. The exact route and time the officers take within the prescribed area can be monitored and correlated with statistics for crime and ASB from that area. We need this information to be sure that the patrols really are effective. And the Home Office rightly require proper evaluation so that the theory is thoroughly tested.

GRIP funding should be available over three years so that by the end of it, we shall have a great deal of good evidence about what works and how well. It is all being evaluated by university researchers.

October 31, 2022

Indian Visitors

Last Monday, I spoke to a group of senior police officers, ten women and twenty men, from the state of Madhya Pradesh in central north India. They were here to take part in a short but intensive training course arranged by the Helena Kennedy Centre for International Justice at Sheffield Hallam University (SHU) and South Yorkshire Police (SYP). Over five working days, they looked at different aspects of policing: digital forensics, problem solving with partners, counterterrorism, public order, patrol tactics, cyber crime, child criminal and sexual exploitation, modern slavery and human trafficking, violence against women and girls, neighborhood policing, and so on. They met police across the county. They had flown from India to Birmingham the day before I met them. If they were jet lagged, they didn't show it, asking many questions.

They were curious about the role of the police and crime commissioner. They were surprised that I appointed the chief constable. In India, the head of the service is appointed by other senior officers, and I guess, they would be fairly wary of any political involvement.

I said we had about 1.3 million people in South Yorkshire. In their state, they had 72 million (according to the 2011 census) spread over a vast area. Many languages were spoken, though Hindi and English were common languages. Being multilingual was normal.

I met the officers again on Friday, their final day with us. The SYP staff officer who had been with them throughout told me about their visits to neighborhood police in each of the districts. Wherever they went, members of the public had been friendly towards the local officers, waving to them, and sometimes greeting them by name. This was something of a revelation to the Indian visitors, but it illustrated the basic principle of British policing: policing by consent. In return, SYP had their own moments of revelation. It seemed, for example, that in an attempt to enable women to come forward and report crimes, Madhya Pradesh has some police stations that only admit women and are entirely staffed by women officers.

The real value of these visits for SYP comes in the interaction that takes place between the officers on the ground talking to those doing something similar elsewhere in the world. One of the SHU lecturers said that whenever he brings together police from different countries, there is an immediate bonding. They recognized that they are all involved in a common enterprise: keeping people safe and beating back crime. And they have a genuine desire to learn from each others' very different experiences.

It is, of course, a legacy of empire that we could communicate in English, and that was probably a major factor in their being here. Otherwise, they might have been training in some other part of the world where policing is done differently. China, perhaps.

Rural Crime

Last week I attended two meetings in the countryside to hear about rural crime. The first was called by a local councilor for Anston and Woodsetts, Tim Baum-Dixon, and the second by the MP for Rother Valley, Alexander Stafford. Rural crimes are of two kinds. There are crimes that can happen anywhere, such as burglary or theft, which also happen in rural places, and there are crimes that can only happen in the countryside, such as the destruction of crops by quad bikes or badger baiting.

I went to each meeting with two police officers who have responsibilities for the off-road biking team and rural and wildlife crime, and two neighborhood team officers. Those who attended the meetings in St. Peter's Church, Thorpe Salvin, and the community hall in Harthill included farmers and two gamekeepers from the Earl of Scarborough's estate, where there are pheasant and partridge shoots, as well as those who live in the villages.

Those at the meetings feared that the issues faced by people who live in villages and on farms is not always given the priority it should. They felt that even the organized crime gangs who operate in the countryside are not always understood as well as the urban gangs. But the Police and Crime Plan that I produce each year giving SYP overarching priorities is very clear that the rural areas must not be forgotten, which is why we need a rural crime team to implement the rural crime strategy. We covered a lot of ground, in every sense! And I listened with great care to what was said and will hold it all in mind in the discussions I have with senior officers about resourcing in the future.

Some things stood out. The police off-road biking team (ORBIT) is highly valued and rated. The presence of police on motorbikes, nimbly going where officers in cars can often not go, is highly disruptive and acts as a considerable deterrent. Despite the squeeze on the public finances that we fear is coming, I hope we can see the biking team enhanced.

Several farmers spoke movingly about how isolated it is living in a farmhouse, especially on dark winter evenings. I think they thought I would have no personal knowledge of this, but in a former life, I was for a short time vicar of Grayrigg (population 242), a remote village in the Lake District, with no shop, no post office, and no pub, though a superabundance of sheep. It was very beautiful. (You can see the big hills as you travel up the M6 between Kendal and Penrith.) But it is very, very dark at this time of year. I recall attempting to find tracks to farmhouses in deep darkness many times and once trying to cross fields to find the west coast mainline after a Virgin train derailed. So I understand why people in a rural area can feel so vulnerable if a crime is committed on their land or property at 4:00 a.m. in the depth of winter.

The value of the meetings were the relationships that were being developed between the police and those who live in this corner of the county on the border with Derbyshire and Nottinghamshire.

November 20, 2022

Psychological Awareness

Each week, I am out and about meeting groups and individuals somewhere in South Yorkshire. Last week, for example, I met, formally, Bawtry Town councilors to discuss policing in their town, and then, informally, I had conversations with the Earl of Scarbrough and his gamekeeper at Sandbeck Park about rural crime.

People want the relevant statistics. They also want to feel, especially in some of our smaller towns and villages, that they are not a police afterthought. That is not something that information alone can convey. A great deal depends on the police officer who is giving it. There is a particular quality that police who engage with the public need to have. I call it psychological awareness, or simply, awareness. What awareness consists of is the ability not just to hear what is said but to listen and to think about it, turn it over in the mind, take it seriously. The officer who does that becomes tuned in to what people are saying and asking at different levels, and as he or she responds, they deal with what lies behind the questions and is unspoken, the need for reassurance.

I don't know whether you can teach awareness, though it is, after all, something we all have to some extent, as human beings interacting with others day to day, especially with family and friends. Perhaps, that's how you do it: treating members of the public as if they were part of your extended family. At any rate, if police officers do not have it, all the statistics in the world, however favorable, will never be enough.

December 5, 2022

Locking People Up

On Friday, the prisons and probation minister Damian Hinds wrote to the Association of Police and Crime Commissioners to say that there was an acute short-term surge in the requirement for places in prisons, and he would be making an announcement in parliament invoking Operation Safeguard. This is an agreement with the police service whereby, in emergencies, the police make available for the prison service up to four hundred additional cells in custody suites. He said the surge in numbers was due to clearing the backlog in court cases that had built up during the period of COVID restrictions, exacerbated by the strike by criminal barristers over the summer. As a result, there were many more prisoners held on remand than usual.

I won't comment on this, save that prison overcrowding has been an issue for many years now, long before COVID and the dispute with the criminal bar. Despite that, ministers have continued to insist publicly that more people should go to prison and prison sentences should be longer. Both of these policies result in demand for prison places to grow at a time when gaols are already full. And the commitment to increase police numbers will also add to the pressures. More police mean more criminals will be caught and receive custodial sentences. More prisons are planned, but that takes time. In the meantime, the shortage of prison places may mean prison governors have to ask for police cells to be requisitioned.

Putting prisoners in custody suites is a disaster. It is bad for the custody suites. If you have ever been in one, you will know that they are busy places where everyone has quite enough to do to process all those who are brought there every day. They, too, face challenges when they are reaching capacity. But it is certainly not a good idea to have offenders locked up in custody cells twenty-four hours a day, where there is little or no capacity for association, education, or recreation. They also have to be fed, and with something a little more substantial than the simple meals, such as pizzas, kept in a custody suite. And we need to think about the well-being and safety of custody suite staff, not all of whom are police officers. Managing prisoners, as well as those who are being processed, is just one more complication.

So, many of our public services seem, at the moment, to be limping along and hoping for the best. We seem to have lost the capacity to plan ahead competently.

But the Good News Is . . .

Some time ago, I wrote about the absurdity of releasing an offender from prison on a Friday afternoon, simply because that was the date when his sentence ended. It was setting someone up to fail. Unless they acted with great speed and were settling somewhere near the prison, it would be quite impossible for many, if not all, the ex-offenders to sort out everything that needed to be done on release: making contact with a probation officer, getting a bank account, securing benefits, finding accommodation, and so on. Yet, one third of all releases fall on a Friday, and in 2022, two out of three ex-prisoners had not secured accommodation when they left. In the diary, I suggested that the judge should be able to say that the prisoner should be released on whichever weekday other than a Friday was nearest to the end of the sentence.

Something like this should now happen if a bill currently before the House of Commons is passed. It had its second reading on Friday. Briefly, the Offenders (Day of Release from Detention) Bill will allow prison governors to bring forward the day of release by up to two discretionary days if it would otherwise fall on a Friday or before a bank holiday.

The bill is a Private Member's Bill, and we should congratulate Simon Fell, the Conservative member of parliament for Barrow-in-Furness, for sponsoring it. At one time, I was an occasional visitor to his local prison, Haverigg, an open prison for men near Millom in Cumbria. We took toys for the visiting children of prisoners.

This is a groundbreaking reform that costs little or nothing but could have far reaching consequences.

December 12, 2022

Keeping Awoke

"Watch, therefore, for you know neither the day nor the hour" (Matt 25:13). That verse sums up the church's pre-Christmas season of Advent: it is all about being alert and awake. We could say "being woke."

People are woke today when they are alert to matters of social injustice, especially racism. Although woke, in this sense, has been around since at least the 1960s, the word only came into most people's consciousness with the more recent Black Lives Matter movement. Activists called on people to stay woke.

But woke has also come to be used in a pejorative sense, if not as a term of abuse, at least by some. People are "woke" if their concern with issues of social justice seems like an obsession, or if their concern is merely apparent, a form of virtue signaling. In September, the home secretary told police chiefs to ignore "wokery" and concentrate on crime.

This may be well-intentioned. We do want the police to focus on crime and not go in for symbolic gestures that are not backed by determined and thoughtful action. But it is not good advice. If it led the police to have less regard for the need, for instance, to have equality, diversity, and inclusion (EDI) policies, that could be disastrous. All good employers know that even if they are not motivated by the ethics of the matter, their company or organization must have clear anti-discrimination policies in place, otherwise, if they are accused of racism, they are immediately on the back foot.

Police chiefs should be motivated by ethics as much as prudence or expediency. We want a police force that reflects our national diversity and welcomes into its ranks people from all backgrounds, sexualities, and ethnicities. If the force does not reflect the diversity of the population it serves, how can it serve the different communities that make up South Yorkshire with the proper degree of knowledge, understanding, and respect? And if it can't do that, it will be harder for it to gain and maintain the trust and confidence of those different groups, something that is crucial if crime is to be overcome.

A good place for the police to start is with their own members. Is diversity recognized, valued, and supported in the force?

I was heartened recently to join a conference organized by South Yorkshire Police's (SYP) Equality Hub for the force itself. The Hub is an overarching group that brings together a range of discrete organizations within SYP that represent many different minorities. These are of many kinds: Association of Muslim Police; Race, Equity, and Inclusion Association; LGBTQ+ group; Women's Network; Neurodiversity Association; Dementia Support Group; Christian Police Association, and so on. SYP needs to understand its own diversity so that it can support and strengthen the well-being of its own minorities and make the force a place where discrimination is not tolerated.

There are some areas where the force needs to be more diverse, more representative of the communities of South Yorkshire. In some respects, it has made substantial progress. The gender ratio in SYP, for example, is now 49.7 percent female, 51.3 percent male. But when we look at the latest figures from the 2021 census on ethnicity in the UK, recently released by the Office for National Statistics, there is clearly much more to be done.[11] The county's ethnic minorities are now 12 percent, whereas the force stands at 3.7 percent.

The chief constable said at the conference why she thought equality, diversity, and inclusion were important issues for the police. This was not being woke, in that derogatory sense, but a recognition that each of these must be addressed if SYP is to be a good place to work and good at what they do. If this is what it means to be woke, then Advent takes on an extra meaning for me this year as I seek to stay woke.

---

11. UK Office for National Statistics, "Population and Household Estimates."

Diary for 2023

What's Happening to Criminal Justice?

January 2, 2023

New Year

Every New Year is a triumph of hope over experience. We wish one another a happy New Year and hope that we have seen the end of whatever was bad in the old. Things can only get better. Or at least, not get any worse. All this we say to ourselves as well as to one another, despite knowing that we have said it so many times before on previous New Years.

But perhaps, we are not in denial after all. We are realists and know that if things are to be better, we have a part to play in making it so, and the New Year offers us a chance to reset the dial and make that fresh start happen. New Year is about renewed commitment and rekindled energy, not serendipity or magic. This year is no exception, including for policing.

This year, the police will be welcoming many new recruits, which is where the hope and energy springs from. In South Yorkshire, we have been recruiting new cohorts for sometime. This year, the first of those recruits will have gained full operational competency and will be able to be deployed across the force and across the county. That is the good news of 2023. Of course, they will have to be funded, not just now, but in the years to come, and that is going to require some hard decisions about where some of that money is to come from, including the question of the level of precept, a decision that I shall have to make in January for 2023–2024.

There is, then, optimism as we start 2023; but it is not joy illimited. The whole of the public sector is about to enter another period of austerity, when every year feels like a crisis, and that will have consequences that will play out over many future years. The current state of the NHS should be a warning to all other areas of public service.

To take one glaringly obvious example, one crucial reason why there is a shortage of nurses and doctors and specialist consultants is because the NHS didn't have a workforce plan all those years ago, when people would have had to begin their training. Now, we have to cope with a crisis while importing nurses and doctors from abroad and making ever greater use of agency staff.

And in the light of what has happened in the NHS, we can see further coming dangers for the justice system, which, in part, begin with policing and the increased numbers of officers. It makes little sense now to increase police numbers if the criminal justice system—the courts, the crown prosecutors, defending barristers, the prisons, probation—are not going to be able to cope with more offenders being caught, prosecuted, and convicted. We have not planned sufficiently, and there is not the capacity in the system. Yet, the whole point of having additional officers is, presumably, to catch more criminals. We are being set up to fail.

South Yorkshire police now has a Futures Board. Its task is to do that hard thinking: what do the economic, social, and cultural changes that are going on around us mean for the future of society and, so, policing? This is one area where answers cannot be written on the back of an envelope or a postcard.

Exercising Restraint

The headline in *The Star* was arresting: "Police Are Using Restraint More."[1] This is another way of saying that the police are using force more; and that made me sit up. Force includes the use of handcuffs or wrestling someone to the ground. So, serious matters. But I wasn't aware of any surge in the use of force, so I looked more closely at what the paper appeared to be suggesting in its headline, which was a big headline over a story occupying half a page.

The report was comparing Home Office figures for the use of force in the year to March 2022 with the year to March 2020, the year before the pandemic really took hold.[2] (Everyone accepts that the time of lockdowns and restrictions distorted normal crime figures and should

1. Ulke, "South Yorkshire Police."
2. Home Office, "Police Use of Force Statistics."

not be used to compare other years.) It had figures for all police forces. The use of force in South Yorkshire had gone up. So given the startling headline, how dramatic was the rise?

I looked for the figures, which were given by the paper in the report. Force had been used 6,845 times in the year to March 2022. This was up from 6,806 in 2019–2020. A rise of—I'm sure you have got there already—1 percent. One percent! You could say, and the headline would have been more accurate, "Little change in police use of force." You could even say "No change," since this is not particularly statistically significant.

We take the use of force very seriously in South Yorkshire. It is something I ask the Independent Ethics Panel to keep an eye on. So, the fact that the use of force has scarcely increased at all, even though there are now more police on the streets than there were in 2019, is the better conclusion to draw. The headline would not be as dramatic: "No Change in Police Use of Force." And it would require the journalists, of course, to exercise—how shall I put it—a little more restraint.

January 9, 2023

Retention, Retention, Retention

The new generations of police officer have new expectations. Unlike police recruits in the past, all police officers now will either have a degree before they start, or they will acquire one in the earliest stages of their training. This is going to have unintended consequences. Some of those are probably unforeseeable at this moment, but at least one can be predicted and, if it is not thought about carefully, will have serious consequences for retaining those recruited.

The force is professionalizing fast. As it does so, police officers are acquiring skills that are prized in many workplaces: educated to graduate level (with all fees paid!), computer and IT literate, highly flexible and adaptable, team players, trained in problem solving, and so on. Highly desirable skills and not just in policing.

In the past, many officers stayed in the force all their working lives, not only because they were committed to public service but because it was not easy to find another job that paid as well and was as secure; police officers cannot be made redundant. But the skilled officers of today and tomorrow will realize that they can move; there are many other reasonably well-paid, if not better paid, jobs open to them, and so they can move with confidence. They will, therefore, balance the job they wanted to do, and the security it continues to offer, with the benefits of moving to other good jobs now open to them. They will remain in policing because they, too, are committed to public service and want to do the job they have been inspired to do; but they have expectations of that job and will not feel trapped if things do not work out as they hoped. They have, and know they have, transferable skills.

Retention is the big issue. It is one thing to recruit an extra twenty thousand officers nationwide. It will be quite another to keep them over a working life.

January 23, 2023

Beyond the Gates

I learned last week about a new initiative at the Doncaster prisons called Employment Boards. This was pioneered by one of the governors Mick Mills and brings together the prisons and local businesses.

Briefly, the Employment Board, chaired by a local business leader, matches offenders who are soon to be released with employers who are looking for specific types of worker. The offender spends time over a twelve-week period, going from the prison on a day release to the chosen place of work. The offender gets to know the business and the business the offender. This means that when the time comes for the offender to be released, he has a secure job to go to, which he knows he can do. Lack of employment is one of the biggest drivers for ex-offenders to fall back into old ways and start to re-offend.

These schemes are still being developed, but so far, in one prison, over 70 percent of those ex-offenders participating were still in their jobs after several weeks. This is really promising.

February 6, 2023

An Inspector Calls

"I congratulate South Yorkshire Police on its performance in keeping people safe and reducing crime."[3] Not my words, though I would echo them, but those of Roy Wilsher, one of His Majesty's inspectors

---

3. HMICFRS, "PEEL 2021/22," 5.

of Constabulary and Fire and Rescue Services (HMICFRS), who led an inspection of the force last year. The inspectors' report was published last Thursday and it was very positive indeed.

During my time as police and crime commissioner from 2014, South Yorkshire Police (SYP) has been on a remarkable journey. In my first years, SYP was reeling from the Jay Report into child sexual exploitation in Rotherham, which said the force had failed many girls between 1997 and 2013, and then the verdicts of the inquests into the Hillsborough football disaster (1989), which blamed SYP for the deaths of ninety-six supporters. Morale in the force, and public trust and confidence in them, was low. Then, in 2016, there was an inspection of SYP by HMI who said the force requires improvement, and put it into special measures. This involved having to go down to London at regular intervals to set out and report progress on a recovery plan.

I appointed Stephen Watson as chief constable with a clear brief: he was to take a firm grip on the organization and give it a clear sense of direction and purpose, which he did. In the last HMI report before he left to become chief constable of Greater Manchester, SYP were graded good overall and outstanding in terms of their ethical leadership. When I appointed Lauren Poultney, the current chief, in 2021, the brief was equally clear and no less demanding: consolidate and take further. This is what the chief, together with all her officers and civilian staff, is doing, and the verdict of HMI could not be clearer.

HMI have five grades for each area of activity they inspect: inadequate, requires improvement, adequate, good, and outstanding. This was their grading for the force:

Outstanding

preventing crime

protecting vulnerable people

good use of resources

Good

recording data about crime

investigating crime

treatment of the public

managing offenders

developing a positive workplace

Adequate

responding to the public

In a nutshell, the force has now set itself a very high bar for the future! But the inspectors noted that this is now a force that does not rest on any laurels but is ambitious to continuously learn and improve its service.

Setting the Precept

With this good report in my hand, I felt able last Friday to go to the Police and Crime Panel, meeting in Barnsley Town Hall, to put before them my proposals for the police budget and the precept (the policing element of the council tax) for the coming financial year, April 2023 to March 2024. I said that if we wanted to keep our force where it now is, among the best performing forces in the country, we would need to give it the funding it needed.

When the government announced the total funding that would be available for policing nationally this coming year, its figures assumed that every PCC in the country would increase the precept by the maximum permitted, which is £15 for a Band D property. There was a realization that the small increase in government grant was nowhere near enough to cover for inflation and increased demands on the service.

In South Yorkshire, we have to be especially careful if we should set a lower precept. This is because we are dependent on something called "special grant," a separate sum of money from the main police grant that comes to us from the Home Office to offset some of the costs of the civil claims against the force from those who suffered as a result of the Hillsborough disaster and the victims of CSE in Rotherham. It is not money we can claim by right. It is a grant that is a matter for the home secretary's discretion. This year, those civil claims are expected to cost us £5.8 million with 85 percent covered by special grant. However, if I were to set the precept at a lower level, the home secretary might take the view that she was not prepared to pay as much special grant, since I had not made the effort to maximize funding through the precept; and many in other parts of the country might well agree with her. So, I proposed the £15 per annum precept increase for Band D properties, a 6.7 percent rise on last year.

However, most people in South Yorkshire will not pay this amount, because most people live in properties that are in lower bands. These are the bands, the percentage of households in those bands, and the extra amount people will pay per week:

Band A (57.0) 19p

Band B (17.3) 22p

Band C (12.3) 26p

Band D (7.2) 29p

Band E (3.7) 35p

Band F (1.6) 42p

Band G (0.8) 48p

Band H (0.1) 58p[4]

In addition, some in Bands A and B will also have discounts and, so, will pay less than 19p and 22p.

The figures above show how hard it is for me to raise big sums even with a maximum permitted council tax increase, because we have so many low value properties in South Yorkshire. There will be some PCCs who will have most of their properties in B and D and above. Other worlds!

The Police and Crime Panel, with councilors from each of the political parties (Labour, Liberal Democrat, Green, and Conservative), were supportive, with only one councilor not voting; and the independent panel member also supported the proposal. In addition, I had undertaken a survey of public opinion, partly gained through an online questionnaire and partly through face-to-face meetings. Only 17 percent of those online said they were not willing to pay more, while 26 percent said they would be willing to pay in line with inflation, which is actually more than what I was proposing. This marks the end of an intense period of activity when we have produced a balanced budget. Even so, it only balances if the force makes substantial savings and we use some reserves.

4. This data was supplied to me by my chief finance officer.

The Emergency Service of First Resort

One of our thoughtful diary readers, Norman Anderson, wrote to me last week about how the police get drawn into dealing with issues when other organizations and agencies fail in some way. He recounted how last year at 11:00 p.m., the main water supply to the cul-de-sac where he lives in Todwick burst and started to flood the neighborhood. He looked on his water bill for an emergency number to ring. There was none. So, he called the police. The call handler, he writes, was calm and professional and gave him the number. But then she said, "Leave it with me and I will sort it for you." Within thirty minutes, a JCB digger had arrived and by daybreak, all was sorted and fresh water restored. "I think that is pretty impressive," he said. And so do I. But it does illustrate the sort of calls that police operatives have to deal with that are not strictly speaking police matters at all. But by default, the police have become a twenty-four-hour service for all emergencies, and sometimes, the only one easily accessible.

March 6, 2023

A Lesson from the USA

What can British policing learn from America's West Point? Not a lot, you might think. West Point is, after all, the academy fifty miles north of New York where the United States trains its military elite. About 1,500 recruits a year come here for a four-year residential course that is physically, intellectually, and emotionally extremely demanding. They work a six and a half day week, rising early and finishing late. There is rigorous study and hard physical activity, with everything being scored. Among many other challenging exercises, the cadets (as they are called) will take part in ruck marches, carrying heavy rucksacks for miles. The idea of such intensive training is to ensure that those who become leaders in the armed forces have the stamina and will power to persevere and succeed; they test for "grit." About fifty cadets a year drop out.

This is an expensive way of determining who does and who doesn't have grit. It is not just the fifty, whose training costs have to be written off, but also the fifty places that were denied others who might have had the necessary quality of mind to stick with it.

The drawback of this highly competitive training course is that it tests physical and intellectual abilities but has no way of testing for stickability, other than to see whether any of the cadets fall by the wayside.

Some cadets were scoring highly on the intellectual and physical tests,but still dropping out. Then a psychologist called Angela Lee Duckworth applied her mind to the problem.

She devised a simple test that could be self-administered and took just a few minutes to complete. It consists of twelve statements that the cadets answered, scoring themselves on a scale of 1 to 5. The statements were similar to these: I am not discouraged by setbacks. I finish what I set out to do.[5]

What the responses do is indicate the key factor around grit, which is the willingness to persevere through failure, to be undeterred by setbacks and adversities, to draw lessons from mistakes and errors, and start again. This is a mindset that conceptualizes failures not as failures but as opportunities to learn and move forward. It is quite different from how well we might succeed at intellectual or physical tasks. And crucially, it is whether recruits have this mindset or not that we need to know.

When these grit tests were administered to a cohort of cadets, the scores turned out to be a far better predictor of who would drop out than the scores the cadets were getting on their West Point course. The tests were tried over five years, with the same results: they were a reliable indicator of who would stay the course and who would fall away. Since these grit tests were used with the military, they have also been administered to other groups, such as those applying to be teachers in very challenging schools, with the same record of success.[6]

So, this is where I think British policing could learn a valuable lesson. At the moment, student officers are selected on the basis of what they have achieved to date (mainly in terms of their education and work experience) and face a testing time, studying and training on the job. But the drop out rate in the first few years is considerable across the country. That is an unrecoverable cost to policing and a waste of public resources. It means that for policing to sustain the uplift in numbers that is currently being set by the government, forces are having to over-recruit. That is inefficient. There is no way of testing in advance whether a potential recruit has stickability or not. But the simple grit test would be a good predictor and could be used as part of the initial selection. If it were used, we could drastically cut the number of recruits who fall by

5. Duckworth, "Grit."
6. Duckworth, "Grit."

the wayside and save a great deal of expense. This is what British policing could learn from West Point.

Dog Bites

Each morning, I read something called the Chief Constable's Log, which lists the more serious crimes and incidents of the previous twenty-four hours. Incidents where dogs have attacked not only adults but also children and babies appear far too regularly. In a previous diary entry, I wrote about what seemed to be a growing number of incidents involving attacks by dogs of certain breeds. Last week was no exception, and a young teenager was the latest to be savaged in this way in Sheffield. He has life-changing injuries.

Many of the dogs in question are XL Bullies, Cane Corsos, and Pocket Bullies, costing anywhere between £200 and £2,000. They are not illegal, not subject to the 1991 Dangerous Dogs Act; but as breeds, they seem now to have form. I know that many postal workers are fearful of those addresses where these dogs are kept. Neighbors, too, have from time to time asked me what can be done. It is hard to do anything on the grounds that something might happen, though too late when it does.

I had thought that people might be more careful about acquiring these types of dog when they had babies and children, but it seems not. Owners have told me that the dogs are gentle and loving and great with kids. Everyone with one thinks that the problem lies with the owners, not the dogs; and they, of course, are exemplary owners. I have come to the conclusion that this is not true. The dogs are the problem. The owners just add to it.

March 20, 2023

Right Care, Right Person

For some time, South Yorkshire police have been preparing for a major change in the way they respond to certain types of vulnerable persons. I have written before about the amount of time police officers are having to devote to looking after people who are having some sort of medical or mental health crisis, or need psychological help or treatment. This is something that has grown considerably and remorselessly over the last few years, in part because other more appropriate organizations and agencies were starved of resources during the times of austerity, but also because the police themselves did not at first realize just how far they were being drawn into these areas of non-crime activity.

But officers became increasingly anxious. They were being sent to deal with matters for which they were not qualified or trained. This posed a risk to the vulnerable person and a risk to the officer who assumed responsibility for them. Sometimes, if they were called to deal with someone in crisis, they might spend the best part of their shift being with them until an ambulance came, or, if it didn't come, taking them and staying with them in A&E until they were seen. And there were also times when, for the person in crisis, the sight of a police uniform raised anxiety levels, leaving them feeling criminalized or stigmatized.

This was a national problem, but now, forces will gradually be resisting and reversing this, using an approach called Right Care, Right Person, first developed by Humberside police. Briefly, it means that incidents will, in the future, be responded to by the appropriate agency and not the police. Staff who answer calls in the force control room have been trained to point callers to those other agencies. Of course, if someone is at risk of serious harm, the police will attend. But otherwise, they should be able to step back from many of the types of calls they have previously been dealing with.

But this will only work if those other organizations are prepared to play their part. So, one of the assistant chief constables, Dan Thorpe, has been preparing to phase in this new approach by ensuring that partners are ready: mental health care providers, social care, Yorkshire Ambulance Service, and so on. Right Care, Right Person will be phased in. If it works, it could see non-crime demand reduce considerably, and that will free up officers to deal with the incidents they have been trained for and not the medical and social issues for which they have not.

March 27, 2023

Casey Review

Last week, Baroness Louise Casey published her review of the standards and culture of the Metropolitan police. The review was, in her words, "rigorous, stark, and unsparing."[7] It was commissioned by the mayor of London following the abduction, rape, and murder of Sarah Everard by

7. Casey, "Baroness Casey Review," 7.

a serving officer in 2021. The review details many other instances of misogyny as well as homophobia and racism within the force. It makes for utterly gloomy reading, stunning members of the public and, in fairness, many police officers as well. It's damning conclusion was that the Met was institutionally racist, homophobic, and misogynistic, together with the suggestion that what was found in the Met might exist elsewhere.

The key word in the review's conclusions was not racist, or homophobic, or misogynistic but institutional. If the Met could not accept that finding, then it was not wholeheartedly accepting the critical finding of the review. But the commissioner, Sir Mark Rowley, could not accept the word "institutional" and other chief constables have distanced themselves from it as well. That will make it hard to convince many in the country that the Met, or any other force, is really going to do what needs to be done to tackle what Casey found. So why the reluctance to use the word "institutional"? I think there are two main reasons.

First, chiefs think that calling any organization institutionally racist, sexist, or misogynistic suggests that this is an issue for that organization alone, when in fact, it is a wider societal issue and has to be addressed by all of us. But that isn't what it means to say that a particular organization has an institutional problem. There are indeed wider issues of racism, sexism, and misogyny in society, but as part of the contribution towards addressing them, each organization must deal with its own issues.

Second, chief officers fear that if they were to say institutional, the public and many rank and file officers would believe they were saying that every officer was racist, homophobic, and misogynistic. I understand the fear, but again, Louise Casey was very clear that this was not what she was saying, though those that are racist, sexist, or misogynist need to be called out and rooted out. She identifies the problem at a different level from that of the attitudes and actions of individuals. She could have called this cultural or systemic rather than institutional, and sometimes does. But her chosen word for her overall summary is *institutional*.

She uses that word deliberately. It harks back in London to the Macpherson inquiry into the murder of the black teenager Stephen Lawrence in 1993. Sir William Macpherson found the police investigation to have been incompetent, partly as a result of issues of race. He said the force was institutionally racist.[8] The Met never accepted that and presumably, therefore, never thoroughly examined themselves in

8. Macpherson, "Stephen Lawrence Inquiry."

the light of it. By using the same word, Casey is forcing the Met to admit that the central problem remains.

An issue is institutional (I prefer the word "cultural") when it is about *the way we do things*. Individual officers do not have to have particular attitudes if the way things are habitually done leads to biases and outcomes that are racist, sexist, or misogynistic. Officers are unconsciously caught up in that. If the organization is to change, it must reflect on these institutional matters. If you don't accept that the problems are institutional, then you fall back on different explanations: it's all about individual bad apples in a society that is itself unreformed. In other words, cultural change cannot just be about promoting certain values, important as that is, but about deep reflection on the way an organization does things.

Embedded in the review is an account of the way the Met handled a vigil that was held in memory of Sarah Everard in the days that followed her murder. It sums up very well why the Met's difficulties are institutional.

A women's group, Reclaim These Streets, approached the police to say they wanted to hold a socially distanced event to remember Sarah. London was under Tier 4 COVID restrictions at the time, and gatherings of more than two were not permitted. The police banned the event. But it was soon clear that women would gather anyway. The force then had choices. There were no easy answers, but in one management meeting, the possibility of allowing a socially distanced vigil overseen by a low key police presence of all female officers was considered, but set aside. Instead, the vigil went ahead without permission, and so without the stewarding that the women's group would have supplied; and it ended with scenes of male police officers wrestling women to the ground and arresting them, video footage of which went viral and did enormous damage to the reputation of the police. In other words, the Met had carried on doing what it always did, the usual institutional response, and was not alert to the feelings of fear and anger that made the women come to the vigil despite the ban and despite any health risks. It was insensitive to women's concerns. This is how institutional misogyny works.

In South Yorkshire, we have had to learn the hard way about how you recover from your mistakes. Our issues were quite different, but the starting point was the same: you have to acknowledge what the victims of your actions are saying to you and learn that lesson first, with no denials, no defensiveness, no ifs, and no buts.

That is not what the response to Louise Casey's report currently looks like, and if that is the case, we shall be back here again at some future point. The only option that will be acceptable then will be the breakup of the Met. We discovered last week that "sorry" is not the hardest word for the police to say. "Institutional" is.

April 3, 2023

The King, the Bundestag, and Parliament

I had a few days away from the office last week and watched part of the King's state visit to Germany. As the King spoke, in German, to the assembled members of the Bundestag, I became aware of something quite astonishing, which we rather take for granted. As the camera showed the rows of MPs in the federal parliament building, what was noticeable was how very white they all are.

What a contrast with the House of Commons. If you look at our government front bench, for example, the three great offices of state, prime minister, home secretary and foreign secretary, are all now occupied by members of ethnic minorities. And following last week's election of a new leader of the Scottish National Party, the first minister of Scotland is also from an ethnic minority. We do not find any of this surprising; yet, if you look at what has happened here and what has not happened elsewhere in Europe, the contrast is remarkable.

But it's not only this diversity among our senior politicians that is so significant; it's also the fact that we are not moved to remark on it. We now take these developments for granted in a way that continental Europeans do not, or do not yet. A German chancellor, whose family origins are in the Indian sub continent, or a French president, who is a practicing Muslim, seems inconceivable at this moment in time. But in the UK and in Scotland, we note it but then move on.

It is, of course, a legacy of empire. More than that, it reverses those old racial stereotypes of empire about which ethnic groups were fit to govern and which not. When we discuss racism in the UK, this is not something I hear remarked upon.

All of which brings me to a puzzle and a problem. Why can't we see the same ethnic diversity that we see in our politicians in our police forces, and in all ranks, including and especially in the higher ranks? I know the force in South Yorkshire, as in other places across the country, has been working hard to try to improve ethnic diversity. The big recruitment drives that have been taking place to increase police numbers provided an opportunity to do just this. But despite all the effort, there has been little progress.

I asked a couple of Muslim friends whether their children ever considered joining the police. They both said that what was important to them as parents was that their children (now all adults) had a good education, did well at school, and, if possible, went to university. They then encouraged them to join the professions, and six of the seven children had: law, medicine, and accountancy. But they had never considered the police. Perhaps, they would have done now with policing professionalizing and requiring either a degree on entry or for a degree to be taken as part of initial training. So far, however, that does not seem to be making the decisive difference we might have hoped for.

The police do need to look like the communities they police. It is part of what gives them their legitimacy, enabling them to police by consent. That includes being able to attract people from all ethnic groups.

April 10, 2023

Unnecessary Deaths

From time to time, Claire Mercer, whose husband Jason was killed in a road traffic collision on a smart motorway and who now campaigns against them, gets in touch. She often ends her emails with a cry of despair: How many more have to die before action is taken?

Last week, another inquest was held following further fatalities on a smart motorway stretch of the M1. Derek Jacobs's van suffered a burst tire and came to a halt in a live lane. A Ford KA ran into the van, killing Mr. Jacobs. It then flipped over and was hit by a coach. The passenger in the car, Charles Scripps, also died.

The assistant coroner, Susan Evans, told the court, "It is immediately apparent that, had there been a hard shoulder, this incident would not have occurred because Mr Jacobs would have been able to pull off the live lane entirely."[9] The collision investigator, Sergeant Paul Moorcroft, said, "It is highly, highly unlikely that this collision would have taken place had there been a hard shoulder."[10]

9. Higgens, "Smart M-Way Crash," para. 5.
10. Higgens, "Smart M-Way Crash," para. 12.

Why the car driver did not see the van in time is not understood, but the comments of the assistant coroner and the police officer could not be clearer: a hard shoulder would have made the difference between life and death. Claire Mercer asked, How many more have to die before action is taken? There is no answer to that because these deaths, and the comments by the coroner, seem to count for little when decisions are being made at the national level.

May 1, 2023

Measuring Crime and Under Reporting

Since 1981, there have been two ways of measuring crime in our communities. First, there is what the police record, and second, there is what is captured in the Crime Survey for England and Wales, commissioned by the Office for National Statistics (ONS). The better measure (in my view) is the ONS Crime Survey. The survey is carried out by a research organization called Kantar Public. They contact a large sample of people in England and Wales and ask them what their experience of crime has been over the previous twelve months. When they did this in 2020/2021, they were in touch with fifty thousand households.

Crime statistics based on police recorded crime are just that: those crimes that are reported to the police and those the police record accurately. But we know that many crimes are not reported and, so, not recorded. Inevitably, therefore, police data is always going to miss a certain amount of crime because of underreporting. We also know that some forces are better than others at recording crime. Our force is rated good for its crime recording. But some forces are less proficient at recording correctly or do not recognized some crimes in the first place. This can be true of hate crimes, for example. The survey, however, picks up not only the reported crime but also the crimes not reported, and, so, not recorded and those not recorded correctly. This is why I prefer the results of the Crime Survey.

But are there some crimes that are likely to be missed more than others, and perhaps missed in both police data and the survey statistics? What are the underreported crimes?

We know that one is Domestic Abuse (DA). There was a time when people struggled to get the police to take DA as seriously as they should. Police officers today have been trained to recognize DA when they are called out to incidents and the definition of victim has broadened to include children in a household.

Nevertheless, many are still reluctant to talk to the police, especially where they fear the reactions of a partner or they worry that children might be taken from them by social services. And a controlling partner may have raised fears that if they go to the police for help and leave the home, they will be in immediate financial peril.

It was only after talking to someone who had been the victim of a coercive and controlling partner that I realized there might be a group of people who are even more unrecognized. The crimes against them might be going more unreported than others. This person told me a little about how the relationship within their marriage eventually became quite toxic. They gradually realized that they were subject to a coercive and controlling partner, with matters coming to a head when they were threatened by them with a knife. They left the marriage but did not report it to the police. Why not? Was it because the threatening person in this marriage was the wife, not the husband?

When we think of DA, we tend to think of women trapped in a difficult or dangerous relationship. We assume the victim is female, and that is usually the case. But this person reminded me that it also happens the other way. And perhaps, men find it even harder to admit to themselves or others, including the police, that they are a victim. If DA is an underreported crime, perhaps even more underreported are those cases, admittedly rarer, where the victim is male.

May 15, 2023

The Prison Population

What is happening to our prison population? I imagine that for most of us, if we think about prisons at all, we doubt whether there is much change as the years go by. The same sorts of people are being locked away now for the same sorts of crimes as they were ten years ago. We might have realized that numbers are rising, at least among the adult (over eighteen) population, which is true, but that may be as far as our understanding goes.

In fact, quite a lot of change is happening, but what struck me most about the latest statistics I have seen is the age of those now in our prisons. Prisoners are getting older, including the much smaller numbers of female prisoners. The over-fifties are, in fact, the fastest growing group in the prison population. There are two main reasons for this. First, prison sentences are getting longer. One consequence is that offenders reach older age while in custody. A second reason is the nature of the offences. An increasing number of older people are being sentenced for sexual offenses, including offenses that go back many years.

What the public may not stop to think about is that all of this has consequences. They can be summarized as: health, purposeful activity, and support.

People in prison age significantly faster than the population as a whole, by about ten years. So, it is not surprising that some of the older offenders have complex health needs. This can be a challenge for prisons: issues such as menopause, poor mobility, dietary needs. It is a challenge for prisons and probation as the prisoners come to the end of their sentence and need to be settled back into the community.

Purposeful activities may also need to be different for the older prisoner, activities that the prison has not traditionally been geared up to meet. And general support can create real headaches. Older prisoners may be a long way from home and those family members who seek to visit and keep in touch. They may not be digitally literate, yet the digital world they will have to return to is moving at an ever faster rate, and they will need to be able to access many of their needs after prison online, including benefits, such as pensions. Having to deal with this falls largely on prison officers who are already under great pressure.

When people tell me to press for longer sentences, I understand the sentiment and the emotion, but I also think about the consequences—the consequences for prisoners but also for prison staff.

(We have four male prisons in Doncaster, and our nearest female prison is New Hall, near Flockton in West Yorkshire.)

May 29, 2023

Joined Up Thinking

Last week, I received a letter from National Highways, from an officer whose job title is national emergency area project sponsor. She tells me that work will start on Monday, June 5, on the M1 between junction 32 at Thurcroft and 35A at Stocksbridge to have new emergency areas added "as part of our National Emergency Area Retrofit." Retrofit reads as if this is something that should have been done before but wasn't; but I may be wrong about that. Altogether, a further twelve emergency areas will be added to the existing eight, so, more than double. The work will not be completed until winter 2024. The left-hand lane will be closed throughout and speed limited to 50 mph. So, massive disruption for a long time.

The letter went on to say this investment in new emergency areas is designed to help road users not only to feel safe but also to be even safer on our roads. If building (at costs undisclosed) more emergency areas will make the roads safer, then why stop at twelve more? For maximum safety, why not join all the emergency areas together? You could call it a hard shoulder.

What Ely Is Telling Us

Last week, there was a riot in the Ely area of Cardiff. This followed the death in a road traffic collision of two young boys who were riding an e-bike. The people of the area believed that the boys had been pursued by the police, hence the riot. The police and the police and crime commissioner were quick to deny this, though some camera footage subsequently came to light apparently showing the bike being followed at some point by a police van. This muddied the waters. We shall have to wait for the investigation to complete before the truth is known. But it shows the level of mistrust that exists between the police and some residents.

Whatever the result of the investigation, what was revealed in the days following the disturbances was the state of some of our most deprived communities. Residents were not slow in coming forward to speak about life in this part of Ely. This is what a deprived community looks like: 66 percent of children are what was called income-deprived, and 46 percent of adults have no qualifications of any kind.[11] A cash-starved local authority struggles to maintain basic services and some, such as youth provision, disappeared a long time ago.

This is the breeding ground for drug-dealing and criminal gangs, where police cannot keep pace. The prevailing mood quickly becomes one of helplessness and hopelessness. It is hardly surprising that young people are drawn into criminality. Ely is not the only deprived community in the country, and parts of South Yorkshire resemble it. We can't say we haven't been warned.

11. Duffy, "Ely."

June 5, 2023

Right Care, Right Person. Right Time?

Just over a week ago, the commissioner of the Metropolitan Police, Sir Mark Rowley, caused a stir by announcing that as from September, his force would not be responding to calls to deal with people having non-emergency mental health issues unless there was a threat to life, the person's own or other people's. He explained that answering these calls was not really police business and was taking officers away from fighting crime for significant amounts of time: ten thousand hours every week. The Met will direct callers to more appropriate agencies; the police will not be answering these calls any more. This policy is called Right Care, Right Person (RCRP).

There is, I think, a widespread acceptance that as public services were reduced back in the decade of austerity, the police began to pick up where other and more appropriate organizations and agencies were beginning to cut back. But this accumulation of extra responsibilities is now impacting on the number of hours the police have to deal with matters that should be their primary concern. The only question is about timing. For reasons I don't understand, the Met decided to take what, on the face of it, seems a unilateral decision simply to serve notice on their partners, the NHS, adult social services, mental health services, that they will no longer be doing what they have done in the past and will be referring callers to these partners instead. Right Care, Right Person. But Humberside took two years to work with partners to plan and prepare for the changes. Why the Met has not done the same is a mystery. And why the mayor of London, who is the PCC, was not consulted first (I am assuming he wasn't) is equally strange.

In South Yorkshire, I am kept in touch with how RCRP is being developed. It is being done carefully and partners are being engaged. Partners, such as the NHS, mental health services, adult social care, and so on, are being consulted. And call handlers are being trained to ensure that calls for service are understood and appropriately directed. The police know full well that they cannot refuse to attend an incident if there is a threat to life, and there may be grey areas.

While I think the general direction is right, the policy must be rolled out with care, taking account of partner preparedness. Right Care, Right Person, yes. But Right Time, too.

DA Matters

As PCC, I give grants to a range of organizations, including those that support victims of domestic abuse (DA). Last week, I visited one such organization to hear about their work with women from minority ethnic groups. I had a long conversation with one woman from a Pakistani Muslim background. She spoke Urdu, so I had to have a translator, though she could understand English.

Mariam (not her real name) had been married for twenty years and had five children. She had lived for most of that time in a West Midlands town and had endured an abusive relationship. Her female relatives had told her that she had to put up with her husband's behavior because that was how men were, and the woman's role was to keep the house and raise the children. In the end, she had taken the children and fled to South Yorkshire, where she had other relatives.

The DA charity had been her lifeline. She had learned there, among sympathetic and understanding women from her own culture and, crucially, religion, that things could be different. For the first time in her life, she felt there was some hope. Life was still very tough, especially financially. But her children were settled and she had found courage and confidence. She now hopes that she can secure an Islamic divorce from a shariah court. This will mean a lot to her.

All those who suffer domestic abuse need support. It is not easy to escape from controlling relationships, especially where there are children and financial dependencies. But for those in some of our minority communities, there are the added pressures that particular cultures can bring. And that is why the support I can give to those DA charities that understand that can be so vital.

June 5, 2023

Chaplaincy: The Acceptable Face of Religion

The chief constable and I recently met with South Yorkshire police chaplains and the lead chaplain, the Rev. Derek Pamment. Derek is also priest-in-charge of Wadsworth, Loversall, and Balby in the Doncaster district. He was appointed in August 2022 and is seeking to increase the number of voluntary chaplains from all faiths and denominations. Two new recruits were male and female Muslims: Imam Mohammad Ismail and Ameena Blake.

I have had an interest in chaplaincy for many years and wrote a chapter about the place of chaplaincy in public life in *A Handbook of Chaplaincy Studies* (Ashgate, 2015). I made the observation then that in a more secular age, chaplaincy could only be justified, and could only be funded from the public purse, if it fulfilled two conditions.

First, chaplaincy had to add value to the work of an organization. A British Army general told me on one occasion that after years of not thinking too much about chaplaincy, the armed services quickly realized the value during the Iraq and Afghanistan conflicts. Chaplains accompanied men and women, many of whom were quite young, to the front line. They were on hand to calm nerves, help maintain morale, and give comfort and reassurance. This might involve some religious practice or simply conversation. As the general put it, at one time, chaplains would have been an afterthought; now, they made sure they were on the second plane out. And chaplains were also back home standing with families when they were anxious or distressed. The key was building good, pastoral relationships. In similar fashion, there has been a steady valuing of chaplaincy in many other institutions, from hospitals, to prisons, and the police.

As well as adding value, chaplaincy also has to follow the British model of chaplaincy, which is to say, chaplains must be willing and able to help people of any faith or of no faith. I call this the British model because it is not the chaplaincy model found universally. In some countries, military chaplains, for example, are paid by their denomination and offer themselves only to those of their church. But in this country, we have evolved a quite different approach. The police chaplains are available to anyone who turns to them, and so, public funding of them is justifiable.

The South Yorkshire voluntary police chaplains, ordained and lay, men and women of all faiths, will gradually increase in number and be available as and when needed: at certain incidents, when officers or their families need support, enabling services and ceremonies. In the future, they will be wearing distinctive jackets with Police Chaplain on the back.

What I find interesting from a sociological perspective is the way that, as society has become less religious, chaplaincy has become more valued. You could almost say that chaplaincy is the acceptable face of religion in secular Britain.

Worrying

I was driving along one of our residential streets, which had cars parked closely together on both sides. The speed limit was 20 mph, though the parking effectively lowered that. Suddenly, a children's buggy appeared from behind one of the cars, pushed out into the road a few cars further on from where I was driving. There was a small child in it. The buggy was pulled back out of sight, almost as quickly as it had emerged. Meanwhile, I had braked and slowed. Cautiously, I moved forward, and immediately, a dog on a lead ran out from the same spot before it, too, was pulled back. When I drew alongside the place where all this happened, I saw what I assumed was the mother of the child, holding with her left hand the buggy and the dog on the lead. In her right hand, pressed to her face, she had a mobile phone and was talking animatedly into it. As I looked towards her, she gave me a cheerful smile, as if to say, "Thank you."

I don't know what gets taught in baby classes these days, but I would like to think that whoever runs them, or health visitors, can impress on parents the dangers of being in charge of a buggy, a baby, and a dog while talking into a mobile phone. It's not only car drivers who can be distracted by them.

June 12, 2023

West Meets East

This week, I am speaking to a group of senior police officers, men and women, from India. As part of their training, they are spending a week at Sheffield Hallam University and with South Yorkshire police. I met a similar group last year when I was intrigued to learn that they had some police stations that were specifically for women, for women to report crime, for female suspects, staffed by women officers. Was there something we could learn from this? One of my staff told me that while holidaying in Goa on the Indian west coast last year, he saw a pink police car, indicating female officers were in it, presumably to give reassurance to women and girls.

June 26, 2023

Funding Victim Services

Each year, I receive from the Ministry of Justice (MoJ) a sum of money to commission services, principally for victims of crime. These services are delivered by organizations in the voluntary sector. They include, for example, those that support victims of sexual assaults (rapes) and domestic abuse and those trying to overcome addictions. Last year, this core grant came to £1.8 million.

But sometimes, the government makes other sums of money available on a one-off basis to enhance the work of these organizations. This seems to be a growing trend. This funding, however, usually has to be applied for on a competitive basis. There is no guarantee that the bid will be successful. While all additional funding for these vital services is welcome, it does involve my staff and staff in other organizations, in both the public and voluntary sectors, in a lot of extra work writing the bids that may, in the end, come to nothing. In addition, because the funding is, usually, for one year only, it may have a limited effect.

To give some idea of the funding and work involved in making and securing these bids, I set out below what we received last year from the various funds. We succeeded in most of our bids.

- Safer Streets Fund 4: £737,560. This was Home Office funding to reduce antisocial behavior in hot spot areas in Barnsley and Rotherham with additional CCTV and lighting in parks.

- National Independent Domestic Violence Advisers (IDVAs) and Independent Sexual Violence Advisers (ISVAs) Fund: £590,574 (MoJ). An additional six ISVAs, three Children's Independent Sexual Violence Advisers, nine IDVAs for those with complex needs, ethnic minorities, LGBTQ.

- Funding for additional IDVAs and ISVAs: £427,092. This enabled the recruitment of additional IDVAs and ISVAs across South Yorkshire to support victims/survivors, including those who were disabled and those who were male.

- Perpetrator Phase 4: £656,069. Home Office funding towards a program to change the behavior of domestic abusers and increase victim safety.

- Community-based services for victims of Domestic Abuse or Sexual Violence: £636,564 (MoJ). Support includes counseling and specialist support for older people, children, and male victims of domestic abuse.

This is over £3 million of funding for vital services to people in South Yorkshire, which would not have come into the county without a great deal of painstaking work, often against tight deadlines, by people in my office, in the local authorities, and in the voluntary sector. Their work is not always as appreciated as it should be.

Apology Accepted

(In 2012, Sheffield City Council entered into a Public Finance Initiative called Streets Ahead with a contractor, Amey, and the Department of Transport, to repair and then maintain all the city's roads until 2035. However, this involved the felling of some mature trees in some streets, and this sparked bitter and sometimes violent protests for several years.)

The Sheffield Trees controversy was a traumatic time for the city of Sheffield, considerably damaging the reputation of the city council and upsetting many residents. It was also blown out of all proportion as the story was told nationally and, indeed, internationally. I had friends who live elsewhere in the country commiserating with me because I lived in a city that was now without trees! I was alarmed because, as the dispute became more fractious, the police were increasingly drawn in. My attempts to reason with senior councilors and officials were rebuffed.

The council commissioned an inquiry into the dispute, chaired by Sir Mark Lowcock, which reported earlier this year. He found that the council had not conducted themselves well and, among other things, said they should apologize to residents generally and to some individuals and organizations specifically. Last Monday, the council did that with a remarkably full and frank acceptance that it had made mistakes, needed to say sorry, and hoped for a new era of properly listening to and engaging with citizens with openness and transparency. It was an astonishing statement, noticed by the national media as well as the local. The new leader of the council, Councilor Tom Hunt, was interviewed on BBC Radio 4 *Today* along with a spokesperson for the Sheffield Tree Action Groups (STAG), who were also criticized in the report for some of the more extreme behavior of some protestors.

The apology to the police and myself is in the report presented to the council's Strategy and Resources Policy Committee, June, 19. The relevant paragraph is this: "Agenda Item 5. 18.b. South Yorkshire Police and the South Yorkshire Police and Crime Commissioner, Dr Alan Billings."[12]

The inquiry made it clear that the council placed the police in an invidious position during the dispute. At times the council placed undue pressure on the police and did not do enough to find alternative solutions to the dispute or to play a visible role on the streets during the protests. "The Police and Crime Commissioner called for a political resolution to the dispute several times: his advice should have been heeded."

Apology accepted. Time, now, to move on.

July 3, 2023

Moral Dilemmas

Not all moral dilemmas are resolvable. Or rather, we are sometimes forced to make a choice between two incompatible courses of action, neither of which we find completely satisfactory. Take the case of Carla Foster. I was recently asked by several people in South Yorkshire to make a statement in support of Ms. Foster, a resident of Staffordshire, who had been sentenced to two years and four months in prison for aborting her unborn child after the legal time limit of twenty-four weeks. She was between thirty-two and thirty-four weeks pregnant. This was during the COVID period when, it was said, she had misled the British Pregnancy Advisory Service about the length of her pregnancy, and they had posted an abortifacient to her. Ms. Foster already has three children, and she wanted to limit the size of her family. So, she took the drug. Those who contacted me were of the opinion that a grave injustice had been done to Ms. Foster.

There were two principal arguments. The first was that it was hard to see what purpose would be served by sending her to prison when there were three children who needed their mother; the judge need not have given her a custodial sentence. I don't know what discretion the judge had, or what he took into account in passing the sentence. I simply note that there were those who did not see this as justice, whatever their views on abortion.

---

12. Sheffield City Council's Strategy and Resources Policy Committee for June 19, 2023.

The second argument was the familiar one, that as long as the baby was in the woman's body, this was her body, and no one had a right to tell her what she could and couldn't do with it. One person said it was evidence that we were still a patriarchal society in which men made the rules and women were (unfairly) expected to obey them.

There was a good deal of public sympathy for Carla Foster for the first of the above arguments: What good did prosecuting her and sending her to prison do? But the public mood is not in favor of extending the time limit for legal abortions and is, if anything, inclined to be more restrictive now than even a few years ago. In any case, there is a law, the Offences Against the Person Act of 1861, and Ms. Foster had broken it and pleaded guilty. Don't we all have a duty to uphold the law? Hence, the moral dilemma. The police, of course, have to enforce the law. But what can we say about the general legal and moral arguments?

The moral issues surrounding abortion have divided public opinion in this country all my life, though, in that time, we have gone from a total ban to the qualified acceptance that we now have, what some would call a fudge. There were those who opposed abortion in all, or almost all, circumstances, arguing that from the moment of conception the unborn had a right to life. There were those who argued that abortion was a woman's right. But most people were somewhere in the middle, arguing that it should be allowed in some circumstances because, without it, backstreet abortions would continue with obvious dangers to women. So, abortion became legal in 1968 (David Steel's Bill), and in 1990, the twenty-four week limit was set on the basis that after twenty-four weeks, a foetus was viable outside the womb.

This was a pragmatic solution to a difficult moral question, on which people were divided. Abortion remained a crime, which was a way of asserting the value of human life, including the life of the unborn, though with allowable exceptions. The tragedy for Carla Foster was that she waited so long to make up her mind and fell foul of the law, unlike the 230,000 women whose abortions last year were legal. The danger of allowing abortion at any point in a pregnancy, however late, is that it could lead some to ask the obvious question, and some, like the ethicist Professor Peter Singer, have asked it: Why do we draw an arbitrary line at birth? If a mother decides that she cannot cope with a very impaired child, for example, why not permit infanticide? There may be some logic in this, but do we seriously want to go down that road?

My own view, then, is that abortion is one of those moral dilemmas where the majority of people probably find themselves somewhere between those who regard it as morally indefensible in all, or almost all, circumstances and those who believe it is a decision for the pregnant woman to make at any stage of pregnancy. For us, the pragmatic stance of British law is where we are most comfortable, or least discomforted, and if this is a fudge, then so be it.

But I am not sure how this would help the judge.

Lessons from Treeton

The Baptist church in Treeton was packed with over one hundred people last week. The parish council had called a meeting to discuss crime in the village, principally burglaries and car thefts. People were, to varying degrees, frustrated, angry, and fearful at what they saw as an outbreak of crime. There had certainly been something of a spike recently. Someone is currently under arrest for some of the crime, and we wait to see the outcome.

The parish council had asked me, the local neighborhood police team, a local ward councilor, and the MP Alexander Stafford to the meeting. We each made a few remarks, but the main purpose was to hear from people themselves.

There were specific issues that I will take forward, but the meeting did raise questions that are of concern to similar-sized villages across the county. First, a number of crimes in a village this size (there are 3,189 residents) can have a much greater impact on a community's sense of safety and security than the same number of incidents in a part of a town or city with a similar number of people. Since January, there had been six residential burglaries (and six attempted burglaries), seven thefts of vehicles, and two thefts from vehicles. In a city, this might not be noticed much beyond the affected roads, but in a village, everyone is quickly aware of what has happened, and the anxiety levels are amplified as a result. This is something the police need to consider. Ensuring village communities feel safe may require a different kind of bespoke activity from bigger urban areas. I will be speaking to senior officers about this.

Second, the audience was very clear about what would make them feel more secure. They spoke about the visibility of police officers and about CCTV. There was some recognition that a police officer could not be posted in every street every minute of the day or night. All recognized that police numbers had been drastically cut during the years of austerity. But if numbers are now gradually coming back with the new recruits, was there not scope for officers to show themselves more, on foot as much as in a vehicle? There is now some research that backs up this idea that a visible presence, such as regular patrolling, has a deterrent effect. It must be something that senior officers take to heart: people want it and the research supports it.

The meeting clearly thought that CCTV was important not so much for its potential as evidence after a crime has been committed as its deterrent effect. "If criminals see cameras at the entry to our village, they will think twice before stopping off here," was how one person put it. Again, there may be some truth in this, and the local authority officers who were present, together with the Treeton parish councilors, can follow that up.

But something important was going on in that meeting that we all might have missed. "What are the police doing for us?" one man asked. What he seems to have overlooked is that five or six years ago, if such a meeting had been held, there would have been no neighborhood police officers present because neighborhood policing had disappeared. The neighborhood teams were abandoned as South Yorkshire police sought to cut costs and balance the books. Now they are back and everyone in the chapel saw and heard from Carl and Nathan, the two constables for whom Treeton is their patch. (There is also a police community support officer.) Having these officers get to know the village and the people, and vice versa, is a huge step forward from where we were even a few years ago, and as new recruits come through, we hope to see more high-visibility jackets joining them.

July 10, 2023

Is Counseling the Only Answer?

As part of my role as police and crime commissioner, I commission services that support victims of crime. I also give grants to organizations in the voluntary sector that work with victims and survivors. One of the areas of growing demand is counseling. While funding is an issue, and perhaps always will be an issue, shortage of counselors seems to compound matters. And there are counselors and counselors. It is often the more experienced and specialized counseling that is most needed.

It doesn't take too much imagination to realize that a child who has suf-fered sexual abuse from a close family member is going to need a very different approach from that of an adult who has been assaulted by a stranger. But is counseling always the right response?

My attention was caught recently by some research that seems to suggest that counselors can be brought in too quickly. Dutch social scientists, who studied 236 survivors of different kinds of traumatic events, found that where emotional debriefing is given too quickly, vic-tims were more likely to go on and show signs of post-traumatic stress disorder, needing even more help.

They compared the victims who received immediate counseling with those who received none and were left to cope for themselves. They found that the former had poorer mental and emotional health outcomes than the latter. This was attributed to what they called "hyper arousal": the counseling raised awareness of the traumatic event in ways that did not happen with those who had no help.

There may also be cultural factors in play when it comes to coun-seling. For example, when I taught at Lancaster University in the 1990s, I met a counselor who was studying for an MA. She had been involved in helping the families of those who were bereaved when PAN AM Flight 103, going from London to New York, was blown apart by a ter-rorist bomb and fell on the Scottish town of Lockerbie in 1988. All the passengers and crew were killed, as well as people on the ground. Griev-ing relatives came from over twenty-one countries, with many different religious and cultural backgrounds, to see the place where their loved ones had died. She was one of the counselors who sought to help them. When she and her colleagues met a family of Buddhists, they were quite disconcerted. Her training had led her to believe that people impacted by trauma needed to express their emotions; the Buddhists were stoic and said little, turning inward. She was forced to rethink her practice. It's possible, in the light of the Dutch research, that the offer of counseling was, in any case, too soon. I am also old enough to recall the Aberfan di-saster of 1966, when a spoil heap fell on the village and buried 28 adults and 116 children. The people of Aberfan, in Wales, refused counseling, closed ranks, and supported one another.

Perhaps, we live now in a less cohesive society, which no longer has as many of these religious or cultural resources to draw upon. Perhaps, we are less resilient as a result and so are in greater need of the help of professional counselors when traumatic events happen. At any rate, the demand for help for victims and survivors of crime is considerable, and I commission what I can to help. But I note the growing difficulty that the statutory and voluntary sectors have in finding suitably qualified and experienced people.

July 24, 2023

Operation Civitas

We have been awarded £1.05 million by the Home Office to do more to tackle antisocial behavior (ASB) in South Yorkshire. ASB is a national problem, and although police recorded ASB has been falling in the county, it is still blighting many lives and communities. It ranges from fly-tipping (a local authority responsibility) to the noise, nuisance, and mayhem caused by people on quad bikes. Although much is already being done to combat it, this additional funding is very welcome.

The present award has to be divided between our four local authority areas of Barnsley, Doncaster, Rotherham, and Sheffield; the actions collectively are called Operation Civitas. We are required to identify ASB hot spots and direct activities to them. Police and partners have drawn up lists of twelve hot spots in each district, and these will be subject now, among other things, to increased patrolling by the police and other uniformed authorities. This additional high-visibility patrolling has already begun. On Friday, I met local councilors, the police, a council official, and a representative of the social housing provider for one of these areas, Highfields, in Adwick Town Hall, Doncaster.

ASB is a serious matter because it is so relentless and causes great distress to many individuals and communities. The councilors in Adwick gave me a graphic account of everything that blights this part of their ward: the rubbish that is dumped, the fires deliberately started, the windows smashed, the vehicles damaged, including police cars. They also explained the serious underreporting, because people fear reprisals if they do.

I hope the additional measures police and partners will be taking will have a deterrent effect and lead to a reduction in ASB in the months ahead in the forty-eight hot spots identified across the county. We shall also be monitoring what happens so that we can learn more about what works. We want to see ASB reduced and not simply displaced and moved elsewhere.

Honesty Pays?

Driving through and between a number of South Yorkshire small towns and villages over the past few weeks, I began to notice something I had not really thought about before: honesty boxes. These are where people sell homegrown produce, leaving it displayed and unattended at the farm or garden gate with a suggested price, and rely on the honesty of passing customers to put the right money in the box.

I say honesty "box," and some were: brightly or beautifully painted, in some cases. But several of the receptacles I saw were not boxes at all: cracked saucers, tin cans, even an old hat. The produce included eggs, honey, vegetables, and fruit. In every case, there was no one to be seen. The sellers relied completely on the honesty of the customers. I imagine it was most helpful if people had the right money and did not need change. (I have yet to see a machine for accepting credit cards.)

What I find interesting is that I have never had anyone report thefts from honesty boxes as a crime. This seems surprising, given the cost of living crisis and the fact that we have had thefts from food banks. So, do honesty boxes work? Are people honest? I have not heard anything to the contrary. Or is this just another case of underreported crime?

August 7, 2023

Support and Accountability

Some years ago, I was a trustee of a national charity called Circles. It was probably not the most popular charity in the country since its aim was to help sex offenders reintegrate into society. These were men who had served a prison sentence for serious sexual crimes. They had been placed on the sex offenders register and released back into the community, subject to conditions and under supervision by the Probation Service and the police.

The charity, which was largely funded by the Ministry of Justice, worked with volunteers who acted as mentors to the offenders. The full name of the charity is Circles of Support and Accountability, because it aims to offer help but also to ensure that the offender is held to account. It is called Circles because a small group of volunteer mentors plus the offender form a circle of support and accountability. The group meets together regularly to talk issues through, and one of the volunteers offers individual support to the offender, who is called the core member.

The volunteer will meet the core member, probably weekly, to have a chat, go to a cafe, take a walk, and generally be friendly and supportive. They will continue this relationship for a year or so.

The first days and months after a long sentence are a real struggle for anyone leaving prison, but these offenders will have restrictions placed on them that will make it even harder to resume normal relationships. They are among the hardest of ex-offenders to bring back into society, for obvious reasons. It may be a condition of their release, for instance, that they are never alone with a woman. It will not be easy for them to speak to those they meet about their past or the reasons why they were in prison. They may have been rejected by their family and previous friends. There may be little sympathy for them or hostility towards them in their community. Some have been known to be attacked.

Part of the accountability role is exploring all of this with the offender. The charity is not trying to minimize the gravity of the offense or do anything that leads the offender to deny his past. The volunteers are trained to help the men acknowledge the past and the sexual impulses that they may still have and to manage their behavior. If there is to be change, there has to be real self-awareness, an understanding of what they are really like, with all their flaws and failings.

The offenders themselves often talk about how hard their journey has now become. One I recall spoke about his fears and anxieties: fear of meeting people, fear of going out, fear of himself, fear of having his past revealed, and anxiety as to whether he had the strength of mind and will to move forward. Another spoke about the sheer burden of shame he felt and his anger, directed at himself, because, to some considerable degree, he had blighted the rest of his life.

The volunteers come from all sections of society, though when I was involved, quite a few were students who simply wanted to do something worthwhile outside of their studies and personal life. They do not necessarily have or need any particular expertise, other than the desire to make a difference and a willingness to cope with disappointment if things do not go entirely smoothly.

The ultimate aim of the charity's work is to see behavioral change and, as a result have, fewer victims.

When I have been to community meetings after a high profile sex case has been in the news, I often have people tell me that the offender should be locked up and the key thrown away. I don't usually mention my past involvement with Circles, but I do try to get people to think beyond that immediate reaction. Sex offenders do serve terms of imprisonment, but then come out. What should happen next? The worst of all worlds would clearly be to leave them with minimal support with the risk that they fall back into old ways. These offenders need help if they are to re-integrate into their community in any meaningful way. But that must be support with accountability. Circles has it exactly right.

August 14, 2023

Syndromes

From time to time, the director of sales and marketing for the Civil Service College Limited sends me unsolicited details of courses they run to support people in their working lives. They vary from the useful to the unbelievable. Last week, I received the latest in their personal development series: Overcoming Imposter Syndrome. Imposter Syndrome is explained as "a condition where we feel we don't deserve the position or responsibility we have . . . and have the feeling that we are a fraud." The blurb asserts that Meryl Streep, Albert Einstein, and Maya Angelou all suffered from this condition.

I think what they are getting at here is something I have some personal knowledge of, though I wouldn't call it imposter syndrome. One of my sons was once a professional actor, and when he lived at home, we went through the emotions he went through: waiting for the phone to ring about an audition, dealing with rejections, the nerves before the performance, anxiety about the reviews. And all the while, knowing that past success did not guarantee future work. Yes, I'm sure Meryl Streep did sometimes feel a failure. My other son was a scientist. As it happens, a theoretical physicist, where having your theories tested by others was a regular part of the life scientific. Yes, you had to be humble and learn from the insights of others. And when I wrote books, I knew how vulnerable you immediately made yourself. As well as articles in journals, I learned to live with reviews on Amazon.

But leaving all that aside, the Overcoming Impostor Syndrome course, we were told, would enable us to overcome our feeling that we don't deserve the job we are doing. There seems to be no understanding that if such a syndrome exists and the actress, the scientist, and the author all suffered from it, perhaps that was one of the reasons why they achieved what they did. A bit of imposter syndrome keeps us on our toes, doesn't allow us to be complacent, makes us keen to learn from others. It's a good thing.

Now the opposite, "Aren't You Lucky to Have Me Working For You" Syndrome, really is a problem. But I doubt whether such people would ever sign up for a course to overcome that affliction.

The Silly Season

Across the country, prisons are full, dangerously so, some would say. Yet, we know that if we want better outcomes, we need fewer prisoners. We need this for good rehabilitation. We need it for the sake of prison staff who have to manage prisons and safeguard those in them. But here, public perception is often well adrift of the reality; the pressure from the public will be for more offenders going to prison and those found guilty of serious crimes spending more time in them.

Yet, this is already the reality. More people are going to prison than ever, and sentences are getting longer. In 2022, for example, more than three times as many people received sentences of ten years or more than was the case in 2008. And for more serious, indictable offenses, the average sentence is now five years and two months, two years longer than it was in 2008. Those serving mandatory life sentences for murder are spending more of their sentence in custody. In 2001, this was thirteen years. It is now eighteen. And judges are also imposing longer minimum terms. In 2001, this was thirteen years. In 2021, it was twenty-one.

We also send more people to prison than anywhere else in western Europe. The figures per 100,000 are these: England and Wales, 141; Spain, 116; France, 108; Italy, 96; Sweden, 74; Germany, 67; Norway, 57.[13]

But the public do not believe any of this. When polled, around two thirds of the population thought that sentencing was not tough enough, by which they meant that the sentences were too lenient. Over the past twenty-five years, sentences on average have got longer, but 56 percent of those surveyed thought they had reduced. And if we exclude from the figures those who didn't know one way or another, 75 percent said sentences were shorter today.[14]

How can we reduce prison numbers? Two answers suggest themselves, but neither will get past public opinion. On the one hand, we can stop sending some people to prison for very short sentences. The

13. These figures were provided by my analyst.
14. This data was also provided by my analyst.

evidence is that these very short sentences are less effective at reducing crime than well-managed community sentences, not least where an offender has mental health issues or has been prolific.

The other possibility would be to release some carefully selected prisoners earlier; but again, public opinion is unlikely to accept this without a careful case being consistently made by those who could influence public opinion.

It is, then, hard to see how numbers will come down if the pressure from the public is for a greater use of custodial sentences and longer terms. So the prison population will continue to get more numerous, but, along with that, older and sicker, and hope will drain away. And we know what that means for offenders and prison officers alike. We create a perfect storm.

As we approach a general election, it will be a brave politician who tries to explain these realities. If anything, we must prepare for the opposite.

August 21, 2023

Angling for All

It was a warm and sunny day when I visited one of the projects we are supporting with a community grant. This is money seized from criminals that we re-cycle back into the communities that have been impacted by crime. Angling for All takes place at the Bolton Brickyard Pond, a park between Bolton upon Dearne and Goldthorpe. As the name suggests, the pond was originally a deep pit at a brickworks, which was flooded and turned into a fishing lake by local mine workers when the works closed. After the coal mines also closed, some fishing kept going, but much of the pond became overgrown and out of use. In recent years, a number of ponds have been created and brought back into use by dedicated local people. I was meeting one of them, Lenny Fowler, who leads the project we are supporting.

Briefly, each evening, and during the day in the holiday period, he meets any young people that want to learn how to fish and shows them the basics. For some time, he and other volunteers have cleared away the brambles and lakeside vegetation, suppressed the lilies that would otherwise entirely cover the ponds, and provided short platforms on which the young anglers can stand to fish. Now, he coaches them, providing some with rods, though most of those I met seem to have saved and bought their own.

My interest, of course, was in what this project is doing for young (mainly) boys who might otherwise be getting into trouble.

The grandmother of one came up and spoke. She told me how the young lad had some issues at school. He seemed unable to focus. A mother said her son "couldn't keep still for more than a few minutes" and went on to describe patterns of behavior that we would probably call ADHD (attention deficit hyperactivity disorder). Yet, here they were fishing. For hours, they would stand with their fishing rods, affixing wriggling and brightly colored maggots, casting their lines, scooping up the catch in a keep-net, and doing all the things anglers do. Whatever ADHD is, it seems highly contextual. These boys had no difficulty focusing on fishing, taking instruction, and getting on with one another.

A lady who comes regularly to the ponds with a group of dog walkers told me what a difference the presence of the young anglers had made to the area. It had once been a haunt of youths who were up to no good and who frequently intimidated those who walked along the paths. Now, it was a pleasure to take an evening stroll and watch the young people. The day I was there seemed idyllic, with swans and other birdlife, a beautiful lakeside setting. And several bream were caught.

The leader gives his time voluntarily. By day, he works in a referral unit, so he knows how to handle those who do not find school an easy place to be. I have no doubt that as the years go by, many young people will have cause to thank him for the work he is doing. I also have no doubt that if we can't support people and projects such as this, there are those in the community who are watching and will lead these young people in a very different direction.

August 28, 2023

Unintended Consequences

Some years ago, I was a board member of the Youth Justice Board (YJB). The YJB oversees the criminal justice system as it applies to those age ten through eighteen. At that time, we were locking up three thousand young people at any one time in secure accommodation and young offender institutions (prisons) (YOIs). We worked hard to reduce the numbers. We were successful, with numbers falling to a few hundred. It meant that some prisons could be closed. These were the intended and good consequences.

But last week, I met someone whose local YOI was closed. He was sent to another. But this was much further away from where he lived and his mother and siblings; and public transport to reach it was very poor. It plunged him into despair. He was seventeen.

The intended consequence of reducing the number of young people sent to prison was good. The unintended consequence that saw young offenders separated from their family support by greater distances was not. As the years have passed, young people sent to custody have got farther from home.

September 4, 2023

Victim Voices

The voice of the victim is very powerful. And rightly so. We are all moved by those who have been the victims of crime, especially some of the more heinous crimes. And in recent times, there have been a number of high profile victims, from the mother of Olivia Pratt Korbel, whose daughter was murdered by Thomas Cashman, to the parents of the babies killed by Lucy Letby, their nurse at the Countess of Chester Hospital. As we draw nearer to a general election, those voices are especially influential over politicians. For obvious reasons, MPs will want to pay particular attention to those who command widespread public sympathy and support.

Last week, we saw this result in the government promising to make changes to the law so that a judge can require a convicted criminal to attend court for their sentencing, something that both Cashman and Letby had refused to do. A level of reasonable force could be used to effect this.

I understand why the parents felt angry that those who murdered their loves ones refused to come to court for the sentencing. They wanted to look those convicted in the face for the last time. They wanted them to hear how their crime had impacted them and their lives. They wanted them to hear the judge sum up the horror of what they had done and express something of their and the public's revulsion and condemnation. They wanted the convicted to feel something of the pain that they felt. And for this not to happen seemed to leave a just outcome somehow incomplete, a further source of pain. So, the government has decided to give judges the power to compel convicted criminals to come to court to hear the victim impact statements and to receive their sentence.

But did the MPs, from all parties, get this right? Many have commented subsequently on the difficulty of having to force the unwilling into the dock. These particular victim voices, powerful as they were, and as fully deserving sympathy as they were, were not the only ones. There was another victim last week who spoke but urged caution: Bryn Hughes. His thoughts deserved a hearing as well, for not only was he the father of a murdered woman, he was also a former prison officer. Commenting on the proposal to allow the use of force to bring those convicted into court for sentencing, Bryn Hughes said he had seen it from both sides of the courtroom.

His daughter, PC Nicola Hughes, together with PC Fiona Bone, two Manchester police officers, were ambushed and killed in a gun and grenade attack in 2012. He understands the pain of the victim. But he was also a prison officer who sometimes had to bring prisoners to court. He knows only too well how some of them might behave if they really were resisting being brought back for sentencing. Trying to force them up the narrow staircase into the dock would not be easy. They could kick and bite prison officers. Once in court, they could be disrespectful to the victims and the court, making comments or gestures, spitting, or just turning their backs. They could become the center of attention for all the wrong reasons, leaving the grieving families with more pain to have to deal with.

It did occur to me that if there was a real risk that something like this might happen, a judge might take the opposite course of action to the one ministers are contemplating, decide not to have someone brought to court for the sake of the victims, and to maintain the dignity of the court.

I found what Mr. Hughes said very compelling. But I don't think he was listened to or consulted.

These powers will be granted to judges, though they seem to have them already. They will have the final decision on whether a convicted murderer should be compelled to come for sentencing. At that moment, the decision has to be whether justice is served by this or not.

The Missing Children

I recently wrote about an occasion when South Yorkshire police found in the Meadowhall Shopping Centre fifty-five children who were not in school. Most were there with a parent or family member, so this was condoned absence rather than truancy. Nevertheless, it raises questions about what the schools knew and what the parents and others thought they were doing. But leaving that aside, it did make me wonder just how big a problem we have with children missing from school and what becomes of them. After all, as well as missing valuable days of education, they may be making themselves very vulnerable and open to exploitation, sexual and criminal.

The problem goes beyond South Yorkshire. According to Dame Rachel de Souza, the children's commissioner, last year, just under one quarter of pupils were persistently absent from the classroom in our region. And this absenteeism is reflected across the country.

So, when the commissioner called a round table for professionals in Yorkshire, the Humber and North Lincolnshire to discuss this, I joined. This was in the Guildhall in Hull, though I participated by remote link. Those at the table represented organizations and agencies she thought could contribute to bringing about 100 percent school attendances.

The statistics for persistent absence by secondary-school-age children in our four local authority areas show a marked increase since the pandemic. Comparing 2018–2019 with 2022–2023, we find this percentage rise in persistent absences: Doncaster, 17.1 to 32.2; Barnsley, 15.3 to 30.5; Sheffield, 15.3 to 28.5; Rotherham, 15.0 to 28.3. Overall absence rates had also risen by approximately 4 percent in each district.[15]

It would seem that during the lockdowns, some young people formed habits of not going to school that proved hard to break afterwards.

The commissioner had undertaken an attendance audit, during which children had pointed out what was going wrong in their lives that led to non-attendance. The issues sometimes lay within the school but sometimes not. There were children who lived in poor housing, children who struggled with public transport, children who were carers, children who had health problems, children in care, children who found little in the curriculum to engage with, children who were excluded. One persistently absent 9-year-old boy said, "My mum gets sick quite a lot. If my dad has to go to work to earn some money, then I need to stay home and look after my mum and little brother."

Children with special education needs (SEND) were especially at risk as a result of lack of support, while the demand for children and

---

15. These figures were given verbally at the round table by Dame Rachel de Souza, the children's commissioner.

adolescent mental health services had risen dramatically; and as a result, there were long waiting lists, with some unable to get onto a waiting list in the first place.

It was a pretty bleak picture and not one that was going to change quickly, even when the issues had been identified.

As well as having a general concern, I was also focused on what all this could mean for the criminal justice system in coming years. If children are not in school, they fall behind with their education, and the more this happens, the more difficult it is for them to progress into a job, an apprenticeship, or college. They may be on the streets and vulnerable or online and equally vulnerable.

A recent joint study from the Ministry of Justice and the Department for Education showed that in 2019–2020, 81 percent of children who committed offenses had a history of non-attendance at school. For serious violence, the figure was even higher at 85 percent.

Last week, the government was much exercised with the problem of decaying school buildings. Ministers exuded, quite rightly, a real sense of urgency. Everyone had to act quickly to prevent a disaster occurring. We need the same sense of urgency towards those who ought to be in those buildings but all too often are found to be missing. This is a serious way of preventing crime.

October 2, 2023

Values

Every school I visit has a set of values. They are often clearly displayed, posted on noticeboards, or painted on walls. They sometimes pop up on sweatshirts. They vary hugely, though there are some commonalities. All primary schools seem to have some version of kindness or friendliness. Secondary schools generally have something along the lines of ambition or excellence. Both primary and secondary will have tolerance or respect, or something that means the same thing. But there are many other values: empathy, happiness, resilience, compassion, confidence, fairness. The lists go on. (Whether they are always mutually reinforcing or compatible is not something I stop to think about.) I wondered when this need to set out the school's values so explicitly started. I don't remember anything like this when I was at school.

At least that was what I at first thought. But on reflection, I realized that my school and others at that time, did have values. I went to a boys' grammar school, and the grammar schools often captured them in succinct Latin mottos. Mine was "Labore et Honore." By work and honor. And we sang them in songs that were frequently repeated in morning assemblies. One of my favorites, which I still remember, was called "Treasure," and the first verse went like this:

> Daisies are our silver,
> Buttercups our gold.
> These are all the treasures
> We can have or hold.

I don't think that was very aspirational. I can see why no head teacher would want it sung now. Though it does commend an appreciation of the natural world, which is very relevant today, even if it also suggested turning away from material things. (Despite singing that our gold was the buttercup, we still managed to produce a good quota of bankers: the present governor of the Bank of England being one.)

In those first decades after World War II, many values were overtly Christian and, again, sung in Christian hymns every single school day. These hymns were often about putting others before oneself, self-sacrifice, and so on. It was thought that these were the values that got us through the war and were needed to bring post-war renewal: unselfishness, sacrifice, hard work, not clock-watching, putting others first. We sang,

> Not for ever in green pastures
> do we ask our way to be;
> but the steep and rugged pathway
> may we tread rejoicingly.

These were the default values. Fast forward to the present period, and we find that the values that people want to speak about now are not these older values of hard work and sacrifice but almost the opposite, and they are not confined to schools. All organizations have them, including the police. They are about personal well-being, life-work balance, and so on. A well-being champion in my office summed them up in a wonderful post last week: when you're saying "yes" to others, make sure you're not saying "no" to yourself. That captures the essence of so many of the modern values very well. The new default position.

And this made me wonder whether the police service is not trying to hold together two sets of different values, which will sometimes be in considerable tension. I put it no higher. On the one hand, there is an appeal to those older values of public service: putting the interest of others before one's own, self-sacrifice. This was a theme, perhaps the theme, running through the police memorial service in the cathedral on Saturday. But it is not easy to square that with the values of contemporary society as illustrated in the post above or those of work-life balance or even well-being. For policing, if not for society more generally, something has to give.

October 9, 2023

Youth Violence

I met this week a prison officer who was telling me about her experiences of what is happening to youth custody, the young offender institutions (YOIs). Although we are sending fewer young people to prison than we did when I was a member of the Youth Justice Board more than a decade ago, those who do have custodial sentences tend to be those who have committed more serious and violent crimes, which probably doesn't make the task of rehabilitation in YOIs any easier. I recalled a conversation I once had with a boy in a young offender institution. He had been convicted of stabbing another boy. I wanted to understand why he carried a knife. Our conversation went something like this:

> Me: Didn't you realize that you might cause him serious harm?
>
> Him: That was the point.
>
> Me: But didn't you realize you might get hurt yourself or end up here, in prison?
>
> Him: That was a risk I had to take.
>
> Me: Why?
>
> Him: Because it was better than ending up slashed or dead.

As long as some young boys think like that, the cycle will not be broken. The bigger task, then, is supporting families and then communities so that all our young people, wherever they live, feel they are in a safe place. And that is a much bigger task than the interventions targeting individuals, important though they are.

No Escape

By the end of last week, I felt I wanted to get away from crime, so my wife and I went to the ballet at the Lyceum in Sheffield to see Romeo and Juliet. Wonderfully energetic dancing to Prokofiev's music, as you would expect from a Matthew Bourne production. But it ended with the death of the two young lovers. From stabbings! And there was blood everywhere.

November 25, 2023

Signs of the Times

For several weeks now, South Yorkshire police have been managing pro-Palestinian protests. Numbers on those protests in Sheffield, at least, have gradually increased, from 50 to 100 to 500 to over 1,000, with other smaller protests as well.[16] These marches and rallies have been mirrored not only across this country but around the world. UK police forces, our own included, have learned to distinguish between the Palestinian flag, which it is lawful to display, and the flags and symbols of Hamas or Hezbollah, which are unlawful (they are proscribed organizations) and which chants and slogans may constitute a hate crime.

So far, at the time of writing, there have been few incidents here and few arrests. I have not felt the need to ask our Independent Policing Protests Panel to turn out to observe. Few arrests, however, does not mean none, and there may be more if the humanitarian pauses in Gaza come to an end and hostilities are renewed with a new intensity. Passions may become more inflamed.

Islamophobic and anti-Semitic hate crimes have risen across the country, with anti-Semitism showing the biggest increase. But while hate incidents impact both communities, the pro-Palestinian marches affect them as well, though differently, and I've been reflecting on that.

For members of the Muslim community, whatever their ethnicity, the protests have brought them together and given them a new confidence as British citizens. For them, the attack by Israel on the Gazans is an attack on the ummah, the worldwide community of Islam. They want to stand together in solidarity. This was the burden of the speeches in the ceasefire debate in the House of Commons by Muslim MPs, and the many more that have been delivered at rallies up and down the country; speeches and

---

16. These numbers were provided by the police in briefings.

sentiments that have been supported by others who are not Muslims. In contrast, there have been few rallies in support of those Israeli families who have had loved ones massacred or kidnapped.

(We might note in passing that the protests have also shown to the country as a whole the salience of religion for the identity of a large group of British citizens, something that may have been true of a more Christian nation in the past, but is not true now.)

These pro-Palestinian rallies have also had an impact on the much smaller Jewish community, too, something different from the effect that hate crimes have. Hate crimes can be seen as the work of a few; but the rallies point to the attitudes and sensibilities of many. The realization of this by some Jews is having an effect that is below the radar. It is not something that can be recorded and is very difficult to capture. Again, I think it goes to the question of identity.

While the protests have strengthened the identity of Muslims as confident British citizens, my guess is that they are having an opposite effect on the Jewish community. They have seen the placards and heard the speeches at the rallies, including some that strayed into the territory of supporting a proscribed organization. They note how those speeches mainly bypass or ignore the events of October 7 and focus only on Israel's military response or the wider issue of Palestinian rights. This must leave some in the Jewish community wondering how they are viewed by significant numbers of UK citizens. It has led some to question their very identity as British citizens.

The Jewish journalist Tanya Gould summed this up rather bleakly last week when she wrote that the events of October 7 have forever changed her relationship with her country. She feels ill at ease, unsure whether the one country in Europe that does not have a roll of names at Yad Vashem (the museum in Jerusalem listing those killed in the holocaust) is as welcoming now as it was when we resisted the Nazis.

We can define and deal with hate crimes, and it is important to do so. But they may not tell the whole story or indeed the most important story. This underlying feeling of unwelcome by at least some in the Jewish community is no less pernicious.

December 4, 2023

No Crisis at Christmas Here

From time to time, people write to me about the homeless. Why don't the police do something? I am never quite sure what the something is that the police are supposed to do, but whatever it is, it is unlikely to solve the problem permanently.

In many ways, we know what the answer to homelessness is. Far from being a lifestyle choice, those who have no roof over their heads are generally people who, through a series of misfortunes in life, some of their own making but many not, find themselves without a home, without a job, without friends or supportive family, and probably with an alcohol or drug problem as well. Where do you even start to help someone in that position?

One answer is Emmaus, not the place but the organization. Emmaus is a charity whose stated aim is to support people to "work their way out of homelessness," so that homelessness can be ended altogether. Last week, I went to the Emmaus project in Sheffield. It's in an old cutlery factory beside the canal, not far from the Quays and the city center.

When you go inside the building, and the public are welcome to drop in, there is a cafe, a shop selling wooden items made by the companions (as Emmaus calls them) as well as books and bric a brac, a furniture store selling refurbished tables and chairs and beds, and workshops. It's like a vast Aladdin's cave.

At any one time, there are up to sixteen people living on the project. Some have been literally on the streets, while others have been sofa surfing. They are given a small bed set with a shared kitchen and have work provided through the various activities of the project. When I was there, some companions were out in the van collecting unwanted furniture, others were repairing items or selling them in the shop; some were working in the kitchen or on lathes in the woodwork shop; and so on. Everyone was doing something productive and useful.

Emmaus is a practical answer to the problem of homelessness. It provides a stable home for as long as someone may need it, which can be anything between one or two years, on average. It gives training. It gives support. It provides companionship. And those who take part have to be drug and alcohol free, something that is strictly enforced.

This was a return visit for me. I dropped into Emmaus some years ago when I was first police and crime commissioner. Last week, I was there to see how they were getting on with a £10,000 grant we had given and to assure them of our continuing support. I was anxious to know that they had managed to survive the pandemic, which they had.

We calculated that in the time I had known them, the project has helped as many as six hundred people, mainly men, to find a way out of homelessness.

As I came away, I thought about the number of charities and initiatives that do something for the homeless, not least at Christmas; but there are few that offer the potential of a permanent way forward. If we had more Emmaus projects (they are found in a number of towns across the country), perhaps I would have fewer calls asking why the police weren't doing something about those wrapped in duvets in shop doorways on cold winter nights.

Maya Angelou Wrote

"I've learned that you can tell a lot about a person by the way she handles these three things: a rainy day, lost luggage, and tangled Christmas tree lights."[17]

December 11, 2023

Hillsborough Law

Last week, the government said it would not accept a so-called Hillsborough Law. This is what the families, bereaved as a result of the Hillsborough football disaster in 1989, have wanted ever since the former Bishop of Liverpool, the Right Rev. James Jones, published his report summarizing their experiences. In it, he recommended what is now known as a Hillsborough Law. But it looks like another long wait, something that in itself encapsulates what they have been through at every stage.

It was not until 2016 that the second set of inquests were held, which found that ninety-seven people had died as a result of police negligence. The families had battled for almost thirty years to have the truth told about what happened on that day and subsequently. They had met a lack of transparency and obstruction by various authorities at every

17. Angelou, "Maya Angelou."

point along the way. It is hardly surprising that the bishop summed up their experiences by titling his report "The Patronising Disposition of Unaccountable Power."[18]

I have lived with the consequences of the Hillsborough disaster and the 2016 inquests verdicts for almost my entire time as police and crime commissioner (PCC). As well as having to be sure that the police force now fully understands and accepts what went wrong for the families, which I believe it does, we have also had to ensure that those who were bereaved and those who suffered in other ways were and will be properly compensated. I had hoped that all the civil claims might be settled before I finished my final term as PCC; but that is not going to happen. In the meantime, as we set the budget each year (something I am currently doing with the chief constable), we have to set aside millions of pounds for the families and others. Hillsborough, as with any major failing by a public body, casts a long shadow.

I have always had the greatest of sympathy for the families and realize that, having had the truth about what happened at the football ground and afterwards laid bare, what they most want to see now is for lessons to be learned, so that others might never have to experience what they have done. They want the Hillsborough Law. Such a law, the Public Authority (Accountability) Bill, would create a legal duty of candor on public authorities and their officials (not just the police) to tell the truth and to proactively cooperate with official investigations and inquiries.

It is true that the Criminal Justice Bill, announced in the King's speech, will provide for a duty of candor for police officers, and there are many codes of conduct already in existence which cover the behavior of ministers. But given the public's unease around what the COVID inquiry is revealing, it is hardly surprising that the families, given their experiences, want to see a clear duty set out unambiguously in legislation that will apply to all public officials. I am pleased that shadow ministers have pledged to support this should they become the next government.

As one of the family members said, "I'm so tired fighting. . . . I just want to be able to get on with my life." After thirty-four years, that does not seem to be asking too much.

---

18. Jones, "Patronising Disposition of Unaccountable Power."

December 18, 2023

Blue Light Carols

Last Wednesday, the annual police and fire carol service was held in Sheffield cathedral; but this time it was rather different. For the first time, it was a service for all three emergency services: police, fire and rescue, and ambulance. The head of each service gave a short Christmas message at different points. The partnership director of the Yorkshire Ambulance Service, Adam Layland, spoke about those in the different emergency services who would be on duty over Christmas and their families who supported them. We gave them all an appreciative round of applause. The chief constable and fire chief reminded us that next year marks the fiftieth anniversary of the two South Yorkshire services.

We sang "Silent Night" and "O Come All Ye Faithful," and the police lead chaplain, the Rev. Derek Pamment, prayed for all those for whom Christmas would not be an easy time, including those displaced by war. Afterwards, the cathedral gave us mulled wine and mince pies.

It was a warm and happy occasion with some good conversations between those in the different blue light organizations. There were, though, poignant moments in the service when we realized that the land of conflict into which the Christ child came, and that we once called the Holy Land, is the same place of conflict that we see today. One of the carols had the words,

> *O hush the noise of mortal strife,*
> *and hear the angels sing.*

I wish you a very happy and peaceful Christmas and New Year.

Diary for 2024

Towards a General Election

New Year 2024

Policing Face to Face

THIS IS GOING TO be a year of technology for the police service. Of course, over the years, many public bodies have been using some of the same technologies as the police. We have become used to CCTV in public spaces, for instance. There are now something in the region of five million surveillance cameras across the country, mainly operated by local authorities. London alone has 942,000. Just before Christmas, I sat in a newly commissioned CCTV van in Wombwell Park in Barnsley, where two council operatives were able to bring up live pictures on half a dozen screens from 165 cameras across the borough![1]

But the technology that will come to the fore this year for policing will be facial recognition software (FR). This will enable the police to match the facial images they capture day-to-day on cameras or mobile phones with data banks of existing photographs in order to identify suspects. There is a lively debate going on among ministers, the police, and police and crime commissioners about what databases should be available to the police. The criminal justice bill going through parliament will allow the police to run searches on millions of driving license holders. The policing minister has suggested going further and allowing access to passport data as well. Between them, this would capture photographic images of almost everyone in the country.

1. iFacility, "How Many CCTV Cameras."

At the moment, there has been little urgent public debate around this. When it happens, we are likely to divide into two camps. There will be those who say, if this helps the police to identify criminals and we have nothing to hide, then we have nothing to fear. This can only be a good thing. On the other hand, there will be those who will feel that this is a step too far, an invasion and erosion of privacy, and a move towards the Big Brother state.

FR is not new. There are two types. Live facial recognition is where the police can compare in real time an image of someone captured by a live camera with an existing police watch list. These watch lists could be, for example, photographs of wanted offenders or missing persons. Then, there is retrospective facial recognition where the matching happens after the fact, when a burglar or car thief, say, is caught on CCTV.

If we look at figures supplied by the Met, between 2020 and 2023, thirty-four people were apprehended as a result of live FR. And in October 2023, 149 thieves were identified as a result of retrospective FR. Many of the bigger retail stores, such as the Co-op, are already using FR themselves to stop known thieves coming into their shops. There are clear benefits to policing from the use of FR. But, as with all technology, and especially as we begin to use it more widely and use more databases, there are questions and risks.

Although the technology is far more reliable than it once was, it is still possible to identify someone incorrectly. A study by Essex University Human Rights Centre found the technology was inaccurate in almost 80 percent of cases they reviewed in the Met in 2019—though the technology has improved immeasurably since then.[2] There have been particular issues with the identification of black female faces. It would hardly be safe to rely solely on FR if people were being arrested, let alone charged, if "success" rates were so low. Perhaps FR should only ever be one piece of evidence anyway. It should be said that there have been no unsuccessful prosecutions in the UK so far as a result of FR, though that has not been the case in the USA; so, we have been warned. We can see the benefits, but are there unintended consequences that we need to think about?

For this reason, I have decided to strengthen the Independent Ethics Panel (IEP) by appointing a new member who has expertise in this area. Dr. Jamie Grace is a lecturer in public law at Sheffield Hallam University who has specialized in the use of technology in policing. The

2. This data was in a briefing note supplied by my analyst.

IEP has already produced some guidelines and given some preliminary thought to new technology, which is developing very fast. They will now help me and South Yorkshire police think further about the use of new technology, beginning with FR, so that we can have the benefits while understanding and mitigating the risks.

January 6, 2024

Political Churn

Some years ago, I realized that far fewer people are interested in politics than I would like to think. I was walking down the street in a town in the Lake District with David Blunkett. I lived there and he was on holiday. A woman saw us from the opposite side of the road and dashed across, camera in hand. (This was a time before mobile phones had cameras.) Could she have a photograph? "Of course," he said. So we stopped, turned towards her, and smiled our best politicians' smile. "No, no, no," she cried. "Not you. The dog." She just wanted a picture of David's very fine guide dog. She hadn't recognized him at all. She had no interest in politics.

But this year, whether any of us like it or not, we are going to hear rather a lot about politics, local and national, because there are going to be a number of elections. In May, there will be council elections in some places, police and crime commissioner (PCC) elections (though not in South Yorkshire, where the May mayoral election will see the mayor take on policing functions), and, almost certainly, a general election. I will no longer be a PCC by the time the general election comes, but, as far as policing and the criminal justice system goes, I will watch it with the usual mix of hope and dread, two sides of the same coin.

The hope is that if there are to be new initiatives, the government will allow the ministers and the policy to remain in place for a decent length of time. The dread is that we shall see, as we have done in the last few years, ministers and policies come and go with nothing ever being in place long enough to see whether it works well or not.

Take the secretaries of state for justice. In my nine years in office, these are those I remember, though I am not absolutely sure about the order and some only stayed a matter of months: Chris Grayling, Michael Gove, Liz Truss, David Lidington, David Gauke, Richard Buckland, Brandon Lewis, Dominic Raab, and the current secretary of state, Alex Chalk. Home secretaries also came and went—seven, I think—with one,

Grant Shapps, only surviving a few weeks. Then there were the junior policing, crime, and justice ministers working to them.

The point about this litany is that with each change of minister, there comes the risk of a change of policy. So, in criminal justice, we have more authoritarian ministers who want such things as more and harsher sentences and more law enforcement (Grayling, Truss, Raab, for example), followed by ministers who are liberal and not convinced and want to see fewer short sentences and better rehabilitation (Gove, Lidington, Gauke, Buckland), all within the same political party, though this is not a party political issue because the same pattern of ministers and policies coming and going applies to governments of all colors.

So, policy moves this way and that. No one ever stays long enough to see policies thoroughly embedded and no policy is pursued long enough to know how effective it has been. As a result the question, "Which works more effectively in reducing crime: more emphasis on enforcement or on rehabilitation?" can never be definitively answered.

This, in turn, often leads to a lack of proper scrutiny. Ministers know they will not be in the job long, so they want policies introduced quickly. This does not give time for the policy to be thoroughly considered, taking expert advice, and for alternatives to be looked at. The best (i.e., worst) example of that during my time was the decision by Chris Grayling to break the probation service in two. It was introduced and became policy. It was disastrous for the service and had to be restored. But he had long since gone.

January 13, 2024

Child Abuse: A Better Understanding

There is a danger in our part of the world of thinking that child sexual abuse and exploitation (CSAE) is all about the sexual abuse of children who are picked up by grooming gangs on the streets of our towns and cities. There is, of course, abuse of this kind. But a recent report has revealed something far wider than that and with growing areas of abuse that we may not have realized.

The National Analysis of Police-Recorded Child Sexual Abuse and Exploitation Crimes Report has never been attempted before. It analyzes data from forty-two police forces across England and Wales and includes profiles of both the victims and the perpetrators.[3] It is invaluable in helping the police to understand what is going on, how crimes are changing and what steps a force will need to take with partners and the public to safeguard children better in the future.

A few of the key points that jumped out at me were these.

First, offenses are on the rise. In 2022, there were 107,000 cases of CSAE. This was an increase of 7.6 percent over the previous year and a quadrupling over the decade. Twenty-five percent of these related to indecent images of children. Some, perhaps many, young people (mainly males) are, in effect, criminalizing themselves by sending intimate photographs of girlfriends or ex-girlfriends to others on their mobile phones, though not realizing they are committing an offense by doing so.

Second, the number of online recorded incidents of sexual abuse continues to grow. It currently accounts for one third of all child sexual abuse and exploitation. We could probably have anticipated this, given the fact that in the last few years every teenager in the country seems to have become glued to a mobile device or laptop for large parts of the day. The majority of reports of CSAE (52 percent) involve children aged between ten and seventeen offending against other children. The most common age is fourteen. The report authors say this is a growing and concerning trend. It may also be related to the fact that growing numbers of children find it easy to access pornography on their devices.

Since the report was written, we heard of the shocking case of the under-sixteen-year-old girl who spent much of her leisure time online in a virtual world with others. In that virtual world, her virtual self, her avatar, was violently assaulted and raped by other virtual characters. She was deeply traumatized, as if the attack on her had been in the real as opposed to the virtual world. This has left a number of questions for the police and crown prosecutors: what crimes, if any, have been committed if everything was virtual and there was no physical contact? If there were crimes, how do you get hold of the others involved when they could be anywhere in the world?

The New Year suddenly seems as dark a place as the old.

3. NCVPP, "2024 National Analysis."

January 20, 2024

Firearms: UK and US

One thing I have never failed to notice since doing this job is the contrast, when it comes to carrying firearms, between the police in this country and the police overseas. However, it was only when David Hartley, one of the assistant chief constables, passed me a note about armed police last week that I realized just how stark the contrast is.

Fewer than 5 percent of British police officers are trained in the use of firearms and only 2 percent of patrolling officers are armed. Or, putting that the other way round, 98 percent of officers in this country patrol unarmed. When I speak to friends in the USA about this, they find it almost unbelievable.

It is a remarkable statistic and one that relies on two things. The first is that officers in this country police by consent. By and large, when the police are maintaining law and order in a town center or an outlying estate or a country village, they can count on the public being supportive. Without that, in so many situations, they might struggle—which is why they must always work hard to maintain that trust and confidence.

The second is that we are not people who feel the need to arm ourselves. Again, I contrast that with what my friends tell me about America. Although none of them have weapons in the house, at least they have never said so, they all have neighbors that do. Their neighbors argue that this is for protection.

If that sounds familiar, it's because this is what scared young people say in this country when challenged about carrying knives. This, I believe, is the principal reason for young people having knives. And, of course, the more young people carry blades, the more other young people become frightened and are tempted to do the same. It becomes a perfect circle that is very hard to break. In turn, this is another very good reason why we need to stop young people feeling they need to carry knives, because, as they get older, they may graduate to carrying firearms.

In the USA, it is hard to stop people wanting to have weapons in the house for similar reasons, and that is why, whenever someone takes a gun into a school or public place and fires at random, it is not seen as a reason for *banning* weapons but a reason for *buying* them: a gun for self-protection. The perfect circle where violence breeds violence. And it is the reason that there are 71,600 firearms dealers in the US.[4] So far, we have been spared that.

February 5, 2024

Vetting Better

In March 2021, a serving police officer, Wayne Couzens, kidnapped a young woman, Sarah Everard, on a London street, and subsequently raped and murdered her. After Couzens had been arrested, it came to light that he had worked for forces other than the Met, and his behavior there had caused some concern. Yet, he had been able to move between forces without any of these concerns being followed up. Similarly, after the serial rapist and police officer David Carrick had finally been apprehended for his crimes, it was found that his conduct had also been called into question over a number of years, but nothing had been done about it.

These high profile cases and others caused a national outcry, and in January 2023, both the home secretary and prime minister called on the police to take steps to ensure that no one else was currently working for the police who should not be. The National Police Chiefs' Council began a search of all workforce records, and last week, the results of this historic data wash of everything on the Police National Database was made public.[5] The records of all officers, staff, and volunteers were screened.

This has been a huge undertaking. It has involved forty-two forces in England and Wales plus six other forces, such as Police Scotland and the Police Service of Northern Ireland. (North Yorkshire was not included because it has been doing this on a monthly basis for some time: Operation Prism.) There have been 307,452 checks. This is the biggest exercise of its kind ever undertaken in this country and, quite possibly, any country. The data searched is the information held before February 2023; there has to be a cut off point. The findings, national but also local, were published last week.

Nationally, 306,991 of the searches caused no concern. But 461 were scrutinised further. Of these, no further action was required in 97 cases. Of the remainder, 88 have led to disciplinary investigation, 128 management intervention, and 139 triggered vetting clearance. But 9 led to further criminal investigation, mainly to do with matters of drugs,

---

4. This information was in a briefing note supplied by my analyst.
5. National Police Chiefs' Council, "Results Published."

sex, or fraud. While every instance of a police officer being investigated for a crime is shocking, these are, thankfully, relatively small numbers, given the total numbers of police officers, staff, and volunteers we have across the United Kingdom. I am pleased to say that there were no cases in South Yorkshire that needed further action.

After the shocks of the Couzens and Carrick crimes and the lax way they had been able to operate for years without being appropriately challenged and stopped, we can all be reassured that the police are now in a better place than we might at one time have thought. I am very reassured by the South Yorkshire results.

But this is a snapshot in time. If we are to prevent those who exhibit poor or potentially criminal behavior going unchallenged in the future, we must find ways of continuing to screen on a regular basis. North Yorkshire police may have something to teach us all.

Holocaust Memorial Day Reflections

I was asked to speak at a vigil in the Cutlers' Hall, organized by Sheffield City Council and the National Holocaust Centre and Museum, to mark the annual Holocaust Memorial Day. This is part of what I said:

> *Hatred is a moral failure; but it starts with a failure of imagination. An inability to put yourself in the shoes of others. To see things from their perspective. To feel what they feel. They then become alien and other. We feel nothing for them. They are nothing to us. Those resentments and hatreds diminish our humanity and wreck our communities.*
>
> *The opposite is empathy, the ability to make the imaginative leap. To see as others see and feel as others feel. You don't have to agree with them or like them. But you get them. Developing the imagination. This is the key preventive work. But how do you do it?*
>
> *Interestingly, Judaism seeks to do it in the annual Passover ceremony. Around the Passover meal, the story of the exodus of the Israelites from slavery in Egypt to freedom in the promised land is recounted. The story of what happened, perhaps three thousand years ago, is retold down the generations, partly so that Jews will not take their freedom for granted; but also because it develops their empathy for others. It's a reminder of what it was like being poor and oppressed then, in order to empathize with those who are poor and oppressed now. "Don't pervert the justice*

*due to the foreigner or the fatherless," say the Scriptures. "For you
were once a slave in the land of Egypt."*

*If discrimination begins with hatred, a moral failure, and if
it is overcome by developing the imagination and the ability to
empathize, that is not a police matter but a matter for all of us.
How do we expand our collective imagination so as to deepen our
capacity to empathize. One way is through hearing other people's
stories, as we are doing this evening. We have to do that because
we can't enforce our way to the peaceable society.*

February 12, 2024

Good News

Last year, the Home Office made £2.4 million available to us so that
we could intensify patrolling in areas blighted by antisocial behavior
(ASB). We had to identify these places and get Home Office agreement;
so, quite a lot of work. It is now six months since these forty-eight hot
spots were identified and patrolled at different times twice a day. Altogether, the police have patrolled for just over 5,527 additional hours.
In addition, in some places, a further 1,076 hours have seen some joint
patrolling with local authority wardens.

The first results of the exercise have now been analyzed, and they
are looking very promising. ASB has been substantially reduced across
all hot spots in all districts. The biggest reductions have been in Sheffield,
where ASB is down 34 percent.[6]

There have been other pluses as well. As the officers have patrolled,
they have come across crimes being committed or have been alerted to
them by local people. As a result, during this time, the patrols have made
forty-seven arrests and conducted ninety-one stop-and-searches.

The Home Office was persuaded to fund these actions because of a
theory, the so-called Koper Curve. (Professor Christopher Koper is a criminology professor at George Mason University and a prominent supporter
of evidence-based policing.) This came out of work by the Minneapolis
police department. They realized that as much as 50 percent of their calls
for service were being generated by 5 percent of places. So, they focused
their patrols on this very small number of blocks. They also came to realize that the deterrent effect was achieved not just by being present but by

---

6. This data was supplied in a police briefing note.

turning up unexpectedly through the day. The patrols had to be regular but random. If they became predictable, their effectiveness was diminished. It was better to patrol for, say, twenty minutes, then return at an unexpected time than to patrol solidly for a couple of hours. It is some of these principles that South Yorkshire police have been borrowing.

What we should also notice is a further benefit of these hot spot patrols. If officers make a determined effort to speak to people as they walk around, residents in the street or businesses along the way, this has the added effect of building confidence in a community. In many ways, this is a return in modern form to what officers did in the past, when there were more of them per head of population.

Flexible Release

Many months ago, I wrote about how difficult it was to ensure that a prisoner could access the various services they needed if they were released from prison on a Friday. Just before Christmas, this was changed. What I argued for in that distant diary will now happen, as far as most prisoners are concerned. Where an adult prisoner is due for release on a Friday or the day before a public holiday, they can be released one working day earlier. Children and young people will be released two days earlier. This is a relatively simple change with little or no cost implications. I am glad it has happened. I just wonder why it took us so long to get there.

February 26, 2024
PCC Functions

What is the most important part of the role of the Police and Crime Commissioner (PCC)? As I come towards the end of my term (and time) as PCC, I think I can give an unequivocal answer.

I could have said appointing a chief constable. That is a considerable responsibility because you know that, while a police force has many good people working for it who all play a key part in making the organization function efficiently and effectively, poor leadership at the top can quickly demoralize the whole. I have appointed two chiefs, very different people, though each making vital contributions to SYP.

I could have said producing the Police and Crime Plan. That matters because it sets the priorities for the force. I could have said that the most important thing I do is set the revenue budget and the (council tax) precept. That, too, is a responsibility that should weigh heavily on all PCCs, not least when an election comes into view. It would be very tempting but wrong for a PCC to cut the budget, and so, the precept, if he or she thought that would win a few votes. The PCC must set a budget and precept that gives adequate funding to the police service. Getting the finances in good shape is an important part of the job.

I could go on and speak about giving grants, the commissioning of victims' services, the work of the Violence Reduction Unit or the Local Criminal Justice Board, and so on. But the work that I think is the most important part of the PCC's role is that of holding the police to account.

This can be misunderstood. People write to me from time to time and want to know why I don't condemn the police for this or that. Media statements have their place, but it is a limited place. If a PCC is taking to the air waves or making pronouncements all the time, we would soon grow tired of it, and any impact would have diminishing returns.

Holding to account is about ensuring that a police force takes responsibility for what it does or decides not to do, and taking all that it does with proper seriousness. The temptation for any organization is to guard its reputation and not admit to shortcomings. Again, we see this with the Post Office. Holding to account means encouraging the force to recognize when mistakes have been made and to say what they are, at first to themselves, because you cannot put right what you don't first acknowledge: you have to name it. A PCC can help this process by talking, asking questions, encouraging, and supporting, both personally and through his or her officers who engage with the force. If the professional relationship between a PCC and senior officers is good, and that takes time and patience to build, holding to account happens naturally, as part of the weekly interactions; it is not something forced. But it is the most important thing I do.

Interestingly, in the government's response to the consultation on transferring PCC functions to the mayor, in the list of functions to be taken on by the mayor, while all the things I mention above are listed, holding to account is not explicitly referenced at all.

March 5, 2024

Protests and Ritual

The prime minister Rishi Sunak has called some of the pro-Palestinian protests that have taken place across the country, though especially in London, examples of mob rule and a threat to democracy. Last week, police chiefs were called to Downing Street and told that when protests were held outside MPs' homes, for example, there should be an immediate police response. This type of demonstration, the prime minister felt, was going too far.

As with many things in British life, we depend here to a large extent on people behaving with self-imposed levels of what seem reasonable and fair. A protest outside a public building, such as a town hall, or an MP's office, is one thing, whereas gathering in the street where an MP and their family and neighbors live, seems quite another. The MP might have stepped into the public arena, but his or her eight-year-old daughter didn't and neither did his or her next-door neighbor. But common sense, even common decency, gets overridden when someone believes their particular cause trumps everything else and nothing should be off limits. This is the tendency that, I believe, we have seen developing over the past year or two, and especially since the conflict between Hamas and Israel began. It can create a climate in which a few can think that violence can be justified. It is now routine for all of us involved in public life to think every day about our own personal safety and that of our staff.

But there is something else happening with the pro-Palestinian protests that I had not understood before. A government minister made me think about this when he said that there was no point in holding these weekly mass protests, since we all knew what the issues were now; and they may even be counter-productive. I am sure that is true, in which case, there may be other less conscious reasons why the protestors carry on. I look for a more psychological or sociological answer.

There is a word for acts that we go on repeating: it is ritual. The protests have become forms of ritual, and ritual is performed for the benefit of those taking part: it binds people together. This may be especially necessary when the people who come together do not otherwise have a great deal in common. So, they perform a common ritual. (Think of the way each school day in the USA begins with pupils pledging allegiance to the flag.) The more they perform the ritual, the deeper the bonding.

Ritual transforms individuals into a cohesive community. The more they act as one, the more they feel as one, and the more they think as one. It also means that an attack on the group, and I mean verbal rather than physical, is taken personally, as an attack on the individual.

I am not sure whether the movement that has been created will endure once a ceasefire is agreed or hostilities end in Gaza. If it does, the values that are being committed to and that bind people together will become clearer. But what it will mean for our politics and community life longer term is, as yet, unclear. Unclear to me, at any rate. In the meantime, the police, being operationally independent of both home secretaries and PCCs will have to rely on their own professional judgments.

March 12, 2024

Rape Trials

Lord Justice Edis, a Court of Appeal judge, said that where rape cases had been waiting to come to trial for more than two years, this was an unacceptable state of affairs. It seems that there are 181 such cases nationally. He would, therefore, ask for these to be prioritized in Crown Courts and for them to be heard before the end of July this year. Some of them would be retrials and some involved children.

The announcement can only be welcomed. The idea that victims and defendants have had their lives on hold for more than two years because of court backlogs is appalling. But it will have consequences. We don't know at the moment how many such cases there are in our area. But however many, it will lead to some disruption in Crown Court timetables. Victims, defendants, and witnesses in other serious trials may now find that their dates have been put back in order to accommodate the rape trials. We know that the longer it takes to get a case to court, the more risks are run: the memories of witnesses and victims fade or they start to withdraw their cooperation. If more distant courts have to be used, victims and witnesses may struggle to get there.

Is it achievable? We also know that there is a shortage nationally of barristers who are eligible to work on cases of serious sexual offending and of judges who are similarly qualified to hear them. In London, because of concerns around pay, a large number of these barristers have said they may not be willing to continue working with such cases. Yet, we need these rape trials to be heard as a first step if large numbers of women are to regain trust in the criminal justice system.

Theresa May

The former prime minster announced that she would be leaving parliament at the next election. This stirred some memories for me. At one critical point during my early years as police and crime commissioner, I was in contact with Mrs. May a number of times while she was home secretary. In 2016, the inquests into the Hillsborough football disaster came to an end, reaching the conclusion that decisions by South Yorkshire police (SYP) had led to the death of ninety-six supporters, eventually ninety-seven. It was also found that in attempts to deflect attention from its own misconduct, SYP had spread stories about the behavior of Liverpool supporters that were not true. Trust and confidence in SYP sank. Parliament and the media were very hostile. The shadow home secretary Andy Burnham told MPs in the House of Commons that the force was rotten to the core, and MPs had applauded. We then faced civil litigation for compensation from the families of those who had died and from other victims. This threatened our ability to meet those claims while maintaining the day-to-day funding of the force. In fact, without help, we could not pay the compensation and secure balanced budgets. It was a nightmare! I wondered what I had taken on.

But Mrs. May agreed to give us special grants that would meet 85 percent of the civil claims; we still had to find the rest. She met me a couple of times in London and rang me twice out of the blue when I was at my desk in Sheffield to see how I was personally bearing up and to offer moral support. So, whatever my views on Mrs. May's politics, I will always be grateful for that financial help and those kind words over the phone in 2016.

Orgreave

Mrs. May also seemed receptive, at one point, to the idea of some sort of inquiry into the miners' strike, or at least the incidents at Orgreave in June 1984, forty years ago this year. But unfortunately, she went off to be prime minister and the new home secretary, Amber Rudd, firmly ruled this out.

But when I became PCC, I promised the Orgreave Truth and Justice Campaign (OTJC) and the former mining communities in South Yorkshire that I would do whatever I could to help bring the archives from that period together. The archives are those of SYP and, so, their cooperation was needed. We have had that cooperation.

I was, therefore, somewhat taken aback when *BBC Look North* ran with a story just over a week ago in which it was alleged that SYP were still "covering up" and not opening the archives to the public. The real story could hardly be more different. This is the outline of what has been done. I have met with the OTJC ever since becoming PCC to keep them abreast of progress. All SYP buildings were searched for files relating to the strike. (These go back to the days of physical recordkeeping and storage, so dusty boxes in dusty cupboards.) The archives were brought together and deposited in Sheffield City Council archives. (They include paper files but also photographs, DVDs, and other old technology.) I funded an archivist to work full-time first on reading through and cataloguing all the material, then on digitizing it so that it is available electronically. This cost £340,000 and took a couple of years or so. Finally, the archive is now being redacted so that any material that is not aligned with GDPR requirements (protecting privacy) cannot be read. (There are, for example, some personal medical records in the archive.)

Storing, cataloging, digitizing, and now reading through 83,000 pages, and redacting comes at a price, so we need to balance these costs against the day-to-day needs of the force. This work will be finished next year. Throughout these years, we hoped that the government would agree an inquiry and this work could be nationally funded and the pace quickened.

So, I think the real story of the Orgreave archives is not one of continuing cover up or not wanting to open up the archive, as the BBC presented it, but the very opposite. I guess, SYP making steady progress in opening the Orgreave archives to the public is not such a good story or headline.

March 19, 2024

Last Post

This is the last diary entry I shall write as police and crime commissioner (PCC). I am standing down when my term ends in May. But in any case, there will be no more PCCs here, since the functions of the PCC will transition to whoever is elected mayor of South Yorkshire on May 2. In addition, because of the election, we are about to enter a pre-election period called "purdah," when politicians cannot write or make announcements that could be construed as using our position to favor one or other of the candidates. A combination of term end and purdah means this is the last time I shall be writing.

I started to write a diary when COVID locked us all down, and I could not get out and about meeting people in the way I had done previously. It was a way of keeping in touch. Now, it is time for me to stop and find my way into life's long grass.

Down the years, numbers of you have responded to the diary, sometimes supporting, sometimes disagreeing with what I wrote, and occasionally correcting my grammar (former teachers!). I was puzzled that responses came from different parts of the country and even from abroad, until I realized that the *Yorkshire Post* sometimes reproduced them.

What Has Changed?

Some journalists and broadcasters have been asking me about what I have achieved in the nine years I have been in this position. I think that is the wrong way of framing the question. There is very little that I do alone or directly. There are always many people involved in change and improvement of public services, and I am rarely, if ever, the principal decision-maker. So, I am mindful of that in what I write below.

Improvement

The most satisfactory change has been the improvement of South Yorkshire police (SYP). In 2016, they were rated by HM inspectors as requiring improvement. In the latest inspection, they were graded as outstanding in three categories, good in five, and adequate in one. This makes them one of the top performing forces in the country. This matters. It gives us, the public, confidence in our force, it supports police morale, and it means that people want to join; recruitment is not a problem here as it is for some.

The main direct contribution a PCC can make to this is to ensure that the right person is appointed as chief constable. I have appointed two in my time. And another is to develop ways of holding the force to account that are supportive but also challenging. There have been times when we have had to ask difficult questions, times when we have had to give encouragement.

Victims

A second area is, without question, the treatment of victims. When I became PCC, in the wake of the Jay Report into child sexual exploitation in Rotherham, I had a visit from the father of a young woman who had been groomed and sexually abused and ignored by the police. I knew little or nothing about CSE. We agreed to set up a Victims, Survivors, and Their Families Panel to advise me and, ultimately, to advise the police. They taught me and, I believe, the police the importance of listening to victims of crimes and not assuming you know everything or that there is nothing new to know. I now see the fruit of that in the way the police approach all their work, from domestic abuse to antisocial behavior. They don't always get it right, but we are in a different world from 2016. In some areas, such as CSE, SYP is one of the leading forces in the country.

Having said that, I think this is an area that needs constant scrutiny because, as we know, all organizations have a tendency in some situations to put their own reputation ahead of the needs of victims: think of the sub-postmasters and the unwillingness of all police forces to use the term "institutional" when considering issues of organizational culture.

Media

This takes me to a third area where results have been decidedly more mixed: relationships with the media. People need to have trust and confidence in the police and criminal justice system. We need the media if we are to help the public understand both the good work that is being done but also the constraints and obstacles. But in the almost ten years I have been PCC, I have seen a withering of the human resources in both the print and broadcast media. It is increasingly rare to find anyone now who specializes in criminal justice, especially the statistics of crime, and so, with a few honorable exceptions, reporters can sometimes get the wrong end of the stick or cause unnecessary anxieties. My regret looking back is that we have not done more to help the media, and so the public, make sense of all the data. We need the data and have never had so much, but data does not interpret itself. "Where is the knowledge we have lost in information?" T. S. Eliot asked in 1934.[7] We are slow learners.

Optimism

But let me end on a note of optimism. One of the last things I have done is to speak to a group of new recruits at their attestation ceremony— when they take an oath before a magistrate and receive their warrant cards. There were fifty-six recruits, men and women, at Robert Dyson House, the police training center at Wath-on-Dearne. The average age was probably somewhere in the early twenties. Hearing them repeat the oath with such conviction was encouraging. They not only swore to keep the King's peace and prevent crime but also to uphold human rights and accord equal respect to all people. This is what these young officers committed to, and it is against these high standards that I have sought to hold South Yorkshire police to account during my three terms of office. Now, it is up to the new mayor.

My term of office ended on May 2, 2024, when the elected mayor for South Yorkshire assumed responsibilities for policing.

7. Eliot, *Rock*, 7.

Bibliography

Aminlogic. "My Quote Review: A Quote About Life from Vivian Greene." Medium (blog post), Dec. 28, 2024. https://medium.com/@aminlogic/my-quote-review-a-quote-about-life-from-vivian-greene-79513c9bad83.

Angelou, Maya. "Maya Angelou: In Her Own Words." BBC News, May 28, 2014. https://www.bbc.com/news/world-us-canada-27610770.

Blunkett, David. "Why I Am So Uneasy About Police 'Taking the Knee': Former Home Secretary David Blunkett Has Fought Racism all His Life. But Here He Takes a Provocative Stance After Officers Knelt Before Crowds of Protesters." *Daily Mail*, June 4, 2020. https://www.dailymail.co.uk/debate/article-8389795/Former-Home-Secretary-DAVID-BLUNKETT-uneasy-police-taking-knee.html.

The Book of Common Prayer (1662). Cambridge: Cambridge University Press, 1878.

Casey, Louise. "Baroness Casey Review: Final Report." Metropolitan Police, Mar. 2023. https://www.met.police.uk/SysSiteAssets/media/downloads/met/about-us/baroness-casey-review/update-march-2023/baroness-casey-review-march-2023a.pdf.

Countryside Alliance. "Rural Charter." https://www.countryside-alliance.org/rural-charter.

Duckworth, Angela Lee. "Grit: The Power of Passion and Perseverance." Apr. 2013. https://www.ted.com/talks/angela_lee_duckworth_grit_the_power_of_passion_and_perseverance.

Duffy, Steve. "Ely: What Do We Know About the Cardiff Suburb?" BBC, May 25, 2023. https://www.bbc.com/news/uk-wales-65683002.

Eliot, T. S. *The Rock*. London: Faber & Faber, 1934.

Gesch, Bernard, et al. "Aylesbury Study: Reducing Incidents Among Young Offenders Through Nutrition." Think Through Nutrition, Feb. 25, 2002. https://thinkthroughnutrition.org/ttn-aylesbury-study.

Gilman, Charlotte Perkins. *The Yellow Wallpaper*. London: Martino Fine, 2018.

Global Health and Human Rights Database. "Airedale NHS Trust v Bland." Nov. 19, 1992. https://www.globalhealthrights.org/wp-content/uploads/2013/01/HL-1993-Airedale-NHS-Trust-v.-Bland.pdf

Goodhart, David. *Head, Hand, Heart: The Struggle for Dignity and Status in the 21st Century*. London: Penguin, 2021.

Hales, Samuel T., et al. "Understanding Sexual Aggression in UK Male University Students: An Empirical Assessment of Prevalence and Psychological Risk Factors." *Sexual Abuse* 34.6 (2021) 744–70. https://doi.org/10.1177/10790632211051682.

Higgens, Dave. "Smart M-Way Crash that Killed Two 'Would Not Have Happened with Hard Shoulder.'" *The Independent*, Apr. 5, 2023. https://www.the-independent. com/news/uk/sheffield-mercer-yorkshire-ford-north-east-b2314782.html.

His Majesty's Inspectorate of Constabulary and Fire and Rescue Services (HMICFRS). "PEEL 2021/22: Police Effectiveness, Efficiency, and Legitimacy." Feb. 2, 2023. https://s3-eu-west-2.amazonaws.com/assets-hmicfrs.justiceinspectorates.gov.uk/ uploads/peel-assessment-2021-22-south-yorkshire.pdf.

Hillsborough Independent Panel. "The Report of the Hillsborough Independent Panel." Sept. 12, 2012. https://www.gov.uk/government/publications/the-report-of-the-hillsborough-independent-panel.

Home Office. "Police Use of Force Statistics, England and Wales: April 2021 to March 2022." Official Statistics, Dec. 12, 2022. https://www.gov.uk/government/statistics/ police-use-of-force-statistics-england-and-wales-april-2021-to-march-2022/ police-use-of-force-statistics-england-and-wales-april-2021-to-march-2022.

iFacility. "How Many CCTV Cameras Are in the UK?" https://www.ifacility.co.uk/how-many-cameras-are-in-the-uk/.

Independent Office for Police Conduct. "The Operation Linden Report, June 2022." Jun. 1, 2022. https://www.policeconduct.gov.uk/publications/operation-linden-report-june-2022.

Jay, Alexis, et al. "The Report of the Independent Inquiry into Child Sexual Abuse." Independent Inquiry Child Sexual Abuse HC 720 (Oct. 2022) E02778684. https:// www.iicsa.org.uk/document/report-independent-inquiry-child-sexual-abuse-october-2022-0.html.

Jones, James. "'The Patronising Disposition of Unaccountable Power': A Report to Ensure the Pain and Suffering of the Hillsborough Families Is Not Repeated." House of Commons, Nov. 1, 2017. https://assets.publishing.service.gov.uk/media /5a82c1cce5274a2e8ab5931d/6_3860_HO_Hillsborough_Report_2017_FINAL_ updated.pdf.

Law Enforcement Action Partnership. "Sir Robert Peel's Policing Principles." https:// lawenforcementactionpartnership.org/peel-policing-principles/.

Macpherson, William. "The Stephen Lawrence Inquiry: Report of an Inquiry by Sir William Macpherson of Cluny." Presented to Parliament by the Secretary of State for the Home Department by Command of Her Majesty, Feb. 1999. https://www. gov.uk/government/publications/the-stephen-lawrence-inquiry.

National Centre for Violence Against Women and Girls and Public Protection (NCVPP). "2024 National Analysis of Police-Recorded CSAE Crimes Report." Dec. 2025. https://www.vkpp.org.uk/assets/National-Analysis-of-Police-Recorded-Child-Sexual-Abuse-and-Exploitation-CSAE-crimes-report-2024-for-England-and-Wales-Totality-3-V2.pdf.

National Police Chiefs' Council (NPCC). "Results Published in Policing's Largest Integrity Screening Project." Jan. 23, 2024. https://news.npcc.police.uk/releases/ results-published-in-policings-largest-integrity-screening-project.

Office of South Yorkshire Police and Crime Commissioner (OPCC). "Big Falls in Crime Across South Yorkshire in 2020." https://southyorkshire-pcc.gov.uk/news/big-falls-in-crime-across-south-yorkshire-in-2020/.

Reja, Mishal. "Trump's 'Chinese Virus' Tweet Helped Lead to Rise in Racist Anti-Asian Twitter Content: Study." ABC News, Mar. 18, 2021. https://abcnews.go.com/Health/trumps-chinese-virus-tweet-helped-lead-rise-racist/story?id=76530148.

Sheffield's Student Union. "Homework Club Action Group with Link Learning Communities." https://su.sheffield.ac.uk/making-change/change-lab/homework-club.

Turner, Justice. "Ms Cheryl Pile v Chief Constable of Merseyside Police." Queen's Bench Division, Case no. E64YJ153, Sept. 18, 2020. https://vlex.co.uk/vid/ms-cheryl-pile-v-849501495.

UK Office for National Statistics. "Population and Household Estimates, England and Wales: Census 2021." June 28, 2022. https://www.gov.uk/government/publications/census-2021-first-results-england-and-wales/population-and-household-estimates-england-and-wales-census-2021.

Ulke, Alastair. "South Yorkshire Police Use of Force Rises Since Pandemic—but Barely at all Compared to England Rates." The Star, Dec. 28, 2022. https://www.thestar.co.uk/news/crime/south-yorkshire-police-use-of-force-rises-since-pandemic-but-barely-at-all-compared-to-england-rates-3967223.

Woolf, Virginia. Killing the Angel in the House. London: Penguin, 1995.

Yorkshire Evening Post. "Cost of MPs Security Rises by £2m Following Murder of Yorkshire's Jo Cox." Dec. 12, 2017. https://www.yorkshireeveningpost.co.uk/news/politics/cost-of-mps-security-rises-by-aps2m-following-murder-of-yorkshires-jo-cox-596386.

Young, Frank, and Shaun Bailey. "Parents Have Their Say on Cannabis: Civitas Polling on the Use of Cannabis and the Views of Parents." Civitas, July 2022. https://civitas.org.uk/publications/parents-have-their-say-on-cannabis/.

www.ingramcontent.com/pod-product-compliance
Lightning Source LLC
Chambersburg PA
CBHW061727270326
41928CB00011B/2144